VOICES

EMILY BRYSON AND CHRISTIEN LEE

NATIONAL
GEOGRAPHIC
LEARNING

Australia · Brazil · Canada · Mexico · Singapore · United Kingdom · United States

National Geographic Learning,
a Cengage Company

Voices Level 3 Student's Book, 1st Edition
Emily Bryson and Christien Lee

Publisher: Andrew Robinson

Managing Editor: Derek Mackrell

Development Editor: Kirsty Hine

Director of Global Marketing: Ian Martin

Product Marketing Manager: Caitlin Thomas

Heads of Regional Marketing:

Charlotte Ellis (Europe, Middle East, and Africa)

Irina Pereyra (Latin America)

Justin Kaley (Asia)

Joy MacFarland (US and Canada)

Production Manager: Daisy Sosa

Media Researcher: Leila Hishmeh

Art Director: Brenda Carmichael

Operations Support: Hayley Chwazik-Gee

Manufacturing Manager: Eyvett Davis

Composition: Composure

Audio Producer: Tom Dick and Debbie Productions
and NY Audio

Contributing writers: Katherine Stannett and
Jon Hird (Endmatter)

Advisors: Anna Blackmore, Bruna Caltabiano,
Dale Coulter, and Mike Sayer

Student's Book with Online Practice and Student's eBook
978-0-357-45881-5

Student's Book
978-0-357-44436-8

National Geographic Learning
200 Pier 4 Boulevard
Boston, MA 02210
USA

Locate your local office at **international.cengage.com/region**

Visit National Geographic Learning online at **ELTNGL.com**
Visit our corporate website at **www.cengage.com**

Printed in Singapore
Print Number: 01 Print Year: 2022

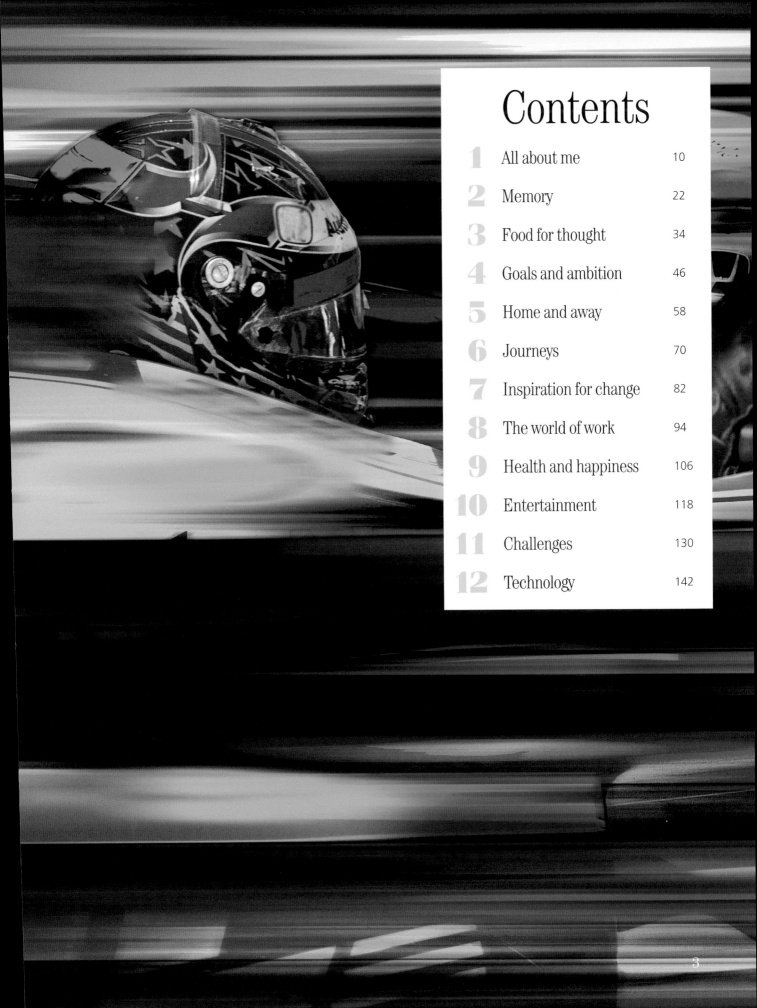

Contents

Scope and sequence

		GRAMMAR	VOCABULARY	PRONUNCIATION
1	**All about me** *Pages 10–21*	adverbs of frequency; simple present and present progressive	personality adjectives	stressing words to express strong opinions; saying long and short sounds (1): /iː/ and /ɪ/
2	**Memory** *Pages 22–33*	simple past; making questions	school subjects	saying regular past form endings (-*ed*); understanding fast speech: how words change
3	**Food for thought** *Pages 34–45*	simple past and past progressive; indefinite pronouns	food	understanding weak forms (1): *was* and *were*; stressing words to express meaning
4	**Goals and ambition** *Pages 46–57*	future plans; *will* and *won't* for promises, offers, and spontaneous decisions	motivation	understanding weak forms (2): prepositions and articles; saying words beginning with /p/ and /b/
5	**Home and away** *Pages 58–69*	zero and first conditionals; comparatives and superlatives	extreme adjectives	understanding contractions of auxiliary verbs; saying /f/ and /v/
6	**Journeys** *Pages 70–81*	present perfect with *ever* / *never*; verb patterns: -*ing* and *to* + base verb	air travel	saying long and short sounds (2): /ʌ/, /æ/, and /ɑː/; noticing difficult consonant sounds

4

READING	LISTENING	WRITING	COMMUNICATION SKILL	CRITICAL THINKING	USEFUL LANGUAGE
an article about personality; skimming	an explorer talks about her personality; listening for opinions	a personal profile; adapting your writing style	talking to people you don't know	recognizing the purpose of a text	asking how often; expressing agreement and disagreement
a blog post about memory; understanding reference (1): recognizing synonyms	an explorer talks about how she remembered things at school; dealing with unfamiliar vocabulary	a story; giving reasons	showing interest when listening	thinking about the quality of information	responding actively in conversation; adding interesting details to a story
an article about where foods come from; understanding how a text is organized	an interview with a restaurant owner; listening for reasons	a recipe; giving clear instructions	making your reasons clear	recognizing direct and indirect ideas; solving possible problems	giving reasons
an online article about a climber; scanning	a podcast about motivation; recognizing fillers	an online forum; using apostrophes	giving encouraging feedback	categorizing	giving encouraging feedback; talking about goals
a review of a TV series; finding meaning (1): using context	explorers talk about memorable places they have stayed; understanding the key points	online messages; being clear and friendly in messages	showing flexibility	identifying a writer's opinion; prioritizing	being a flexible guest and host; arranging a stay
an article about unusual ways to get to work; understanding reference (2): pronouns and determiners	a bird expert talking about bird journeys; using information you already know	an email to a travel company; choosing informal or more formal language	understanding other English speakers	choosing the best option	checking understanding; using informal and more formal language in emails

Scope and sequence

READING	LISTENING	WRITING	COMMUNICATION SKILL	CRITICAL THINKING	USEFUL LANGUAGE
five texts about important inventions; finding meaning (2): using definitions	a conversation about cleaning up the environment; predicting the content	a blog post; using paragraphs and topic sentences	persuading people	finding connections	talking about things that inspire you; persuading people; introducing topics
an article about the changing world of work; understanding cause and effect	an explorer talks about her work; making mind maps	a résumé; proofreading and checking information	making a good impression at an interview	combining information from different sources	using positive language at an interview; writing about your skills and experience
an article about living without pain; identifying supporting examples	an explorer talks about his health; staying positive when you don't understand	a gratitude journal; keeping the reader interested	saying "no" when you need to	reflecting on how things make us feel; finding positives in negative situations	saying "no" politely
two folktales; understanding sequence in a story	an explorer talks about what he does for entertainment; listening for general meaning	a review; giving opinions	showing you value people	identifying the moral	showing that a relationship is important; describing a show
three different text types about social media challenges; recognizing genre and message	an explorer talks about working in extreme conditions; listening for signposts	a report; writing factual information	asking for help	connecting a topic to personal opinions and experiences	asking for help; writing reports
an article about art and technology; recognizing paraphrase	explorers talk about technology; taking notes when you listen	an online returns form; giving only necessary information	taking turns on a group video call	drawing conclusions	managing a group video call; describing a problem

Meet the explorers

ABBY MCBRIDE

Lives: U.S.A.
Job: I am a sketch biologist—this means I study wildlife and draw pictures of it. I travel all over the world and describe my adventures in ecology and conservation with words and pictures. I spent 2018 in New Zealand studying seabirds.
What do you like to cook? Anything with chocolate! (I was a pastry chef for two years.)
Find Abby: Unit 4

ARIANNA SOLDATI

Lives: Germany
Job: I am a volcanologist—this means I study volcanoes. As a National Geographic Young Explorer, I studied a volcano on La Réunion, a tiny island in the Indian Ocean. I'm also very involved in teaching people about science.
What do you do to relax? I paint volcanoes, and read novels and poetry.
Find Arianna: Unit 1

ALEXIS CHAPPUIS

Lives: Indonesia
Job: I am a marine biologist and scientific diver. I explore underwater environments and document them with photography. I am particularly interested in deep coral reef ecosystems that we do not know much about yet.
Do you have any fears? What are they? I worry that we don't do enough to protect our planet and the wonderful biodiversity that lives on it.
Find Alexis: Unit 5

BRIAN KASTL

Lives: U.S.A.
Job: I am a conservationist—this means I am trying to save animal life. I am a PhD student at Berkeley, California and my research is on saving endangered coho salmon (a kind of fish) in California.
What do you always take with you when you travel? When possible, my bike or surfboard!
Find Brian: Unit 3

ANDREJ GAJIĆ

Lives: Bosnia and Herzegovina
Job: I'm a shark research scientist—I work in the conservation of sharks and study the diseases caused by sea pollution in the Mediterranean and other marine environments. I'm also a biology professor, author, and underwater photographer.
What do you always take with you when you travel? Laptop (so I can work), camera, passport, notebook, and chopsticks
Find Andrej: Unit 4; Unit 10

ELLIE DE CASTRO

Lives: Philippines
Job: I'm an archeologist—this means I am interested in what we can learn about our own history from what we find in the ground. I spend most of my time thinking of ways to give children access to their own heritage—and for them to enjoy it!
What advice would you give someone who wants to explore the world? Be open to other ways of living, to ask, and listen!
Find Ellie: Unit 5

ANNE JUNGBLUT

Lives: U.K.
Job: I'm a microbiologist and polar scientist—this means I study the ecology of the cold North and South Poles. I am trying to learn how to respond to climate change in these regions. I am a research scientist at the Natural History Museum in London.
What's your favorite place you've ever been to? Antarctica
Find Anne: Unit 8; Unit 11

FEDERICO FANTI

Lives: Italy
Job: I am a paleontologist and geologist—this means I study the history of life on Earth, looking at fossils and rocks. I am also a professor at the University of Bologna in Italy.
Describe yourself in three words: Curious, stubborn, scientist
Find Federico: Unit 9

GINA MOSELEY

Lives: Austria
Job: I am a professor of geology at the University of Innsbruck. I study caves to understand our climate over the last 500,000 years. As a member of the Greenland Caves project team, I have explored ancient cave sites in the Arctic Circle, and I am developing the first cave-based record of past climate change for Greenland.
What did you want to do when you were younger? Fast jet or helicopter pilot
Find Gina: Unit 2

PAOLA RODRÍGUEZ

Lives: Mexico
Job: I am a coral reef researcher—this means I study how this tiny tropical sea creature will be affected by climate change and look for ways to protect and restore it.
What did you want to do when you were younger? Ice skater
Find Paola: Unit 12

IMOGEN NAPPER

Lives: U.K.
Job: I am a marine scientist—this means I study what happens in the sea. I specialize in plastic pollution. I am working to identify technology that can catch the tiny plastic fibers that enter the water when clothes are washed.
What do you do to relax? Play my guitar (badly)!
Find Imogen: Unit 7

RUBÉN SALGADO ESCUDERO

Lives: Mexico
Job: I'm a photographer. I have lived in and traveled to many different countries. In 2014, while I was living in Myanmar, I started my project Solar Portraits, showing the lives of people who have access to electricity for the first time through solar energy.
What advice would you give to someone who wants to explore the world? Do it! You will never regret it.
Find Rubén: Unit 8

ISAÍ MADRIZ

Lives: Chile
Job: I am an entomologist, zoologist, and marine biologist, and I'm especially interested in the freshwater insects of Patagonia. I combine hiking, cycling, and rafting to explore rivers and lakes to search for some of the rarest insects on the planet.
What's your fondest memory? I have so many! Probably one of my favorite memories is of my grandma teaching me how to milk a cow.
Find Isaí: Unit 12

SALOME BUGLASS

Lives: Ecuador
Job: I am a marine ecologist in the Galápagos, Ecuador—this means I study where and how marine creatures live. I'm researching life on underwater mountains found in deep-sea environments, where it's very dark and cold, but also calm and beautiful.
What's your best memory? My first ever dive.
Find Salome: Unit 6

NORA SHAWKI

Lives: Egypt
Job: I am an archeologist—this means I study people and places from the past. I spend my time digging and doing research. Now, I am working in the Delta in Egypt to save areas from modern building and development.
What advice would you give to someone who wants to explore the world? Talk to people. You learn so much about a culture from talking to real people in real places.
Find Nora: Unit 2

TSIORY ANDRIANAVALONA

Lives: Madagascar
Job: I am a paleontologist—this means I study the history of life on Earth. I have a special interest in shark fossils. I co-founded an organization to inspire young people to take an interest in science and technology and encourage the next generation to make positive change for my home country, Madagascar.
What did you want to do when you were younger? I wanted to be an archeologist or a detective.
Find Tsiory: Unit 3

Chef Soufiane Lezaar has a collection of more than 10,000 objects in his apartment in Tangier, Morocco.

1

All about me

GOALS

GOALS

- Skim an article about personality
- Practice talking about daily habits
- Talk about people's personalities
- Listen for opinions in an interview
- Learn strategies for talking to new people
- Write a personal profile

1 **Work in groups. Discuss the questions.**

1 Look at the photo. What can we say about the person who lives here?

2 What do you think your home says about you?

WATCH ▶

2 ▶ 1.1 Watch the video. Circle the words below that Arianna uses to talk about herself.

NATIONAL GEOGRAPHIC EXPLORER

ARIANNA SOLDATI

careful	curious	excited	friendly	funny
happy	kind	polite	shy	

3 **Make connections. Discuss the questions. Give reasons for your answers.**

1 Which of Arianna's three words also describe you?

2 Do the other words in Exercise 2 describe you?

1A
Knowing me, knowing you

LESSON GOALS
• Skim an article
• Recognize the purpose of a text
• Talk about personality

READING

1 Work in pairs. Discuss the questions.

1 How do you think we can learn what kind of person someone is before we meet them?

2 When can it be useful to do this?

2 Complete the definitions of the words and phrases in bold with one of these phrases.

| do it often | feel unhappy | make money |
| spend time | think carefully | |

1 To **get to know** someone, you _____ with them and learn about them.

2 To **judge** means to _____ and form an opinion about something.

3 To be **worried** is to _____ because you keep thinking about possible problems.

4 To **tend** to do something means to _____ or be likely to do it.

5 To be **successful** means to do something well or _____ doing it.

3 Look at the Reading Skill box. Skim the article on page 13 to choose the best heading (1–6) for each paragraph (A–F).

READING SKILL
Skimming

To skim is to read a text quickly and not in detail in order to find the writer's main ideas. There are different ways you can try to do this:

• Read the title and any headings.
• Read the first and last sentence of each paragraph.
• Look for repeated ideas.

1 Are personalities in the blood? _____

2 An introduction to personality _____

3 What do footwear and family tell us? _____

4 The usual way to get to know someone _____

5 What's in a name? _____

6 Is your plane seat important? _____

4 Work in pairs. Read the article again. What does the article say about...

1 people with strong names?

2 people with type O blood?

3 being the only child in your family?

4 choosing the aisle seat on a plane?

5 slow eaters?

5 Look at the Critical Thinking Skill box. Work in pairs. Match purposes 1–5 in the box with types of writing a–e. Then discuss what you think the main purpose of the article is.

CRITICAL THINKING SKILL
Recognizing the purpose of a text

Knowing a writer's purpose—or reason for writing—can help you understand and respond to a text. These are some common purposes.

1 providing entertainment

2 giving information about a topic

3 expressing a personal opinion about a topic

4 trying to make someone do something

5 describing the good and bad aspects of something

a a blog post or social media comment _____

b a *for and against* essay or a review _____

c a good story or funny article _____

d an advertisement _____

e a news or factual article _____

SPEAKING

6 Work in groups. Do you think any of the ideas in the text can tell you about someone's personality? Why or why not?

7 What other ways can you think of for how you might learn about someone's personality? Use these ideas or your own.

• someone's clothes or the colors they like
• how someone walks
• how someone talks or laughs

EXPLORE MORE!

Find out more about opinions on the connection between personality and where we sit on a plane. Search online for "personality + sit + plane."

What do **I know** about **you**?

A In general, we know that our personalities—all the parts of our character that make us who we are—come from two things: our DNA from our parents and the experiences we have during our lives. But what is the best way to get to know someone? Can we find out about somebody's personality before meeting them?

B Some people believe our ID cards say lot about our personalities. In some places, parents give their children strong names to help them become strong adults. Can our name change who we become? Probably not. However, in the 1980s a Belgian psychologist found that people prefer names that sound similar to their own. So maybe a name can change what we think about a person.

C In certain countries, some people think we can judge personality from somebody's blood type. For example, they believe that people with type O blood are good leaders and type Bs are friendly. There seems to be no scientific reason for this, but it's possible that people change their behavior because they know their blood type.

D A study in the *Journal of Research in Personality* suggests that just looking at somebody's shoes can tell us whether they are generally calm or worried. Other studies suggest that people with at least one brother or sister tend to be kind to others, while people with no brothers or sisters may find it hard to have good relationships.

E Some studies suggest that your choice of seat on a plane tells us something about your personality. Choosing a window seat may mean that you get angry easily. Preferring the aisle may show that you want to be free. What about eating? Research shows that people who eat slowly usually enjoy life. While quick eaters don't like waiting and want to be successful.

F These theories show that something might be true because we believe it is. But, maybe it's better to get to know someone in the usual way: not from looking at their ID card—or even their shoes—but by talking and listening to them.

ID CARD
Name: Dominique Pereira
Date of birth: 06/06/98
Blood type: B
Occupation: Student

1B
How often do you go out?

LESSON GOALS
- Understand people's daily habits
- Talk about how often you do something
- Talk about your regular activities

SPEAKING

1 Work in groups. Are you someone who likes going out a lot and meeting friends or do you prefer staying home?

2 Work in pairs. Look at the infographic below. Discuss the questions.

1 Who enjoys these activities more—extroverts or introverts?

a thinking   d observing
b talking   e walking
c going to parties   f teamwork

2 Do you think you are an extrovert or an introvert? Why?

LISTENING AND GRAMMAR

3 🎧 **1.1** Listen to two people talking about their habits. Is Eva or Meera more similar to the description of extroverts in the infographic? Why? Discuss with a partner.

4 🎧 **1.1** Listen again and read the sentences. Are they true for Eva, Meera, or both? Check (✓) all the correct answers.

	Eva	Meera
1 They live in a large city.	☐	☐
2 They work long hours.	☐	☐
3 They run every day.	☐	☐
4 They go to work by bike.	☐	☐
5 They go out in the evenings a lot.	☐	☐
6 They do exercise on the weekend.	☐	☐

Are you an extrovert or an introvert?

Extroverts are people who like going out and need other people to feel happy.
Introverts prefer a quiet life and need time alone to feel happy.

Extroverts
After a day at work you want to talk about it.

You have conversations with people you don't know every day.

You have a lot of friends and you often go out.

You are always ready to try something new.

You like working in groups.

You love being the center of attention.

You sometimes speak before you think!

Introverts
After a day at work you usually need time alone.

You are often lost in your thoughts.

You have a few close friends you enjoy spending time with.

You go for walks several times a week.

You occasionally go to parties, but you rarely stay late.

You never want to be the center of attention.

You prefer to think before you act.

5 Read the Grammar box. Work in pairs. Complete tasks 1 and 2.

> **GRAMMAR** Adverbs of frequency
>
> Use **indefinite adverbs of frequency** to give a general idea about how often someone does or feels something. They usually come before the main verb.
> I **occasionally** *meet a friend after work.*
> However, they come after the verb *be* and other auxiliary verbs.
> *I'm* **always** *at work by 8.*
> Use **definite adverbs of frequency** to be more specific. They usually come at the end of the sentence.
> *I go for a long bike ride* **once** *or* **twice a month***.*
> *I meet with friends* **several times a week***!*
>
> Go to page 166 for the Grammar reference.

1 Underline the ten adverbs of frequency in the infographic.

2 Which are the two definite adverbs?

6 Match the beginnings of the sentences (1–6) with the endings (a–f).

1 I have a full-time job and a baby, so _____

2 I hate TV, so _____

3 I am a night person, so _____

4 I usually take lunch to the office, but _____

5 I don't work on Fridays, so _____

6 The traffic is terrible in the mornings, so _____

a I usually go to the gym and meet a friend for coffee.

b I am always tired.

c I occasionally eat out with my work friends.

d I never watch it.

e we are sometimes late for work.

f I rarely go to bed before 1 a.m.

7 Rewrite the sentences using these adverbs in the correct place.

always	occasionally	often
rarely	sometimes	usually

1 We eat out every three or four months.
We occasionally eat out.

2 I get up early every day except Sundays.
_____

3 The baby wakes up five or six times a night.
_____

4 I ride my bike to work about twice a week.
_____

5 My mother does yoga before work every morning.
_____

6 I'm late to class about once a year.
_____

8 Look at the Useful Language box. Match questions 1–3 in the box with a–c below.

> **Useful Language** Asking how often
> **1 How often do you** go on vacation?
> **2 Do you usually** take the train to work?
> **3 Do you ever** work on Sundays?

a you expect the answer *yes* _____

b you are not sure of the answer _____

c you expect an adverb of frequency _____

SPEAKING

9 Use the Useful Language and some of these verbs to make six questions about regular activities in your notebook.

call	dance	eat	exercise
go	plan	swim	watch

How often do you exercise?

10 Work in pairs. Take turns asking your questions from Exercise 9. Use adverbs of frequency when you answer. Write your partner's answers in your notebook.
I run three times a week and I walk almost every day.

11 Work with a different partner. Discuss some things you learned in Exercise 10.
Mei often runs and she walks a lot, too.

EXPLORE MORE!

Search online to find out more about introverts and extroverts.

1C
My best self

LESSON GOALS
- Listen for opinions in an interview
- Talk about present situations
- Stress words to express strong opinions
- Talk about personality characteristics

LISTENING

NATIONAL GEOGRAPHIC EXPLORER

1 Work in pairs. Look at the photos of Arianna Soldati. Talk about what she is doing in each photo, how she might feel, and why. How would you feel in these situations?

2 🎧 1.2 Listen to the interview and circle the correct option for each sentence. Then discuss what you think being your "best self" means. Where do you feel your best self?

1 She speaks *four* / *five* languages.

2 Her second language is *German* / *English*.

3 She feels her "best self" in *Italy* / *the U.S.*

4 She acts *differently* / *the same* in different situations.

Arianna Soldati

3 🎧 1.2 Look at the Listening Skill box. Then listen to the interview again. Who has each opinion (1–5)? Check (✓) Interviewer, Arianna, or both.

LISTENING SKILL
Listening for opinions

To understand what someone's opinions are:
- listen for expressions that introduce an opinion, such as *In my view,…* or phrases that are clearly positive or negative, such as *Amazing!* or *That's not good.*
- listen for reasons and examples that express a positive or negative opinion. For example "*…because it made me happy*" (positive) or "*…it was too expensive*" (negative)
- listen for words that a speaker says strongly. For example "*It was **really** good.*"

	Interviewer	Arianna
1 Being able to speak five different languages is great.	☐	☐
2 People can feel different when they use different languages.	☐	☐
3 It can be a good thing to think before you speak.	☐	☐
4 People can have different personalities in different places.	☐	☐
5 People can act differently when they are with different people.	☐	☐

4 Work in groups. Discuss how your behavior and personality change when you:
- are at work or school.
- are at home with your family.
- go out with your friends.
- speak different languages.

GRAMMAR

5 Read the Grammar box. Underline the examples of the simple present and circle the examples of the present progressive in the excerpt from the interview below.

> **GRAMMAR** Simple present and present progressive
>
> Use the simple present (with or without adverbs of frequency) to talk about regular events, routines, habits, facts, and things that are always true.
> *I sometimes **say** something without thinking.*
> Use the present progressive to talk about something happening or true right now, or an activity happening around now.
> *I'**m learning** German.*

Go to page 166 for the Grammar reference.

[...] Actually, the U.S. is the place where I feel my best self because the culture fits me. [...] And right now I'm living in Germany, like I said. I'm working at the university for a year. The culture is more serious and quiet—in a good way—so I'm naturally trying to act like other people.

6 Look at 1–5 and in your notebook write sentences using the simple present or present progressive. In which sentences can you use either form? How does the meaning change?

1 what / do / right now?
2 how / usually / go / to work?
3 he / teach / me / to play / tennis
4 she / try / to eat / healthy food
5 we / rarely / watch TV / these days

7 In your notebook write four sentences that are true for you. Use the simple present for two sentences and the present progressive for the other two sentences.

PRONUNCIATION

8 🎧 1.3 Look at the Clear Voice box. Listen and repeat.

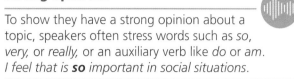

CLEAR VOICE
Stressing words to express strong opinions

To show they have a strong opinion about a topic, speakers often stress words such as *so*, *very*, or *really*, or an auxiliary verb like *do* or *am*. *I feel that is **so** important in social situations.*

9 🎧 1.4 Listen to the opinions. Underline the words that the speaker stresses. Then, listen and repeat the opinions using correct stress.

1 I definitely prefer living here.
2 Absolutely. I talk a lot when I'm at home!
3 Yes, I do like learning new languages.
4 When I'm at work, it really changes how I act.

VOCABULARY AND SPEAKING

10 🎧 1.5 Work in pairs. Circle the correct option to complete the definitions of the personality adjectives. Then listen and check.

1 **Confident** means you *enjoy being with others* / *think positively about yourself*.
2 **Creative** means you have interesting ideas and are good at *making things* / *making friends*.
3 **Friendly** means you *talk a lot* / *are kind and helpful to people*.
4 **Honest** means you tell the truth *only in some* / *in all* situations.
5 **Patient** means you *get angry* / *stay calm* when you need to wait or deal with a difficult situation.
6 **Professional** means you act in a correct way at work and *do your job well* / *work very fast*.
7 **Serious** means you are quiet and careful about things and *don't laugh very much* / *are often sad*.

Go to page 160 for the Vocabulary reference.

11 Choose an adjective from Exercise 10. Describe a person you know to give an example of the adjective, but don't say the adjective. Use stress to emphasize opinions. Your partner should try to guess your word.

A: My sister, Luisa, talks to everyone!
B: Is she friendly?

EXPLORE MORE!

Search online for articles about "how to be your best self." Find some suggestions that you think might be useful. Discuss them with your friends.

LESSON GOALS
- Learn strategies for talking to new people
- Practice saying words with long /iː/ and short /ɪ/
- Express agreement and disagreement

1D
Talking to people you don't know

SPEAKING

1 Work in groups. Discuss whether you enjoy these situations, and why.

1 going to a party where you don't know anybody

2 having a conversation with someone you don't know on a train

3 going out for coffee with a friend of a friend

MY VOICE ▶

2 ▶ 1.2 Look at the Communication Skill box. Then watch the video about talking to people you don't know. Write communication strategies 1–5 in the order the speaker mentions them.

COMMUNICATION SKILL
Talking to people you don't know

It can be difficult to have a conversation with a stranger. These strategies might help:

a _____ Comment on what the other person said and show interest in them.

b _____ Ask the other person questions to learn about their personality.

c _____ Find a connection with the other person, such as something you have in common.

d _____ Introduce yourself to the other person and share some personal information.

e _____ Let the other person talk more. Give short answers to questions they ask.

3 Look at the Communication Skill box again. In pairs, say which strategies you already use and how useful they are. Then discuss which strategies you could use in the future.

4 Work in pairs. Which questions do you think could be useful to ask when you are getting to know somebody? Why?

1 What do you do in your free time?
2 Are you a morning person?
3 What kind of TV shows do you enjoy?
4 Where do you want to live?
5 What is one thing nobody knows about you?

5 In your notebook, write two more questions that can help you get to know somebody. Discuss your questions and reasons with the class.

PRONUNCIATION AND SPEAKING

6 🎧 1.6 Look at the Clear Voice box. Listen and repeat.

CLEAR VOICE

Saying long and short sounds (1): /iː/ and /ɪ/

English has long and short vowel sounds. It's important to say the length correctly because using the wrong length can sound strange or mean other people don't understand.

/ɪ/ I *live* in Brazil.
/iː/ I'm *lea*ving *E*gypt.

7 🎧 1.7 Listen to sentences 1–6 and circle the words you hear.

1 he's /iː/   his /ɪ/
2 sleeping /iː/   slipping /ɪ/
3 feet /iː/   fit /ɪ/
4 sheep /iː/   ship /ɪ/
5 eat /iː/   it /ɪ/
6 heating /iː/   hitting /ɪ/

8 Write five questions using words from Exercise 7. Work in pairs. Take turns asking and answering the questions. Answer using full sentences.

A: What time do you usually go to sleep?
B: I usually go to sleep about 11 o'clock.

9 Look at the Useful Language box. Work in pairs. Take turns reading sentences 1–5 and responding to them about yourself.

Useful Language   Expressing agreement and disagreement

Agreeing with a positive statement
Me too.
So do / am / can I.

Agreeing with a negative statement
Me neither.
Neither do / am / can I.

Disagreeing with a positive statement
Really? Not me.
I don't / can't.
I'm not.

Disagreeing with a negative statement
Really? I do / am / can.

1 My sister can't eat milk or cheese.
   Neither can I. / Really? I can. I love cheese!
2 I live in an apartment in the city.
3 She doesn't really like meeting new people.
4 I'm so sleepy!
5 We stayed in a really cute town last summer.

10 Complete the sentences about you. Take turns saying your sentences and responding to your partner's sentences using the Useful Language.

1 I like _____.

2 I don't like _____.

3 I can _____.

4 I can't _____.

5 In the future, I want to _____.

6 In the future, I don't want to _____.

11 **OWN IT!** Find a partner you do not know very well. Spend a few minutes talking to them. Use the strategies from the Communication Skill box on page 18 and the Useful Language box.

12 Work in groups. Discuss what you learned about your partner and what you have in common.

1E

Me in a few words

LESSON GOALS
• Recognize different writing styles
• Adapt your writing style
• Write a personal profile

SPEAKING

1 Work in pairs. Discuss which types of communication you often write and why.

business letter   essay   personal email
social media post   text message

2 Work in groups. Check the meaning of the bold words in descriptions 1–3. Then discuss which type(s) of writing from Exercise 1 match each description.

1 Uses a **serious** and **formal** style. May use advanced vocabulary and long sentences. Will not usually use contractions such as *couldn't* or *don't*.

2 Uses a **professional** style and is usually serious. Will focus on business, and express ideas in a clear, **direct** way.

3 Uses an **informal** style and is not usually serious. Will generally use simple vocabulary and short sentences. Contractions are common, and may use exclamation points (!) or abbreviations like *msg* for *message*.

READING FOR WRITING

3 Read texts 1–3, on the right. Match each text to one of the following headings. Then read the responses (A–C) and match them with the texts (1–3).

• an ad to share a home _____ _____

• a job application _____ _____

• a social media profile _____ _____

4 Read the texts (1–3) and the responses (A–C) again. In your notebook, write full sentences to answer these questions.

1 What is the writer looking for?

2 What do people reading this need to do next?

3 What should people responding write about?

A How often does the writer paint?

B What skills is the writer trying to learn?

C What does the writer do in the evenings?

---

1 Friendly person wanted to share comfortable apartment downtown. $475 per month. Shared bathroom, kitchen, and living room, but own bedroom. Nobody too crazy, please!

2 You're one step away from joining our exciting social media community. Just write a short description of yourself and click "Let Me In!"

3 To find the perfect job for you, tell us a little about who you are, what skills you have, and what work you enjoy doing. Write no more than 50 words.

A I'm positive, confident, easygoing, and patient. I love going out and meeting new people, but occasionally I like to be alone. I've just started painting. I don't think I'm very talented, but I love it and I do some painting almost every day, so I'm definitely getting better!

B I graduated last year with a business degree. I am working in sales now, but I want to get experience in marketing or advertising. I am very good with computers and social media. I am trying to develop new professional skills, like speaking in public and writing business reports.

C I'm very interested. I live south of the river right now, but I work on North Road, so moving downtown would be perfect! My friends say I'm generous and reliable. I usually like quiet nights at home, but sometimes I like going out! I love exercising. I'm learning karate right now.

5 Look at the Writing Skill box. Work in groups. Look at the texts and responses on page 20 again. Do you think each response (A–C) uses the correct style? Give reasons.

WRITING SKILL
Adapting your writing style

Change your writing style based on:
- why you are writing (the situation).
- who you are writing for (the reader or readers).
- what you want to say (the content).

For example, you might use an informal style when writing a personal profile for social media. You might use a formal style in a business profile.

6 Work in pairs. Look at the steps below and work together to rewrite response A so it is suitable to include in a job application.

1 Add information about education level, and previous and current jobs.

2 Change exclamation points to periods and contractions such as *don't* to *do not*.

3 Give information about professional skills rather than personal hobbies.

4 Mention professional characteristics instead of personal ones such as *easygoing*.

WRITING TASK

7 WRITE Choose <u>one</u> of the writing tasks below that is useful for you. Then write a personal profile in a style that matches the situation. Use the model profiles A–C on page 20 to help.

- You have signed up for a new social media app. Write a short profile of yourself that other members of the site can read.
- You have joined a website for people who want to find a new job. Write a short profile of yourself for companies to read.

8 CHECK Use the checklist. Your profile...
- ☐ describes your personality clearly.
- ☐ uses a writing style that matches the situation.
- ☐ uses a writing style that is suitable for the reader.
- ☐ uses adverbs of frequency correctly.
- ☐ uses present tenses correctly.

9 REVIEW Exchange profiles with another student. Did they include at least three things from the checklist? Give each other feedback. Then make changes to your profile based on your partner's feedback.

Go to page 154 for the Reflect and review.

COLOR
TRANSPARENCY

THIS SIDE
TOWARD SCREEN

22

Catherine Panebianco holds one of her father's slides as part of her project *No Memory Is Ever Alone*, U.S.

2

Memory

GOALS

- Recognize synonyms in a blog post
- Use the simple past to talk about memories
- Deal with unfamiliar vocabulary in an interview
- Talk about school subjects
- Show an interest when listening
- Give details and reasons in a story

1 **Work in pairs. Discuss the questions.**

  1 What can you see in the photo?

  2 Do you have any photos that help you remember when you were very young?

WATCH

2 ▶ 2.1 Watch the video. With a partner, answer the questions.

NATIONAL GEOGRAPHIC EXPLORERS

| GINA MOSELEY | NORA SHAWKI |

  1 What do Gina and Nora remember well?

  2 What do Gina and Nora sometimes forget?

3 **Make connections. Which of these do you remember or sometimes forget?**

movie and book titles	friends' birthdays
important dates	new words in English
people's names	where you put your phone

How to improve your memory

LESSON GOALS
- Understand a blog post about how to improve your memory
- Recognize synonyms
- Think about the quality of information

READING

1 Work in pairs. Look at the title, headings, and photos in the blog post on page 25. What do you think the post might say about the topic? Read quickly to check.

2 Work in pairs. Read the blog post again. How does it answer questions 1–4?

1 What can I eat and drink to improve memory?

2 How often do I need to exercise?

3 How can I relax?

4 When should I sleep to help learning?

3 Look at the Reading Skill box. Then look at the chart below. Complete the pairs of synonyms from the blog post. All the words are in bold in the blog post.

READING SKILL
Understanding reference (1): recognizing synonyms

A synonym is a word that has the same meaning as another word. Writers often use them to avoid repeating the same words and to make their writing more interesting. When you find a word you don't know:

- think what kind of word it is (e.g., noun, verb, adjective).
- look at whether the word seems to mean the same as another word you know.
- look for clues before and after the word.
- use a dictionary.

study	necessary
research	
memorize	strengthen
reduce	affect

4 Look at the Critical Thinking Skill box. Circle two examples of information in the blog post that refer to research that you can check. Then underline two examples that need more information.

CRITICAL THINKING SKILL
Thinking about the quality of information

The writer of the blog post states that certain things improve our memory, but doesn't always give evidence. The post also uses phrases like "studies show" and "experts say," but doesn't always say which. You may need to check some online information on other sites. Look for university research and reliable websites. Also check the date—some information may be old.

5 Complete the sentences with the correct form of a word from Exercise 3. In some sentences, either word from the pair is possible. Which sentences do you want to fact check?

1 _____ shows that eating almonds for lunch can improve memory in the afternoon.

2 Like our overall memory, our ability to remember faces _____ after we turn 34.

3 Happiness is _____ for good memory.

4 Regular TV watching _____ memory.

5 A recent _____ showed that weight lifting can help memory.

6 Closing your eyes _____ your ability to remember a movie.

SPEAKING

6 Work in pairs. Discuss the questions.

1 Which suggestion from the blog post would you find hard to do?

2 Is there anything that you want to try in order to improve your memory?

sudoku | jigsaw | meditation | water

Seven tips to improve your memory

Most of us know that our brains decrease in size as we get older, but did you know that diet and lifestyle affect how well our brains work? Read on to find out more!

1 Food
Research shows that eating a lot of fruit, vegetables, and proteins **improves** memory. Avoid sugary foods such as cakes, cookies, and milk chocolate. Eating oily fish or dark chocolate (with over 70% cocoa) and taking Vitamin D3 can also help **strengthen** your memory.

2 Drink
The body is 60% water, so it's **essential** to drink enough water for the brain to work well. Drink when you are thirsty. In cold countries, experts say to drink 1–2 liters a day, more in hot countries. Studies show that green tea and coffee are also good for our memory.

3 Exercise
The role of exercise is very important, too. A 2011 study by Kirk Erikson showed that regular exercise increases brain size. Another **study** from the University of Iowa in the U.S. found that exercise improved memory in some people. One single training session had the same effect on memory as regular, longer exercise sessions! (Read more about it in the *Science Daily*.)

4 Relaxation
One study by the University of Massachusetts found that eight weeks of daily meditation improved memory. Other forms of relaxation can also positively **influence** memory. Take 5–10 minutes each day to meditate or listen to music. Or just take a bath!

5 Weight
Some studies show that people with a healthy body weight have better memories and had less chance of getting Alzheimer's disease (an illness that makes it hard to **remember** things).

6 Sleep
Age **reduces** our ability to learn, but sleep can help. For your brain to work well, 7–9 hours of sleep is **necessary** for most people. A 2019 study in the *Nature Research Journal* found that students learned better before and after a short sleep!

7 Use
Use your brain to keep it in good condition. Try to **memorize** information like event details and passwords rather than putting it in your phone. You could also learn a language or do brain training such as sudoku, crossword puzzles, and jigsaw puzzles.

EXPLORE MORE!

Choose one of the seven tips from the blog post and find more information about it online. For example, search for "body weight + memory." Add the current year so that you find the most recent information.

Childhood memories

LISTENING AND GRAMMAR

1 Work in pairs. Look at the photos. Discuss the questions.

1 What toys do you remember as a child?
2 Do you know any famous children's toys similar to Pudsey?
3 What sports do you remember doing as a child?

NATIONAL GEOGRAPHIC EXPLORER

2 🎧 **2.1** Listen to Gina Moseley telling two stories about her childhood. Match each story with a photo (A or B). Tell a partner.

3 🎧 **2.1** Listen to Gina again. Work with a partner. Correct the sentences.

1 Gina wanted to go caving, so asked her mom to go with her.
   Gina's mom wanted to go caving, so asked Gina to go with her.
2 Gina and her mom stayed in a hotel near the outdoor center.
3 Gina studied caves at university because of Pudsey bear.
4 When she was thirteen she hurt her arm.
5 The doctors saw her immediately when she arrived at the hospital.
6 The nurses put newspapers on her teddy bear.

A

Pudsey bear helps the BBC raise money for children around the world every year. He always has a bandage over his eye.

B

Caving in Cheddar Caves, Somerset, U.K.

4 Read the Grammar box. Cross out the option that is <u>not</u> correct in each sentence 1–5.

> **GRAMMAR** Simple past
>
> Use the simple past to talk about finished actions in the past.
> I **felt** very scared.
> My mom **wanted** to try caving but **didn't want** to go alone.
> You often use a past time expression with the simple past, e.g., *yesterday, last year*.

Go to page 167 for the Grammar reference.

1 Use the simple past with *last week / yesterday / two days ago / next weekend*.

2 Use *didn't / don't* to make the negative past form of all verbs except *be*.

3 Use *wasn't / aren't / weren't* to make the negative past form of *be*.

4 Regular past tense verbs end with *-d / -est / -ied / -ed / consonant + -ed*.

5 Irregular past tense verbs *end in -ed / have different endings so you need to learn them*.

5 Complete the text with the correct past form of the verbs.

When I ¹_____ (be) about ten, my grandparents ²_____ (move) to Mexico. They ³_____ (live) by the ocean and one year we ⁴_____ (spend) our summer vacation with them. Every day we ⁵_____ (go) to the beach, ⁶_____ (swim) in the ocean, and ⁷_____ (sail) on my grandfather's boat. We ⁸_____ (not think) about school for a month! The best thing was that we ⁹_____ (eat) my grandmother's food at every meal! She ¹⁰_____ (make) fried corn and her cakes ¹¹_____ (be) always delicious. In those days, my grandparents ¹²_____ (not have) a TV so we ¹³_____ (read) books and ¹⁴_____ (play) games in the evening. We ¹⁵_____ (not want) the vacation to end!

6 Look at the audioscript for track 2.1 on pages 183–184. Circle all the examples of regular past forms and underline all the examples of irregular past forms.

PRONUNCIATION

7 [🎧 2.2] Look at the Clear Voice box. Listen and repeat.

> **CLEAR VOICE**
> **Saying past form endings (-ed)**
>
> You say -ed as **/d/** after a voiced consonant.
> **/d/** *loved, realized, changed*
> You say -ed as **/t/** after a voiceless consonant.
> **/t/** *asked, finished, watched*
> You say -ed as **/ɪd/** after -t and -d.
> **/ɪd/** *wanted, needed*
> Put your hand on your neck when you say a voiced consonant. You should feel your throat vibrate (it should make small movements).

8 [🎧 2.3] Listen to the verbs. In your notebook, write if they are past or present forms.

9 [🎧 2.3] Listen again and repeat the verbs.

SPEAKING

10 Work in pairs. Ask and answer questions about childhood or vacation memories. Use these topics to help you.

an accident	an adventure
a favorite book or game	a funny experience
a special person	

A: Did you have a favorite game when you were a child?
B: Yes, I loved playing ball!
A: Where did you play?
B: I played in the yard with my neighbors and at school with my friends.

2C
How to remember new things

LESSON GOALS
- Deal with unfamiliar vocabulary in an interview
- Talk about school subjects
- Make questions using *be* and *do*

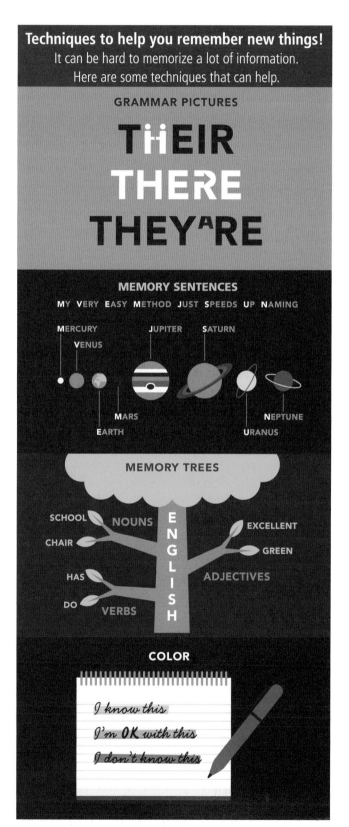

Techniques to help you remember new things!
It can be hard to memorize a lot of information.
Here are some techniques that can help.

GRAMMAR PICTURES

T**H**EIR
THE**R**E
THEY**A**RE

MEMORY SENTENCES

MY VERY EASY METHOD JUST SPEEDS UP NAMING

MERCURY
VENUS
JUPITER
SATURN
MARS
EARTH
NEPTUNE
URANUS

MEMORY TREES

SCHOOL
CHAIR
NOUNS
HAS
DO
VERBS
ENGLISH
EXCELLENT
GREEN
ADJECTIVES

COLOR

I know this
I'm OK with this
I don't know this

SPEAKING

1 Work in pairs. Discuss how you remember lists of things, new words in English, grammar, study notes, and numbers and dates.

2 Work in pairs. Look at the infographic on the left. Discuss which of the ideas you could use to help you remember the things in Exercise 1.

3 Work in pairs. Choose a way to remember some information you sometimes forget. Use the infographic and the ideas you talked about in Exercise 1 to help you.

LISTENING

NATIONAL GEOGRAPHIC EXPLORER

4 🎧 2.4 Listen to Nora Shawki. What technique from the infographic did Nora use to remember things at school? Discuss with a partner.

5 🎧 2.4 Look at the Listening Skill box. Then listen again and try to complete sentences 1–4 on page 29 using one to four words. Work in pairs. What do you think the words and phrases in bold mean?

LISTENING SKILL
Dealing with unfamiliar vocabulary

When you listen, there are often words that you don't know. Try not to worry about these words. There might be a definition, an example, or some more information to help you understand what it means. A word might sound like one in your language or there may also be other words in the sentence that can give you a clue. Listen for phrases such as *like*, *you know*, *such as*, and *for example* to help you.

1 I also try to find a word it **reminds me of** in my own language, English. For example, *rosado* in Spanish _makes me think of_ pink roses.

2 I: Did you use any memory techniques to _____ for school exams?

   N: Well, I'm not very good at memorizing. To **revise** for exams, I color-coded my notes.

3 I **highlighted** everything that looked _____ in yellow pen.

4 I created **mind maps**, you know? Diagrams to link _____.

VOCABULARY

6 Match the school subjects (1–10) with the pictures (a–j).

1 art _____   6 history _____
2 biology _____   7 IT _____
3 chemistry _____   8 math _____
4 drama _____   9 gym _____
5 geography _____   10 physics _____

a b c d e

f g h i j

Go to page 160 for the Vocabulary reference.

7 ∩ 2.5 What school subject from Exercise 6 is each question about? Listen and check. Then, work in pairs. Ask and answer the questions. Say the subject.

1 How did you remember dates? _____
2 What plays did you perform? _____
3 What sports did you do? _____
4 Which countries did you study? _____
5 Did you enjoy drawing and painting? _____
6 Did you use a calculator? _____
7 Are you good with computers now? _____
8 What did you learn about plants? _____
9 Did you learn about electricity? _____
10 Did you mix things together? _____

GRAMMAR AND SPEAKING

8 Read the Grammar box. Circle the correct option to complete sentences 1 and 2.

> **GRAMMAR** Making questions
>
> To make questions with *do* and *did*, use this word order: Question word, Auxiliary, Subject, Base verb.
> **How do you remember** new words?
> If there is no question word, use this word order: Auxiliary, Subject, Base verb.
> **Did you use** any memory techniques for school exams?
> To make questions with *be* use this word order: Question word + *be* + Subject.
> **What were your** favorite subjects?
> You can also use: *be* + Subject + Adjective / Noun.
> **Were there a lot of dates** to remember?

Go to page 167 for the Grammar reference.

1 Questions with *be* / *do* use the question word, auxiliary, subject, *to* + base verb word order.
2 Questions with *be* / *do* go with adjectives and nouns.

9 Put the questions in the correct order.

1 you / did / where / go to school?
   _____

2 was / who / your favorite teacher?
   _____

3 were / what / your best subjects at school?
   _____

4 a forgetful person / you / are?
   _____

5 you / do / learning new things / like?
   _____

10 Work in pairs. Ask and answer the questions in Exercise 9. Ask your partner for more information.

   A: *Where did you go to school?*
   B: *I went to school in Cairo.*
   A: *What did you like about school?*
   B: *I didn't really like school, but I liked seeing my friends.*

2D
Showing interest when listening

LESSON GOALS
- Show interest when listening
- Understand how words change in fast speech
- Talk about the first time you did something

SPEAKING

1 Work in pairs. Take turns asking and answering the questions.
1. Can you remember a time when you went to a special event (e.g., a wedding or a party)?
2. Where was it?
3. Who did you go with?
4. What did you enjoy about it?

2 Discuss the questions with a partner.
1. What did your partner do to show they were interested in your answers in Exercise 1?
2. When you are speaking in your own language, how do you normally show interest when someone is speaking?

MY VOICE ▶

3 ▶ 2.2 Watch the video of two conversations. Which conversation is more successful? In your notebook make a list of everything Hanadi does differently in each conversation.

4 Look at the Communication Skill box on page 31. Work in pairs. Discuss the questions.
1. Which of the things in the box do you do?
2. Which do you like others to do?
3. Are there any things you don't usually do or you find difficult to do?

Showing interest when listening

When we listen to others, some speakers feel more confident when the listener shows an interest while they are listening. We can do this by:

- using facial expressions and body language—nodding your head, smiling; looking happy or sad.
- making listening noises such as *hmm, oh,* and *ah.*
- using expressions such as *Wow!, Awesome!,* and *I'm sorry to hear that.*
- repeating parts of their story (*You fell over!*).
- asking questions (*Did you see them again? What did you do?*).

5 Look at the Useful Language box. Work in pairs. Choose a situation from 1–4 below to have a conversation about. Then choose a new situation and change roles.

Student A: Say the news.

Student B: Respond using the Useful Language. Ask questions for more information.

1 I got the job!
2 My sister is getting married!
3 My cat died yesterday.
4 I fell down this morning!

Useful Language   Responding actively in conversation

Responding to positive information
Good job! / Congratulations!
Awesome! / Cool!
That's nice!

Responding to negative information
Oh, no! / Oh, my!
That sounds painful!
That's terrible! / That's awful!
I'm sorry to hear that!

Showing surprise
Wow! / Oh! / Ah!
Really?

Asking questions
What happened? / What did you do?
Did you like it?
Does it hurt? / Are you OK?

PRONUNCIATION

6 🎧 2.6 Look at the Clear Voice box. Listen to the example. Tell a partner what you notice about how *did you* sounds when we say it fast.

CLEAR VOICE
Understanding fast speech: How words change

Sometimes when people speak quickly, some words mix together and sound different. This can make it difficult to understand. For example, when Hanadi asks *What did you do?*, *did you* / dɪdjuː/ sounds like /dɪdʒə/.

In international communication, it can be a good idea to speak slowly and clearly, but understanding how sounds and words change will help you when someone is speaking to you quickly.

*What **did you** do?* ➔ /wɒdɪdʒəduː/

7 🎧 2.7 Listen to the questions. Which pronunciation is easier to understand, a or b? Discuss with a partner.

1 How did you learn to skate?
2 Did you see her again?
3 How often do you see her now?
4 Do you still go ice skating every Saturday?

SPEAKING

8 **OWN IT!** Work in pairs. Choose a "first" from the list or think of your own idea. Ask and answer questions about the event you chose. Use the techniques from the Communication Skill box and the Useful Language.

your first day... at school / of this English class / the first time you went to another country / rode a bike / drank coffee / spoke in public

A: Can you remember your first day at school?
B: Yes! I remember it clearly!
A: Did you like it?
B: I loved it!
A: Ah! What did you like about it?

2E
A happy memory

LESSON GOALS
- Give reasons
- Add interesting details to a story
- Write a story about a happy memory

SPEAKING

1 Think of a happy memory. Take some notes about:
- when it happened.
- who you were with.
- where it was.
- why it is memorable.

2 Work in pairs. Take turns telling your partner about your happy memory.

READING FOR WRITING

3 Read the story on page 33. What happy memory does it describe? Tell a partner.

4 Look at the Writing Skill box and read the story again. In your notebook, answer questions 1–5.

WRITING SKILL
Giving reasons

The writer uses *so* and *because* to give reasons.
The streets of Jeri were made of sand, so we walked around with no shoes on the whole time.
She also adds reasons in a new sentence.
We went there almost every day. It was too hot to go walking!

1 Why did the writer like the house?
2 Why didn't they wear shoes for a week?
3 What did the writer love about the beach?
4 Why did they have to share their fish?
5 Why does the writer want to go to Jeri again?

5 Look at the Useful Language box. Find the phrases in the story. Work in pairs. Think of a situation when you might use each phrase.

> **Useful Language** Adding interesting details to a story
>
> I have such good memories of the time we had!
> It was wonderful.
> It was small but had a nice little balcony.
> My favorite thing about it was...
> The fish was delicious, but...
> I would love to go there again.

6 Complete the short story below with these phrases.
  a Everyone loved her!
  b I have such happy memories of this trip.
  c I would love to go again.
  d Some of the tickets were really cheap!
  e We couldn't believe it!

> A few years ago I visited a friend in Edinburgh during the famous festival they have every August. [1]_____ We had great fun and saw a lot of amazing plays, dance, and music. [2]_____ My favorite evening was when we went to see a very funny young comedian. [3]_____ On the way out of the theater we met our next-door neighbors from home! [4]_____ We all went for a coffee and ended up dancing. There was such a great atmosphere in the city. [5]_____

WRITING TASK

7 **WRITE** Using your notes from Exercise 1 and the story on page 33 as a model, write a story about a happy memory. Describe why it was happy and include some interesting details and reasons why you enjoyed it.

8 **CHECK** Use the checklist. Your story...
- ☐ describes where and when it happened and who you were with.
- ☐ adds details to make it interesting.
- ☐ describes a favorite thing.
- ☐ uses *so* and *because* to give reasons.
- ☐ uses different adjectives to describe things.

9 **REVIEW** Exchange stories with another student. Did they include at least three things from the checklist? Tell them two things you really liked and make two suggestions for improvement.

Go to page 154 for the Reflect and review.

A few years ago I went to Jericoacoara, in Brazil, for a week with my brother and sister. I have such good memories of the time we had!

I loved the house we rented. It was small but had a nice little balcony and a view of the ocean. The streets of Jeri were made of sand, so we walked around with no shoes on the whole time. It was wonderful.

My favorite thing about Jeri was the amazing, long beach—I've never seen such white sand and clear, blue water. We went there almost every day to swim and relax. It was too hot to go walking!

One evening we made a fire on the beach and watched an amazing sunset. My brother, João, cooked some fresh fish. The fish was delicious, but we had to share two between three of us, because João dropped one in the sand!

I would love to go to Jeri again. It is such a special place.

Enjoying the amazing white sand in Jericoacoara, Brazil

EXPLORE MORE!

Ask a friend or family member to tell you about one of their happy memories.

A street vendor sells a kind of ice cream called *dondurma* in Istanbul, Turkey.

3

Food for thought

GOALS

- Recognize indirect information in an article
- Talk about ongoing events in the past
- Practice words related to eating at a restaurant
- Listen for reasons in an interview
- Learn how to make your reasons clear
- Write clear instructions in a recipe

---

1 Work in pairs. Discuss the questions.

1 Look at the photo. What interests you the most in it? Why?

2 What is your favorite kind of street food? Why?

WATCH ▶

2 ▶ 3.1 Watch the video. Which foods do Brian and Tsiory like? Circle **B** or **T**.

NATIONAL GEOGRAPHIC EXPLORERS

BRIAN KASTL

TSIORY ANDRIANAVALONA

1 cauliflower	T B	4 French fries	T B
2 curry	T B	5 pizza	T B
3 fish soup	T B	6 tofu	T B

3 Make connections. Discuss the questions.

1 Do you like the foods mentioned in Exercise 2?

2 What foods do you never get bored of eating? Why?

3A
Favorite dishes

LESSON GOALS
- Understand an article about where foods come from
- Recognize direct and indirect ideas
- Plan a special meal

READING

1 Think of four countries and one or two well known foods from there. Work in groups. Take turns saying the foods and guessing the countries.

2 Read the definitions. Then quickly find the words in bold in the article on page 37.

1 A _____ is a detailed list of instructions about how to make a food or dish.

2 _____ are foods made from flour and butter. They are often sweet.

3 A _____ food is one that people have enjoyed for a very long time.

4 People add _____, like ginger or chili, to food to make it taste good.

5 To _____ means to do something nice to show that a day is special.

6 To _____ people or things means to feel sad because they are not with you.

7 _____ are the different foods you need to make a dish.

3 Look at the Reading Skill box. Circle which is the best way to summarize how this article is organized (a, b, or c).

READING SKILL
Understanding how a text is organized

Identifying how a text is organized can help you understand the content. Texts can be organized in different ways. For example:
- by topic—what the text is about.
- by sequence—the order things happened.
- by contrasting ideas—how things are different.

a three interesting stories to show how food has changed from 1683 to now

b three surprising stories to show that foods don't always come from the place we think they do

c three contrasting stories comparing foods that are popular in different places

4 Read the article. Circle the correct options to complete the sentences.

1 The first recipe for apple pie comes from *England / Portugal* rather than the U.S.

2 In 1683, people in Vienna, Austria, made pastries that looked like the *sun / moon*.

3 *Most / All* restaurants in Italy do not have spaghetti with meatballs on their menu.

4 Chicken tikka masala became very *popular / spicy* in the U.K.

5 Look at the Critical Thinking Skill box. Then work in pairs to decide if the author gives the information in 1–4 directly (D) or indirectly (I).

CRITICAL THINKING SKILL
Recognizing direct and indirect ideas

Writers sometimes choose to express information indirectly rather than say it directly.
It was raining. (direct)
She needed her umbrella. (indirect)
Recognizing both direct and indirect information can help you understand a writer's message.

1 Where the first recipe for apple pie is from. _____D_____

2 People from Vienna were happy that the attack was not successful. _____

3 People make spaghetti with meatballs using canned tomatoes. _____

4 Chicken tikka masala is a curry. _____

SPEAKING

6 Work in groups.

1 Imagine you are planning a special meal for eight people. Discuss which dishes to serve at the meal. Each person should suggest one dish.

2 Describe your menu to the class. Talk about the dishes you chose and why.

Foods with a story

¹ Every country has some well-known, **traditional** foods. We think of fish and chips as British, for example, and apple pie as American. But the way of cooking the fish for fish and chips probably comes from Portugal. And apple pie? The first apple pie **recipe** is from England, not America.

² When you bite into a delicious, buttery croissant, you probably think you are eating something French. However, the story of croissants probably begins in Vienna, Austria. In 1683, an army attacked the city, but they lost. People made special **pastries** in the shape of a moon to **celebrate** and these became very popular. About 90 years later, Marie Antoinette moved from her home in Austria to France to marry the French king. One story says that she **missed** typical foods from her country, so French chefs made these pastries for her. Over time, these became the croissants we know today.

³ Is anything more Italian than a plate of spaghetti with meatballs in tomato sauce? In Italy, this dish is usually on the menu only in tourist restaurants. Between 100 and 150 years ago, millions of Italians moved to the U.S.A. In their new country, meat, spaghetti, and canned tomatoes were all cheap and easy to find. So people invented a new recipe with these three **ingredients**.

⁴ In Indian restaurants in Britain, a favorite choice is chicken tikka masala, a dish made with **spices** and a creamy tomato sauce. However, several stories suggest chicken tikka masala is not from India. According to one story, a chef in Glasgow, Scotland, invented it in 1971 after a customer said his curry was too dry. The chef quickly made a sauce using some cream and tomato soup. The customer loved the changes, and soon the dish was popular all over the country.

a croissant

spaghetti with meatballs in tomato sauce

chicken tikka masala

EXPLORE MORE!

Search online to find out about some of these foods and which country each one really comes from:
Danish pastries, French fries, Korean tacos, Swedish meatballs, Swiss cheese.

3B
A recipe for disaster

LESSON GOALS
- Understand social media posts about cooking disasters and discuss
- Learn how to use the simple past and past progressive
- Recognize weak and strong forms of *was* and *were*

READING AND GRAMMAR

1 Work in groups. Look at the photo. Make up a story about what happened and why. Then share your story with another group.

2 Read the Grammar box. Then look at the social media posts and underline other examples of the past progressive.

> **GRAMMAR** Simple past and past progressive
>
> Use the simple past to talk about past events that are finished.
> I **made** an apple pie last week.
> Use the past progressive to describe past actions or situations that continued for some time.
> I **wasn't paying** attention.
> When something happened in the past at the same time as another action, use the past progressive to describe the longer action (or the one that started first). Use the simple past for the action that interrupted—or happened in the middle of—the longer action.
> I **was carrying** the lasagne and I **dropped** it.

Go to page 168 for the Grammar reference.

 LittleDave

I had a cooking disaster. I made an apple pie last week. I wasn't paying attention and I used salt instead of sugar by mistake. Sooooooooooo bad! #recipefordisaster

 GiorgioR

I was cooking for my sister's birthday. While I was carrying the lasagne from the oven to the table, I dropped it. The food was OK, but my foot wasn't! #recipefordisaster

 Tanya2697

I was making dinner yesterday and got a call from a friend. We were soon chatting away, and I asked my son to turn the heat off. Five minutes later I smelled smoke and ran back into the kitchen. Dinner was on fire…He thought I said, "Turn the heat up"!
#recipefordisaster #mystorywins

3 Work in pairs. Complete the sentences with one simple past form and one past progressive form.

1 I _____ (start) to feel very hungry while we _____ (wait) for our food.

2 I _____ (not add) enough cheese while I _____ (make) pasta last week.

3 While we _____ (live) in Buenos Aires, we _____ (have) many delicious meals.

4 She _____ (put) three more potatoes on my plate while I _____ (not look).

5 While we _____ (watch) TV, I _____ (decide) to order some pizza.

4 Work in pairs. Look at the diagram, which shows sentence 3 from Exercise 3. Discuss which sentence (a or b) describes it.

living in Buenos Aires

delicious meals   now

a Past actions can happen many times during a longer action.

b Many different past actions can happen at the same time.

5 Choose a different sentence from Exercise 3. In your notebook, create a diagram to show it.

6 Write true sentences using the two verbs in 1–4. Use one simple past and one past progressive form. Then compare with a partner. Are any of your sentences similar?

1 take / meet

I was taking the train to school yesterday
when I met an old friend.

2 eat / find

_____

3 buy / drop

_____

4 walk / see

_____

EXPLORE MORE!

Search online for more stories about people's "cooking disasters." How many of the stories use past progressive verbs?

PRONUNCIATION

7 🔊 **3.1** Look at the Clear Voice box. Listen to the examples. Tell a partner what you notice about the strong and weak forms.

CLEAR VOICE

Understanding weak forms (1): *was* and *were*

Like most auxiliary verbs, *was* and *were* have two pronunciations: weak and strong. The weak form is the usual way of saying these words in an affirmative sentence.

*I **was** making dinner yesterday.* /wəz/

*We **were** soon chatting away.* /wər/

However, the strong form is common in short answers to questions and in negative sentences.

*A: Who **was** cooking?* /wɒz/   *B: We **were**.* /wɜːr/

*She **wasn't** happy about it.* /wɒznt/

8 🔊 **3.2** Look at the underlined auxiliaries in sentences 1–4. Will it be a strong or a weak form? Listen and check. Which form is easier for you to recognize? Tell a partner.

1 He <u>was</u> having sushi for lunch.

2 They <u>weren't</u> interested in eating out.

3 I <u>wasn't</u> happy with the food, but he <u>was</u>.

4 A: Who <u>was</u> looking for the recipe?
   B: We <u>were</u>.

SPEAKING

9 Choose two of the disasters from the list below that happened to you or to a person you know. Practice telling the story of what happened.

a burning something or causing a fire

b cooking something for too long / not long enough

c dropping something on the floor

d forgetting an important ingredient

e using the wrong ingredient

10 Work in groups. Take turns telling your stories. Use the simple past and past progressive correctly.

LESSON GOALS
- Listen for reasons in an interview
- Learn vocabulary for eating at a restaurant
- Practice stressing words to express meaning
- Talk about restaurant experiences

SPEAKING

1 Work in groups. Read the text about different kinds of restaurant customers. Discuss the questions.

1 Do you think the descriptions are trying to be serious or funny? Why?

2 Which type of restaurant customer are you most similar to? Why?

Different Restaurant Customers

Picture takers These customers only order food that looks good in photos. They take photos of each dish and post them online.

Conversation lovers Diners like these don't care about the food because they're interested in talking, not eating. Their meals take a long time because they talk, and talk, and talk, and…

Food experts These restaurant customers usually order only delicious, high-quality dishes. Their meals take a long time because they ask hundreds of questions about the ingredients.

Money savers These kinds of restaurant-goers only order cheap dishes. Their meals take a long time because they check the price of everything and then calculate how much it is all going to cost.

Healthy livers Customers like these only order low-fat, low-salt, and low-sugar food… even if it's also low-taste. They never eat dessert and they leave quickly to get to the gym.

Caroline Bennett

LISTENING

2 🎧 **3.3** Listen to an interview with Caroline Bennett, a successful restaurant owner. Match the beginnings of the sentences (1–5) with the endings (a–e).

1 In the 1980s, Caroline had the chance to

2 In 1994, Caroline decided she wanted to

3 About 20 years ago, Caroline chose to

4 In 2004, Caroline made the decision to

5 A few years ago, Caroline's customers began to

a live in Japan for a year. _____

b open a sushi restaurant. _____

c start a second company. _____

d take a lot of photos. _____

e take tuna off her menu. _____

3 🎧 **3.3** Look at the Listening Skill box. Then listen to the interview again. In your notebook, write answers to questions 1–4.

LISTENING SKILL
Listening for reasons

It's often important to understand the reason why a thing happened or a person did something. Speakers sometimes use specific phrases to give reasons, such as *because (of)* or *one reason was*. You can also think about possible reasons by asking yourself *Why did this happen?*

1 Why did Caroline start a restaurant?

2 Why did she stop selling tuna?

3 Why did she start a second company?

4 Why are many people changing what they eat?

VOCABULARY

4 🎧 **3.4** Work in pairs. Look at the excerpt from the interview. Answer questions 1–7 below. Then listen and check.

"**Raw** fish is really popular now. So people know more about it and they expect their sushi to be both **delicious** and cheap. [...] More people are **vegetarian** or **vegan** than before. And even people who do eat meat may eat it rarely. [...] People want to try new **dishes** and flavors when they eat out. [...] I know somebody who started a pop-up restaurant in her home. She **prepares** food for customers in her own kitchen. She **serves** them in her home, too."

Which word in bold means...

1 very good to eat?
2 not cooked?
3 a type of food served as part of a meal?
4 people who do not eat meat?
5 people who do not eat anything from animals?
6 to bring food to people?
7 to make food ready for people to eat?

Go to page 161 for the Vocabulary reference.

5 Complete the three social media posts with the correct form of the words from Exercise 4.

> I became a(n) ¹_____ a couple of months ago. Not eating meat at all! But I don't think I can become a(n) ²_____ because I like cheese too much!

> Had sushi and sashimi for the first time yesterday. Didn't think ³_____ fish would be so good! Liked watching the chefs ⁴_____ it. The waiters ⁵_____ the food on beautiful plates from Japan, too.

> My friend and I chose the same chicken ⁶_____ at our local Thai restaurant. She thought it was ⁷_____, but it was a little too spicy for me.

PRONUNCIATION

6 🎧 **3.5** Look at the Clear Voice box. Listen and repeat.

CLEAR VOICE
Stressing words to express meaning

To make the meaning of a sentence clear, especially to correct a mistake, you can give extra stress to a word or phrase.
*Excuse me, **I** ordered the salmon.* (="You have given the dish I ordered to the wrong person.")
*Excuse me, I ordered the **salmon**.* (="You have given me the wrong dish.")

7 🎧 **3.6** Look at the conversations between a waiter (W) and a customer (C). Underline which word(s) you think the customer will stress. Then listen, check, and repeat.

1 W: Here you go—two small teas and two pastries.
   C: Actually, we ordered two small coffees and two pastries.
2 W: Here you go—two large pizzas and salads.
   C: Actually, we ordered two small pizzas and salads.
3 W: Here you go—a burger with a green salad.
   C: Actually, I ordered a burger with fries.
4 W: Here you go—one chicken curry and one bowl of rice.
   C: Actually, we ordered two chicken curries and two bowls of rice.

8 In pairs, write your own scenarios like those in Exercise 7. Practice your conversations. Take turns being the waiter and customer. Use stress to express meaning.

SPEAKING

9 Work in groups. Talk about a time when you had a great or terrible meal at a restaurant. Say:
- which type of restaurant you went to.
- where the restaurant was.
- why you went there.
- what food you had.
- how much you enjoyed or hated it.

EXPLORE MORE!

Choose one of the customer types from the text in Exercise 1. Then search online to find a restaurant that might be good for that person. Share what you found with the class.

3D
Making your reasons clear

LESSON GOALS
- Understand and use indefinite pronouns correctly
- Learn ways to make your reasons clear
- Roleplay conversations to practice giving reasons

SPEAKING

1 Work in pairs. Discuss the questions.
1 What is your favorite type of restaurant?
2 When you are choosing a restaurant to eat at, what things are important for you, e.g., the type of food, the prices, the staff?

READING AND GRAMMAR

2 Read the restaurant advertisement. What food do they serve at Paolo's?

_____

_____

> At Paolo's Italian Café, we have something for everyone. We serve delicious pasta, fish, and meat dishes, and you won't find a better pizza anywhere. Nobody makes better desserts and everything's a great price! You can ask for something that's not on the menu because Chef Paolo can make anything! Our food is also available to go.

3 Read the Grammar box. Work in pairs. Underline three more indefinite pronouns in the restaurant ad in Exercise 2.

GRAMMAR Indefinite pronouns

Use indefinite pronouns to talk about people or things in general. Many indefinite pronouns combine *some-*, *any-*, *every-*, or *no-* with *-body*, *-one*, *-thing*, or *-where*.
You can ask for **something** that's not on the menu (*some-* is common in positive statements)
everything's a great price (*every-* is common in questions, positive, and negative statements)
you won't find a better pizza **anywhere** (*any-* is common in questions and in sentences with *not*)
Nobody makes better desserts. (because *no-* pronouns mean *not any-*, don't use *not* with them)

Go to page 168 for the Grammar reference.

4 Work in pairs. Complete sentence pairs 1–6 with these indefinite pronouns.

anywhere	anything	everyone	everything
nobody	nothing	somebody	

1 I think _____ was happy to eat pizza again. = I don't think **anyone** was unhappy to eat pizza again.

2 _____ on our menu is vegetarian. = **Nothing** on our menu has meat or fish in it.

3 I didn't have _____ to eat for breakfast. = I had _____ to eat for breakfast.

4 _____ said the food was too spicy. = I didn't hear **anyone** say the food was too spicy.

5 Can **anybody** help me wash the dishes? = I'd like _____ to help me wash the dishes.

6 We couldn't find _____ that sold vegetarian food. = **Nowhere** we looked served vegetarian food.

5 Work in groups. Discuss possible problems you might have in each situation and why.
- cooking for somebody you don't know very well
- going to a restaurant with friends when everyone likes different types of food
- finding somewhere to eat in a city you don't know very well

MY VOICE ▶

6 ▶ 3.2 Watch the video about a way to communicate more effectively. Then discuss the questions in pairs.
1 Why did Luke have problems in the first two examples?
2 Why did Luke not have problems in the second two examples?

7 Look at the Communication Skill box. Work in groups. Discuss whether it would be helpful or not helpful to explain your reason(s) in situations 1–4 and why.

COMMUNICATION SKILL
Making your reasons clear

Mentioning the reason why you are saying something or asking why another person has said something can be particularly important when you are talking to someone who has a different communication style or speaks a different language. Being clear about your reasons can help you avoid…
- problems with a bad decision.
- making someone else unhappy or uncomfortable.
- a difficult or possibly dangerous situation.

1 You don't want to join some friends who are sitting outside at a café, because it's too cold.
2 You are very late to dinner at your boss's house because your train was canceled.
3 You don't want to meet with your colleagues for Thai food because you can't eat peanuts and are worried that some of the dishes will contain them.
4 You decide not to go to your end-of-year work party because you don't like parties.

SPEAKING

8 Look at the Useful Language box. Then work in pairs to answer questions 1–3.

> **Useful Language** Giving reasons
> The reason is that… / (This is) because…
> You see,… / It's just that… / The thing is,…
> I'd rather… because… / I'd prefer… as… /
> Actually, since… , could… ?

Which phrases would you use to…
1 give your reason indirectly?
2 state your reason directly?
3 explain why you want to do something different?

9 **OWN IT!** Work in pairs. Read the situations below. Create two roleplays. Use the Useful Language box to help you.
1 One of you really wants to eat at a popular Indian restaurant, but the other person doesn't like spicy food.
2 One of you gives the other person a homemade cake, but the other person can't eat it because they can't eat eggs.

3E
Comfort food recipes

LESSON GOALS
- Give clear and accurate instructions
- Solve possible problems
- Write a recipe

SPEAKING

1 Work in groups. Read the definition. Then discuss questions 1 and 2 below.

> comfort food /ˈcʌmfət ˌfuːd/ [noun: usually uncountable] food that makes you feel better, or that reminds you of home cooking or your childhood

1 What is your favorite comfort food? Why do you like it?
2 Do your comfort foods change at different times of year or when you are not well?

READING FOR WRITING

NATIONAL GEOGRAPHIC EXPLORERS

2 Work in pairs. Student A: Read Tsiory Andrianavalona's recipe. Student B: Read Brian Kastl's recipe. Then follow steps 1 and 2.

1 Are there any ingredients the cook can choose to add or not?
2 Tell your partner the ingredients they need to make your recipe, then explain how to make it.

3 Work in pairs. Discuss which dish you would prefer to eat, and why.

Dried fish soup

Ingredients
- 2 whole dried fish
- 1 large onion
- 3 potatoes
- 2 or 3 cups of green vegetables
- a little oil
- 3½ cups of water
- salt and pepper

Preparation
You first need to cover the dried fish in water and leave them for at least half an hour. While the fish are soaking, chop the onion and potatoes. Wash and chop some green vegetables, like sweet potato leaves. Cook the onion in the oil. When the onion is soft, add the fish and half a cup of water, and maybe a little salt and black pepper, too. After about ten minutes, add three more cups of water, the potatoes, and the greens. Keep cooking the soup until the potatoes are soft. Serve it with a plate of rice.

Green curry with tofu

Ingredients
- 1 small onion
- 1 chili
- 4 or 5 cups of mixed vegetables
- 300 grams of tofu
- some oil
- 2 teaspoons of green curry paste
- 1 cup of coconut milk
- fish sauce or soy sauce
- juice from 1 lime

Preparation
Chop the onion and chili. (Do you like spicy food? Use more than one chili!) Also chop the vegetables—they can be any vegetables you like—and the tofu. Cook the onion in oil for three minutes. Then add the chili and cook for one more minute. Add the green curry paste and cook for another minute. Add a cup of hot water, the coconut milk, and some fish or soy sauce, and cook until it boils. Then, reduce the heat and cook for five minutes. Next, add the vegetables and tofu. Finally, add some lime juice and enjoy it with a bowl of rice.

4 Look at the Writing Skill box. In addition to recipes, can you think of some other kinds of writing that need clear instructions? Discuss with a partner.

WRITING SKILL
Giving clear instructions

Recipes and other kinds of descriptions of how to do something need to be clear and accurate. Some examples include:

instruction	examples
• saying how much	*500 grams of sugar / two eggs*
• saying how long or how often	*cook for 40 minutes / leave for one hour*
• giving the order of steps	*first / next / after that / at the same time / before*
• giving more information	*at 200 degrees / chop into small pieces*

5 Read the two recipes again. Underline some examples of the following.

1 information about how much
2 information about how long or how often
3 words that explain the order of steps
4 other information that is important

6 Work in pairs. Look at the Critical Thinking Skill box. Then read sentences a and b. Which sentence can you add to Brian's recipe and which to Tsiory's? Decide the correct place to add them.

CRITICAL THINKING SKILL
Solving possible problems

When writing or giving instructions, think about common problems that people following the instructions might have. Then mention those problems in your instructions and suggest ways to solve or avoid them.

a Make sure you cook the vegetables until they are soft enough to eat.
b Do not stir the pot much because the fish will break into pieces.

7 Work in groups. Read the short recipe, then complete tasks 1–3.

> Break some eggs into a bowl. Add some ingredients such as cheese, mushrooms, and chopped tomatoes. Add salt and pepper. Mix everything well. Cook it.

1 Discuss what dish this recipe might be for and what other ingredients you could add.
2 In your notebooks, rewrite the recipe using accurate information and the ingredients you chose. Mention possible problems and give solutions, too.
3 Discuss your new version of the recipe with the class. Which groups' recipes do you want to eat? Why?

WRITING TASK

8 **WRITE** Using Tsiory's and Brian's recipes as a model, follow the steps to write a recipe.
1 Choose a dish you know how to make.
2 Make notes about how to prepare this food.
3 Write your recipe.

9 **CHECK** Use the checklist. Your recipe...
☐ gives clear instructions about how much to use of each ingredient.
☐ gives clear instructions about how long or how often to do each step.
☐ uses the correct verbs for the preparation of the food.
☐ gives clear information about the order of the steps.
☐ explains information that other people may not know.

10 **REVIEW** Exchange recipes with another student. Did they include at least three things from the checklist? Offer at least one idea for how to improve their writing. Discuss how much you want to try each other's recipes.

Go to page 155 for the Reflect and review.

EXPLORE MORE!

Find a simple recipe online and try to follow it.

Nicholas Dlamini leads the group in the 2019 Tour de Yorkshire bike race, U.K.

4

Goals and ambition

GOALS

- Scan an article about achieving an ambition
- Talk about future plans
- Talk about goals and motivation
- Recognize fillers in a podcast
- Explore ways to give encouraging feedback
- Write comments on an online forum

1 Work in pairs. Discuss the questions.

1 Look at the photo. How do you think the people in the race feel?

2 Is there anything difficult that you want to do? How do you plan to achieve it?

WATCH ▶

2 ▶ 4.1 Watch the video. How do Abby and Andrej answer these questions? Discuss with a partner.

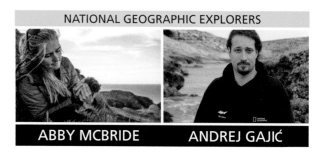

NATIONAL GEOGRAPHIC EXPLORERS

ABBY MCBRIDE | ANDREJ GAJIĆ

1 What do you do to stay fit and healthy?

2 Do you have health and fitness goals?

3 Make connections. In what ways are your fitness habits and goals similar or different from those of Abby and Andrej? Tell a partner.

4A
Achieving your ambitions

LESSON GOALS
• Scan an online article for information
• Categorize information
• Talk about ambitions

READING

1 Work in pairs and discuss the questions.
1 What is an ambition?
2 What ambitions do you have?
3 What steps are you taking toward achieving your ambitions?

2 Work in pairs. Match these verbs a–f with their meanings 1–6.

a achieve	b coach	c concentrate
d give up	e push	f train

1 succeed at a goal _____
2 stop trying to do something _____
3 practice a sport _____
4 think carefully and pay attention _____
5 force someone to do something _____
6 teach athletes _____

3 Look at the Reading Skill box. How is scanning different from skimming? See page 12. How can scanning help you to read? Discuss with a partner.

READING SKILL
Scanning

Scanning a text can help you to find information that you need quickly.
• To find out *when*: scan for numbers
• To find out *where*: scan for capital letters
• To find out *who*: scan for capital letters, names, and job titles
• To find out *what*: scan for information related to what you want to know (e.g., look for *work* or *study* to find what someone does)

4 Scan the online article about Mark Chan on page 49. In your notebook, answer questions 1–6.
1 Where is Mark from?
2 What two things take up most of Mark's time?

3 What is Mark's main ambition?
4 When did Mark first try climbing?
5 Who trains Mark now?
6 Who else does Mark's coach work with?

5 Read the article again. Are these sentences true (T) or false (F)?
1 Mark is confident that he will go to the Olympics.   T   F
2 Mark studies, then trains every day.   T   F
3 Mark plans to live in the U.K.   T   F

6 Work in pairs. Which parts of Mark's life would you enjoy or find difficult?

7 Look at the Critical Thinking Skill box. Then check (✓) the actions 1–8 that are helpful for achieving ambitions.

CRITICAL THINKING SKILL
Categorizing

You can categorize things by thinking about how they are the same or different, for example, deciding if information is true or false, or positive or negative. Putting information into different categories can help you think about and understand it.

1 ☐ give up
2 ☐ listen to friends, teachers, or coaches
3 ☐ give 100%
4 ☐ practice as much as possible
5 ☐ have an ambition
6 ☐ do nothing
7 ☐ worry about failing
8 ☐ take part in races and events

SPEAKING

8 Work in pairs. Discuss the questions.
1 What are you training for or practicing right now, e.g., sports, languages, or hobbies?
2 Which of the things in Exercise 7 do you do when things get difficult?
3 Are you someone who pushes yourself?

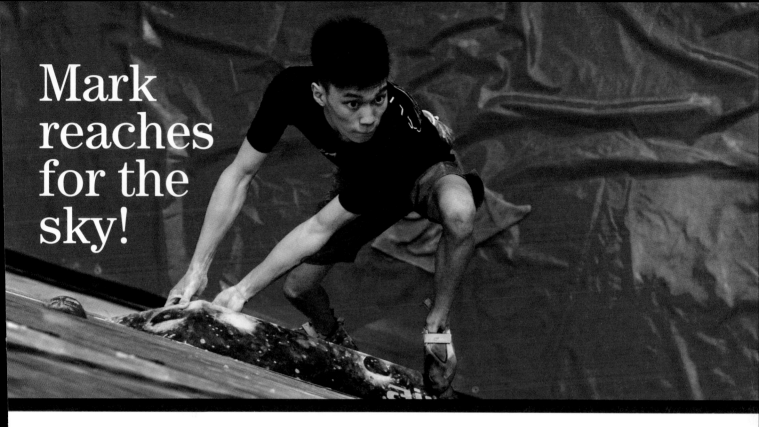

Mark reaches for the sky!

Mark Chan is a hardworking student with a dream. In his free time he loves climbing and he was the first Singaporean to climb in the Youth Olympic Games. His ambition is to climb for Singapore in the next Olympics.

Mark started climbing when he was fourteen years old. His school coach thought he was so good that he introduced him to the Singapore national team. He made the team and that's when he started to push himself.

Mark studies aerospace engineering at college. He says that in Singapore the cost of living is very high, so everyone has to study hard to get a good job. His parents also push him to succeed. It's hard to find time for both school and training. He worries that he won't make the Olympics because he doesn't have enough time to train, but he wants to try.

To do it, Mark trains as much as possible. He races in every climbing competition that he can, and goes to the gym every day after class. He says it's very tiring but that he's "working hard for what I really want." Mark knows that to achieve his goal he has to give 100%. Practice makes perfect, so he often does the same climbing move many times before he gets it right. And he never gives up! Next year, he's moving to the U.K. to train with his coach.

Mark's coach, Ian Dunn, has 40 years of experience and coaches the Great Britain climbing team. He wants to push his climbers and help them succeed. He says that Mark needs to concentrate and "be more confident." He's excited that Mark is going to work with him in the U.K. He thinks Mark's future is "really bright."

Mark plans to train hard. We hope he makes it to the Olympics!

Follow this site for updates!

EXPLORE MORE!

Do you think Mark qualified for the Olympics? Search online for "Mark Chan climber" to find out.

4B
Setting goals

LESSON GOALS
- Listen to people talking about their goals
- Use *going to* and the present progressive for future plans
- Understand weak forms

LISTENING AND GRAMMAR

1 Work in pairs. Discuss the questions.

1 Do you set goals for the future or do you live in the moment?

2 What are the advantages and disadvantages of making future plans or of living in the moment?

NATIONAL GEOGRAPHIC EXPLORERS

2 🎧 **4.1** Listen to Andrej Gajić and Abby McBride. Do they set goals, live in the moment, or both? Discuss with a partner.

3 🎧 **4.1** Listen again. Are these goals Andrej's or Abby's? Check (✓) the correct answers.

	Andrej	Abby
1 protect wildlife with storytelling	☐	☐
2 protect more animals	☐	☐
3 teach people on social media	☐	☐
4 stop using social media	☐	☐
5 go to Patagonia	☐	☐
6 travel to Vietnam	☐	☐
7 work in the U.S.A.	☐	☐
8 practice Spanish	☐	☐
9 learn more about the ocean	☐	☐
10 do more things they love	☐	☐

Andrej Gajić

Abby McBride

4 Read the Grammar box. Then underline another example of each form in the audioscript for track 4.1 on page 185.

GRAMMAR Future plans

Going to
Use *going to* + base verb for plans and future intentions.
I'm **going to learn** more about my science.

Present progressive
Use the present progressive for definite arrangements in the future (sometimes used with a time, day, or date).
I**'m traveling** in South America soon.

Go to page 169 for the Grammar reference.

5 Work in pairs. Look at the pairs of sentences (1–5). Discuss the difference in meaning, if any, between each option, a and b.

1 a They're moving on May 7.
  b They're going to move.
2 a I'm starting a class soon.
  b I'm going to start a class soon.
3 a We're running at 3 p.m.
  b We're going to go for a run at 3 p.m.
4 a He's taking a driving lesson tomorrow.
  b He's going to take a driving lesson.
5 a I'm practicing my English this summer.
  b In the summer, I'm going to practice my English.

6 Complete the questions about future plans using the present progressive or *going to*. Then ask and answer the questions in pairs.

1 What _____ you _____ (do) tonight?
2 How _____ you _____ (study) for your exams?
3 Where _____ you _____ (go) on your next vacation?
4 _____ you _____ (meet) anyone after class?
5 _____ you _____ (learn) a new skill this year?

PRONUNCIATION

7 🎧 4.2 Look at the Clear Voice box. Then listen to the example and tell a partner what you notice about the stressed words and weak forms.

CLEAR VOICE
Understanding weak forms (2): prepositions and articles

Some words, like prepositions (*at, to, for*) and articles (*a, an, the*), are difficult to hear because they're not stressed. This means that, for example, the *to* in *going to* is often weak and difficult to hear.
I'm going **to** meet **a** friend **at** six.

---

8 🎧 4.3 Listen to sentences 1–4 and underline the stressed words. Then listen again and circle the weak forms.

1 I'm planning to write a book.
2 He's going to Brazil next summer.
3 I'm visiting my family soon.
4 She's staying with her parents for another year.

SPEAKING

9 Complete the sentences about your plans. Discuss with a partner.

1 I'm going to learn how to _____.
2 I'm planning to visit _____.
3 I'm meeting _____ next week.
4 I'm hoping to _____.
5 I'm going to try to _____.
6 I'm _____ on the weekend.
7 This summer I'm _____.

10 Work in pairs. Discuss the questions. Think about your work and personal life. Use the future forms.

1 Do you have any short-, medium-, or long-term goals? What are they?
2 Are any of your goals similar to the explorers?

4C
What motivates you?

LESSON GOALS
- Talk about motivation
- Recognize fillers in a podcast
- Learn to make promises, offers, and spontaneous decisions
- Say words beginning with /p/ and /b/

VOCABULARY

1 Work in pairs. Read the definition. Then read the quotations about motivation. Discuss which ones you agree with.

> motivation /ˌməʊtɪˈveɪʃ(ə)n/ [noun: usually uncountable] a feeling of being excited and interested, which makes you want to do something

"However difficult life may seem, there is always something you can do, and succeed at. It matters that you don't just give up."

Stephen Hawking, scientist, mathematician, and author

"Motivation comes from working on things we care about. It also comes from working with people we care about."

Sheryl Sandberg, Facebook executive

"No one will motivate you. Only you can motivate you."

Mark Hunter, sales expert

2 🎧 4.4 Look at the infographic below. Then, complete the sentences with these words. Then listen and check.

challenge	encourage	praise
prize	punish	reward

1 I like to get _____ or hear that I'm doing well from my family and friends.
2 When my brother and I argued, my parents didn't let us watch TV, to _____ us.
3 It's important to _____ a child when they are learning an instrument.
4 I won a(n) _____ for being the best basketball player in my school.
5 I enjoy trying difficult things and always look for a new _____ every year.
6 We are offering a _____ of $100 for information about our missing cat.

Go to page 161 for the Vocabulary reference.

WHAT MOTIVATES PEOPLE

EXTERNAL MOTIVATION

a prize

a reward

praise

avoiding punishment

SELF-MOTIVATION

fun

success

purpose

happiness

52

3 Work in pairs. Use the words in Exercise 2 and the infographic to discuss what motivates you.

LISTENING

4 🎧 4.5 Listen to the podcast about motivation. What is Linzi motivated to do? What does she need help with motivation for? Discuss with a partner.

5 🎧 4.5 Listen again. Circle true (T) or false (F) for each statement.

1 Linzi's parents motivate her.　　　　　T　F
2 Linzi's brother pushes her to work hard.　T　F
3 Research shows that money motivates　T　F
　people for thinking tasks.
4 Linzi is motivated to change the world.　T　F
5 Maria's three motivation rules are　　T　F
　"choose," "improve," and "enjoy."

6 🎧 4.6 Look at the Listening Skill box. Then listen to the excerpts from the podcast and complete statements 1–5 with the fillers.

LISTENING SKILL
Recognizing fillers

Speakers use fillers to give themselves time to think. They use words such as *oh, um, so,* and *like,* and phrases such as *y'know* and *I mean.* Fillers are usually not stressed and are often said quickly and quietly. Learning to recognize fillers can help you focus on the words that give information.

1 _____Well_____, I'll explain! _____, one experiment asked two groups to do the same task.
2 _____, the task was, _____, a puzzle, so people had to, _____, think.
3 Yes, I do. _____, I don't like working all day every day, but I think my research is really important.
4 What, _____, like basketball?
5 Like trying to, _____, help change the world—that makes me feel good, so it's, _____, motivating.

GRAMMAR

7 Read the Grammar box. Are examples 1–3 promises, offers, or decisions (P, O, D)?

> **GRAMMAR**　*will* and *won't* for promises, offers, and spontaneous decisions
>
> Use *will* and *won't* for promises, offers, and for decisions made at the time of speaking.
> Promises: *I won't tell anyone!*
> Offers: *I'll help motivate you.*
> Decisions: *Well, OK, I'll come!*

Go to page 169 for the Grammar reference.

1 A: The gym is closed tomorrow.
　B: I'll go today.　　　　　　_____
2 A: This is really difficult.
　B: I'll help you tonight.　　_____
3 A: Are we still friends?
　B: I'll always be your friend!　_____

8 Write a response to each sentence. Use *will* to make a promise, offer, or decision.

1 I have to cook party food for 40 people.

　_____

2 Please don't tell her. It's a surprise!

　_____

3 I want to learn the guitar.

　_____

PRONUNCIATION

9 🎧 4.7 Look at the Clear Voice box. Listen and repeat.

CLEAR VOICE
Saying words beginning with /p/ and /b/

To make the sounds /p/ or /b/, close your lips then open them quickly to let out the air.

Hold a piece of paper in front of your mouth. It should move more for /p/ than for /b/. Touch your throat. It should vibrate for /b/ but not for /p/.

/p/ *purpose, praise* **/b/** *basketball, brother*

SPEAKING

10 Work in groups. Discuss the best ways to motivate children. Is it different for adults?

Giving encouraging feedback

LESSON GOALS
• Learn to give encouraging feedback
• Practice language to give encouraging feedback and make suggestions
• Practice ways to give feedback

SPEAKING

1 Look at the photo. Work in pairs. Discuss how you feel when you give and get feedback.

2 Work in pairs. Read about Natalia and answer the questions.

1 Do you agree with how Isabella is giving Natalia feedback?

2 What advice can you give Isabella?

Natalia is having dinner with her roommates. One roommate, Isabella, tells Natalia that she needs to clean the apartment more often. She jokes about the time that Natalia cleaned the bathroom but forgot to change the towels. Natalia remembers and knows that Isabella is right. Her other roommates don't say anything and Natalia feels embarrassed and upset. She doesn't clean the apartment the next day because she worries that she won't do it the way Isabella likes.

3 Read the examples of feedback (1–4). Work in pairs. Discuss questions a and b below.

1 You'll need to try harder. You're really slow.

2 That was really difficult. You had a lot of good ideas for your first time.

3 Good idea to use a different color. You're getting better. Keep on trying!

4 Well, that song was awful. You need more practice.

5 So you made a mistake! Don't worry, now you know what not to do!

a Which ones do you think would help you improve next time?

b Which ones would you like to hear?

MY VOICE ▶

4 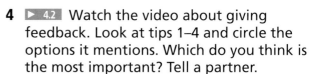 **▶ 4.2** Watch the video about giving feedback. Look at tips 1–4 and circle the options it mentions. Which do you think is the most important? Tell a partner.

1 Encourage people for *working hard* / *trying new things*.

2 Be *positive* / *negative*.

3 Ask each other for *advice* / *feelings*.

4 Give ideas for how to *improve* / *work with others*.

5 Look at the Communication Skill box. Read the feedback in Exercise 3 again and match each example of helpful feedback with the types of feedback in the box. There is not an example of every type of feedback.

COMMUNICATION SKILL
Giving encouraging feedback

When giving feedback, try not to focus too much on what someone didn't do well. Make sure you also tell them how they can improve next time. First, you can give positive feedback for:

• working hard _____
• making small changes _____
• trying new things _____
• learning from mistakes _____
• succeeding _____

Then you can suggest how to improve. Feedback should be a conversation, so try to listen to the other person's opinion as well!

6 Read the Useful Language box. In your notebook, rewrite the examples of unhelpful feedback in Exercise 3 to be helpful. Use a phrase or idea from each section.

Useful Language   Giving encouraging feedback

Introducing the feedback
I can see that you (found that hard).
I noticed that you (didn't get that right).
That's a shame. Sorry (you missed).

Asking for and listening to opinions
What do you think of this?
How did you feel?
I can understand why you say that.

Talking about the positives
That was hard. You spent a lot of time on it.
I can see you worked hard.
Keep practicing! You're getting better!

Making suggestions for improvements
Have you tried (writing everything down)?
Next time you could try (calling them first).

7 Work in pairs. Look at the situations. Discuss how you could give helpful feedback in each situation.
• Your sister came last in a race.
• Your son failed his exam.
• Your neighbor has parked badly, and now you can't move your car.

SPEAKING

8 **OWN IT!** Work in pairs. Discuss how you would give helpful feedback to Wan, Surio, and Rowan. How do you think you would feel giving feedback? How do you think they would feel receiving your feedback?

Wan
You have a test coming up and go to the library after class every day. Your friend, Wan, comes with you. She takes some notes and reads a little, but also spends a lot of time on her phone. You are worried about her. She didn't pass her last test.

Surio
Your best friend, Surio, wants to save money for a vacation, but he isn't very successful. He goes out less now, but you still think he could save more money. For example, he still buys coffee at the school café every day and often buys lunch, too.

Rowan
You are in a soccer team with some friends. You have important games soon. Your team member, Rowan, comes to all the practice sessions and tries hard, but isn't good at passing the ball. Last week he accidentally scored a goal for the other team and also accidentally kicked another player.

9 Work in pairs. Discuss the questions.
1 Think of a time you had a positive or negative experience of *getting* feedback. What happened?
2 Think of a time you had a positive or negative experience of *giving* feedback. What happened? What could you do differently?

EXPLORE MORE!

Find other tips for giving feedback. Search online for "giving feedback."

4E
Language-learning goals

LESSON GOALS
- Read an online forum
- Use apostrophes correctly
- Reflect on your language-learning goals
- Write about language-learning goals

READING FOR WRITING

1 Read the forum posts. Underline the reasons people give for learning English.

What are your language-learning goals?

 Krzysztof_the_student: I'd really like to speak English well. I'd love to understand everything.

Jan 22nd 👍 4

 Andres089: Me too! I want to have conversations in English. I don't care about making mistakes.

Jan 22nd 👍 3

 Abdallah_H: I agree. I also don't need to be perfect…and I don't want to change my accent—it's part of who I am!

Jan 23rd 👍 2

 Shahla92: I work at an international company, so many of my customers speak English.

Jan 24th 👍 2

 Andres089: I speak a lot of English at work, too. I'd love to send emails quickly and understand phone calls.

Jan 25th 2

 Jenny_R: My language goal is just to enjoy learning. I try to study for 30 minutes every day.

Jan 26th 1

 Sofia_smiles: When I started learning English I just wanted to order food, but now I hope to be in the advanced class one day.

Jan 26th 👍 3

 The_Great_Nawal: I dream of being in the advanced class, too. I need C1 level for college. I'll have to do research in English. 🙂

Jan 26th 3

2 Work in pairs. Discuss the questions.

1 Which of the people in Exercise 1 do you think have realistic goals?

2 Whose learning goals are similar to your own? Which are different?

3 What could the people in the forum do to work toward their goals?

3 Look at the Writing Skill box. Then correct the mistakes in the messages below.

WRITING SKILL
Using apostrophes

Forums are informal and people write quickly. Here are some common mistakes with apostrophes.

You're / your: *You're* is the short form of *you are*. *Your* is a possessive adjective: *Is this **your** book?*

It's / its: *It's* is the short form of *it is*. *Its* is a possessive adjective: ***It's** hard to learn a language and **its** rules.*

They're / there / their: See the infographic on page 28.

Apostrophes: Apostrophe + *s* (*'s*) can be used with a noun to show possession or to contract two words. It is not used to show plurals.

*Here**'s** Dorothy**'s** bag.*

 Jin: I'd love to speak very good English. My wifes Scottish and I live in Scotland now. Id like to talk to my wifes family and understand all they're joke's! I need to speak English well to get a U.K. passport, too. 🙂

Jan 27th 👍 2

 Sofia_smiles: You're English is great. Its hard, but we can do this!

Jan 27th

 The_Great_Nawal: Yes! We can!

Jan 27th

 Jin: ☹

Jan 27th

4 Look at the Useful Language box. Find examples of each form (1–4) in the forum posts.

> **Useful Language**   Talking about goals
>
> I dream of (being an English teacher).
> I want / I'd really like to (improve my pronunciation).
> I hope to (move to the U.S.).
> I'd love to (speak more languages).
> I need to (speak English for my work).
> I try to (watch English TV shows).

1 *hope* + noun or *hope to* + verb _____

2 *(don't) want / need / try to* _____

3 *dream of* + verb-*ing* _____

4 *would / 'd* + *like / love to* + verb

_____

5 In your notebook, write 4–6 statements about your language-learning goals using the Useful Language. Use the ideas in the forum posts to help you.

6 Work in groups. Discuss your ideas from Exercise 5. Are any of the language-learning goals very popular or unpopular with other students?

EXPLORE MORE!

Find a forum about language-learning goals online. Search for "language-learning goals forum." Are the comments similar or different from those in your class? Write your own comment.

WRITING TASK

7 **WRITE** Write your own forum post on a piece of paper. Ask a question about language-learning goals. Include a username. Pass your paper to another classmate. Take someone else's paper and answer their question. Continue until you have answered all your classmates' questions.

Do you want to change your accent?
Would you like to use your English to live in another country?

8 **CHECK** Use the checklist. Each forum post...
☐ has a clear language-learning goal.
☐ answers the question.
☐ uses apostrophes correctly.
☐ uses would *like / love to* or *hope / want / need / try / dream of*.

9 **REVIEW** Complete the tasks.

Check each forum post. Does it include at least three things from the checklist? Make any corrections you think it needs. Then, in pairs discuss what you think of the different responses to your questions.

Go to page 155 for the Reflect and review.

A houseboat on Black River, Michigan, U.S. in the fall

5

Home and away

GOALS

- Use context to find meaning in a review
- Use zero and first conditionals to talk about facts, suggestions, and consequences
- Use extreme adjectives
- Understand the key points of a conversation
- Learn strategies to show you can be flexible
- Write online messages about accommodations

1 Work in pairs. Discuss the questions.

1 Look at the photo. What is special about the house?

2 Would you like to stay somewhere like this? Why or why not?

WATCH ▶

NATIONAL GEOGRAPHIC EXPLORERS

ALEXIS CHAPPUIS   ELLIE DE CASTRO

2  Watch the video. Which two places does each explorer think of as home? Why? Discuss with a partner.

3 Make connections. Discuss the questions with a partner.

1 Where do you think of as home?

2 Is there anywhere that you think of as a second home?

A tidy house makes a calm home

LESSON GOALS
- Use context to find meaning in a review
- Recognize the difference between fact and opinion
- Discuss the advantages and disadvantages of being tidy

READING

1 Work in pairs. Are you a tidy person? Do you fold your clothes carefully, like in the photo?

2 Quickly read the review of a TV show on page 61. What is the show about? Did the reviewer like the show? Tell a partner.

3 Look at the Reading Skill box. Work in pairs. Find a word in the review that you don't know. Look at the words around it and discuss what it might mean.

READING SKILL
Finding meaning (1): using context

When you see a new word, look at the text around it to help you understand the meaning before you use a dictionary. There may be examples, words with similar or opposite meanings, or even an explanation in the sentence before or after. It can be helpful to decide if the word is a verb, a noun, or an adjective before you look.

4 Read the review again then match these words with the definitions. One definition has two answers.

a charity	b messy
c pile	d stuff
e throw away / out	f tidy up
g untidy	

1 an organization that helps people   _____
2 with things in the wrong place   _____
3 put things in the right place   _____
4 different things   _____
5 put something in the trash   _____
6 a number of things on top of each other   _____

5 Check (✓) the ways Marie Kondo helps people tidy up.

1 She helps people decide what things they love and want to keep. ☐
2 She tells people what to throw away. ☐
3 She starts by tidying the most untidy place. ☐
4 She tidies up one type of thing at a time. ☐

6 Look at the Critical Thinking Skill box and read questions 1–3. Then underline the information in the review that tells you the answer.

CRITICAL THINKING SKILL
Identifying a writer's opinion

When you read reviews, it is important to notice what the writer's opinion is. Expressions like *For me*, *I feel*, *In my view*, can show that something is an opinion. But often you have to read carefully to decide if something is a fact or an opinion. Look for adjectives describing the writer's feelings, or for reasons and examples that show they agree or disagree with the thing they are reviewing.

1 How do we know that the reviewer found the KonMari method helpful? (paragraph 3)
2 How do we know that the reviewer thinks what Marie Kondo suggests is not easy? (paragraph 4)
3 How do we know what the reviewer's general opinion of the show is? (paragraph 5)

SPEAKING

7 Work in pairs. Discuss the questions.
1 What is your opinion of Marie Kondo's advice?
2 Have you read her books or watched her show? If not, do you want to now?
3 Does the review make you want to tidy up?
4 Do you have any tidying tips?

Tidying Up with Marie Kondo

★ ★ ★ ★ ★

Marie Kondo is a tidying expert and best-selling author who developed her own KonMari method to help people organize their homes. Here we review her TV series.

1 I read Marie Kondo's best-selling book, *The Life-Changing Magic of Tidying Up*, last year, so I was interested to watch her TV series *Tidying Up*. In the show she visits people with untidy homes to help them throw things out and find a place for the things they love. The people in the show are all unhappy about things being messy, but Marie believes that by tidying your home you can take control of your life.

2 Marie Kondo encourages people to throw away things that don't "spark joy"; if it doesn't make you feel happy, don't keep it! I watched people hugging items and trying to decide whether to keep them. I understood their pain—so many items had good memories, were gifts, or "might be useful" in the future.

3 Marie recommends tidying up in a special order, starting with clothes, then books, papers, mixed stuff (those things in your closets, shelves, and boxes that you probably don't need, use, or love!), and, finally, things

that are important to you for emotional reasons. Marie helped a couple with too many clothes. First they emptied everything from their closet into a pile, then they decided what "sparked joy." Finally, they hung items back in their closets or folded them and put them away in their drawers so they could see exactly what they had. After watching, I folded all my clothes using the KonMari method. It's so much quicker to find things now!

4 If something doesn't spark joy, she tells people to put it in the trash, recycle it, or give it to charity, so that someone else can enjoy it. One of Marie's tips is to have a picture in your mind of how you want your house to be. It's hard to imagine a tidy home with three kids, but it helped me make decisions about what I wanted to take to my new place.

5 Many of the people in the show said that they felt Marie made their lives calmer and more organized. I loved this show. Watch it! It will change your life!

EXPLORE MORE!

Search online for "Marie Kondo KonMari tips." Find out more about Marie and how to tidy your home.

5B
If you are in town, call me!

LESSON GOALS
- Understand an email about living in Seoul, South Korea
- Use zero and first conditionals to talk about facts, suggestions, and consequences
- Understand contractions of auxiliary verbs

READING AND GRAMMAR

1 Work in pairs. Look at the photo. What can you say about the city from looking at this photo?

A view of Seoul, South Korea, from Namsan Park

New Message

Hi Rawan,

I thought I'd let you know how we're getting on in Seoul. Well, we're really enjoying our new life! My job here is going well and the kids seem very happy in their school.

Seoul is a great place to live. It's a big city, but if you like being outdoors, there are plenty of green spaces. We love bike riding by the Han River, and you can go windsurfing on it, too!

If we want to go hiking, we take the subway to Bukhan Mountain. It's close to the city and the views are spectacular. It's not a problem if you haven't got a car here. One of the great things about Seoul is the transportation. It's very well organized and fast. If you have a T-money card, it's pretty cheap. I try and leave early for work because if you use the subway at rush hour, it's very busy!

The food is great, too, and we love all the street food. If you enjoy good, healthy food, you can eat really well. I think my favorite is kimchi (spicy pickled cabbage). When I don't want to cook, I just order takeout. Many places deliver 24 hours a day!

You should come visit. I'd love to show you around. Everyone says the spring is a beautiful time to be here.

Best wishes,
Stella

2 Read the email. Work in pairs. Answer the questions.
1 Why does Stella write Rawan?
2 How does Stella feel about living in Seoul?

3 Read the email again. Work in pairs. Discuss what Stella says about each topic.

education	food	nature
technology	transportation	

4 Read the Grammar box. Circle the correct answer to complete the sentence below.

> **GRAMMAR** Zero conditionals
>
> Stella uses the **zero conditional** to talk about facts.
> *If* we **want** to go hiking, we **take** *the subway to Bukhan Mountain.*
> And actions that happen after or as a result of other actions.
> *When* I **don't want** to cook, I just **order** *takeout!*

Go to page 170 for the Grammar reference.

Use the zero conditional to talk about *imagined situations / things that are generally true.*

5 Complete the conditional sentences with the correct form of the verbs.

1 When it _____ cold and rainy, we sometimes _____ (be, go) to the movies.

2 When my brother _____, he _____ (visit, like) to sing karaoke.

3 It _____very hot, if you _____ (get, not have) air conditioning.

4 If I _____ tired, I _____ (be, take) the train to work.

5 If I _____ where to visit, I _____ (not know, ask) the tourist information office.

LISTENING AND GRAMMAR

6 🎧 **5.1** Listen to the conversation. Why is Goran excited? Tell a partner.

7 🎧 **5.1** Listen again. Match the sentence halves.

1 Goran will work ○ from home,

2 Goran's kids will ○ learn Spanish,

3 Goran will video ○ call friends and family,

4 Hazem will visit, ○

○ a if his children miss them.

○ b if his manager allows him to.

○ c if they go to school in Colombia.

○ d if Goran buys his ticket.

8 Read the Grammar box. Circle the correct words to complete the sentence below.

Use the first conditional to talk about things that are *likely / unlikely* in the future.

> **GRAMMAR** First conditionals
>
> The speakers use the **first conditional** to talk about possible future situations.
> *If* we **miss** people, we**'ll call** *them.*

Go to page 170 for the Grammar reference.

9 Correct the mistakes in the first conditional sentences.

1 If we live there, it will being too quiet.

2 If the weather is bad, we don't go back next year.

3 They'll be very happy if they're going on vacation.

4 If you aren't hungry now, we order food later.

PRONUNCIATION AND SPEAKING

10 🎧 **5.2** Look at the Clear Voice box. Listen to the example. Tell a partner what you notice about the difference between *I* and *I'll.*

> **CLEAR VOICE**
> **Understanding contractions of auxiliary verbs**
>
>
>
> Sometimes it can be difficult to hear auxiliary verbs. Listen carefully for contractions like *'ll* (*I'll, she'll, it'll,* etc.)—they are often weak.
> *If* **I** *go to Cuba,* **I'll** *come see you!*

11 🎧 **5.3** Listen to four sentences. In which sentences can you hear *'ll*? Listen again and write the sentences in your notebook.

12 Complete the sentences so that they are true for you. Use conditionals. Then discuss in pairs.

1 If I move to another country, _____.

2 When it's sunny, _____.

3 If you love good restaurants, _____.

4 Please call me _____.

5C
That was the weirdest place!

LESSON GOALS
- Use extreme adjectives
- Understand the key points of a conversation
- Use comparatives and superlatives
- Say /f/ and /v/ clearly

VOCABULARY

1 When you are away from home, what kind of accommodations do you like or dislike staying in? Discuss with a partner.

2 🎧 5.4 In your notebook, rewrite the paragraph by replacing the regular adjectives with these extreme adjectives. Listen and check.

amazing	disgusting	enormous	filthy
freezing	spectacular	terrible	tiny

I once stayed in a strange little place—a ¹**very small** hut on the side of a ²**very big** mountain. The bed was uncomfortable and the bedroom was ³**very cold**. It was ⁴**very dirty** and the food I found in the fridge tasted ⁵**very bad**! The funny thing is, I don't remember the experience as ⁶**very bad**. I actually had a ⁷**very good** time and the views were ⁸**very good**.

Go to page 162 for the Vocabulary reference.

3 Describe to a partner a place you have stayed or visited. Use the extreme adjectives from Exercise 2.

LISTENING

LISTENING SKILL
Understanding the key points

It isn't always possible to understand every word when you listen, but you can try to listen for…
- words that the speaker repeats, says more loudly, or pauses after.
- words with similar meanings.
- stories and examples.

4 🎧 5.5 Listen to the audio. Circle the best summary (a or b) of the key points.

1 When Alexis stayed in Venezuela…
   a the beds were uncomfortable and he felt salty all the time.
   b he slept badly, but the showers were good.
2 When Alexis visited Indonesia…
   a he stayed in a hotel with no electricity and his hosts were very funny.
   b his hosts were very kind and he slept on a very comfortable mattress on the floor.
3 When Ellie stayed in Switzerland…
   a it was freezing cold, but her accommodations had spectacular views.
   b her hostel was beautiful, but the walk there was too cold and difficult for her grandmother.
4 When Ellie travels for work…
   a she prefers sleeping on the floor at a friend's house to being in hotels.
   b she loves sleeping in interesting places like tents, hammocks, and benches.

GRAMMAR

5 Read the Grammar box. Look at sentences 1 and 2 on page 65. Circle which one is comparative (C) and which is superlative (S).

> **GRAMMAR** Comparatives and superlatives
>
> Use comparatives to compare two different things.
> *It was **more memorable** than staying in a hotel.*
> Use superlatives to say that something is better / worse / more extreme than anything else.
> *It was **the worst** sleeping experience of my life!*
> Use *less* and *the least* to say the opposite of *more* and *most*.
> *Their homes are often **less comfortable** than a hotel.*

Go to page 170 for the Grammar reference.

1 I chose the bigger room. C S
2 It had the most beautiful view in the whole hotel. C S

6 Complete the sentences using a comparative or a superlative. Use *less / least* or *more / most* and add *the* or *than* where necessary.

1 There were parties every night. It was _____ (noisy) street in the city!

2 They like staying in _____ (unusual) accommodations that they can find.

3 There's usually no one there. It's probably _____ (crowded) place in town!

4 _____ (good) memory I have is the night we camped on the beach. It was amazing!

5 I was shocked by the campground's prices! It was _____ (expensive) the hostel.

6 Washing in cold, salty water was _____ (bad) being dirty.

PRONUNCIATION

7 🎧 5.6 Look at the Clear Voice box. Listen and repeat.

CLEAR VOICE
Saying /f/ and /v/

Touch your top front teeth to your bottom lip and blow air out of your mouth to make /f/. Your throat doesn't vibrate. To make /v/ do the same, but try to make your throat vibrate.
/f/ *funny*
/v/ *very*
very funny

8 🎧 5.7 Listen to the words. Underline the word you hear.

1 have	half	4 leaf	leave
2 save	safe	5 live	life
3 love	loaf	6 wives	wife

9 🎧 5.8 Listen and repeat the words.

SPEAKING

10 Work in groups to plan a trip to Ho Chi Minh City, Vietnam. Choose accommodations from the ads below. Persuade the others in the group why it's the best.

The capsule hotel is the closest to downtown. I think the apartment is more comfortable.

Riverside bed and breakfast
- From $30 per night
- Single, twin, or double rooms
- River view
- 20 mins from downtown (taxi)
- Private bathroom, Wi-Fi, air-con, fridge, TV, restaurant

Beautiful apartment
- From $60 per night
- Whole apartment with living room, kitchen, bathrooms
- 2 bedrooms (sleeps 4)
- Park view
- 5 mins from downtown (taxi)
- Wi-Fi, air-con, TV

Central capsule hotel
- From $13 per night
- 2.5 square meters
- All single
- No view
- Downtown
- Shared bathroom and entertainment room, USB, Wi-Fi, TV

5D
Showing flexibility

LESSON GOALS
- Show you can be flexible
- Talk about experiences of being a guest
- Learn phrases to show you are a flexible guest or host

SPEAKING

1 Work in pairs. Answer the questions.
1 What makes you feel welcome when you stay somewhere?
2 What do you try to do to be a good guest?
3 Do you have any memorable experiences of being a guest in someone's home?

LISTENING

2 🎧 5.9 Listen to two conversations between a guest and a host. Why might the host be upset? Discuss with a partner.

3 Work in pairs. Have you had similar experiences? What do you think the host and guest could do differently?

MY VOICE ▶

4 ▶ 5.2 Watch the video about being a good guest. What general advice does it suggest? Discuss with a partner.

5 ▶ 5.2 Watch again. Check (✓) which advice from 1–7 the video gives.
1 Make yourself at home in every house. ☐
2 Talk to your host to find out what they want you to do. ☐
3 Help your hosts as much as possible. ☐
4 Understand that people do things differently. ☐
5 Think about your host's feelings. ☐
6 Take the opportunity to try new ways of doing things. ☐
7 Always change the way you do things for your host. ☐

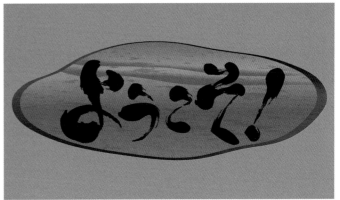

Welcome signs from around the world

6 Look at the Communication Skill box and situations 1 and 2 below. What could Soheila and Enzo do differently? Discuss with a parter.

Showing flexibility

Everyone has different ways of doing things. When you stay with someone, talk to them and find out what they'd like you to do. Show that you are happy to try new ways of doing things, if you can. This is a helpful skill for many situations and helps build good relationships with people.

1 Soheila stays with a friend. When she gets up, she takes a long shower. Her friend is annoyed because she can't get in the bathroom and when she does, there is no hot water left!

2 Enzo stays with an uncle. He gets up early to make his uncle breakfast. His uncle is upset because Enzo woke him up, the kitchen is a mess, and he never eats eggs for breakfast.

SPEAKING

7 Look at the Useful Language box. What phrases could you use if you are in the situation described after the box?

Useful Language Being a flexible guest and host

Asking
When do you usually get up? I can get up about the same time if it helps.
I'm a little cold. Could I turn the heat on?

Offering help
Can I do anything to help you?
Do you want me to do the dishes?

Saying "yes" or "no" to an offer of help
OK. That's very nice of you. / Thanks for offering. I appreciate it. / You're very kind.
It's OK. / Don't be silly! You're my guest! / Thanks for the offer, but I'm OK.

> You are staying with a friend of a friend. Their house is very hot. Usually, you don't sleep well in hot rooms. They have air conditioning, but they don't offer to turn it on. The window is open, but it's hot and noisy outside.

8 Work in pairs. Look at the list. What are you usually flexible about when you stay at someone's house? What can't you change or do you find difficult to change?
1 daily routine (e.g., meal times, bed time)
2 diet (e.g., vegetarian)
3 comfort (e.g., tidiness, hot water, television)
4 people (e.g., talkative, quiet)
5 sleeping arrangements (e.g., bed, sofa, temperature, light, noise)

I don't mind sleeping on the sofa, but I can't eat meat. I'm vegetarian.

I'm happy to sleep in a cold room if I have enough blankets.

9 **OWN IT!** Work in pairs. Discuss situations where you might need to be flexible with other people. Then roleplay the situations below. Then change roles. Use the Useful Language.

Student A: You are a guest.
Student B: You are the host.

1 You stay with a family member that you don't know very well. Their house is a little untidy and they are very busy, so when they're out you would like to cook or clean for them to help out. However, you are worried they might think you think their house is dirty or their cooking isn't good and get upset.

2 You are staying with your best friend for one night. The last time you saw your friend was two years ago, so you have a lot to talk about. You are on vacation, but you know your friend has important things to do the next day. You want to spend as much time with your friend as you can. You'd love to take them out for breakfast in the morning, but you're worried that your friend won't have time.

Can I do anything to help you? I would love to help out around the house or cook dinner for you, if that's OK with you.

We have so much to talk about! I know you're really busy tomorrow, but can I take you to breakfast in the morning?

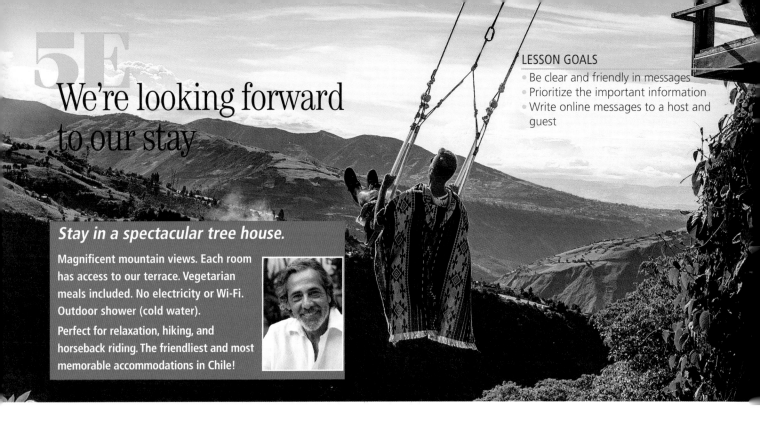

We're looking forward to our stay

Stay in a spectacular tree house.

Magnificent mountain views. Each room has access to our terrace. Vegetarian meals included. No electricity or Wi-Fi. Outdoor shower (cold water).

Perfect for relaxation, hiking, and horseback riding. The friendliest and most memorable accommodations in Chile!

SPEAKING

1 Look at the ad above. Work in pairs. Discuss what is unusual about these accommodations.

READING FOR WRITING

2 Read the messages. Complete the chart below with the information.

Location		Dates (Hajer)	
Beds		Dates (Hajer + friend)	
Keys		Bus Arrival	
Towels		Host arrival time	
Activity		Check-in time	

April 2	**Hajer** I would love to stay at your place. I am coming to Chile in July to do some hiking. Could I stay with you July 5–20? Also, my friend will join me July 10–15. How many beds are there in each room?
April 2	**Alonso** My place is perfect for hiking and I have a room with two beds. If you make a reservation now, you can have that room. It has the best view!
April 2	**Hajer** Great. Will make a reservation now. Thanks
April 2	**Hajer** I am looking forward to my stay. My bus arrives at 2 p.m. on Friday. What time can I check in and how do I pick up the keys? Also, do you provide towels?
April 2	**Alonso** Check-in is usually 4 p.m., but you can check in early at 2:30 p.m. There is a small box with the key. It's behind the trash can in the backyard. The code is 8743. I will give you towels. I will be back around 6 p.m. Looking forward to meeting you!
April 2	**Hajer** Great. Thanks. See you in July!

3 Look at the Writing Skill box. Underline all the questions and circle the friendly comments in the messages.

WRITING SKILL
Being clear and friendly in messages

In messages about arranging a stay, it's important to be friendly, brief, and clear. Hajer asks questions, but also says friendly things like *I would love to stay at your place.* Alonso gives helpful information and says he's looking forward to meeting Hajer.

4 Look at the Useful Language box. Write questions to ask about the things below.

Useful Language Arranging a stay

Asking to stay
Can / Could we stay with you?
Do you have any vacancies from June 20–30?

Asking for information
Is breakfast included?
How do I check in?
What time do we need to check out?
Are there good beaches nearby?
Do you know if we can take bikes on the bus?

Asking permission
Is it OK if I arrive after 11 p.m.?
Can we bring pets?

Being friendly
I'm looking forward to my stay. / I'm looking forward to meeting you.
Your place looks perfect.
I would love to stay for a week.

- good walks nearby
- best way to get there
- available dates
- nearby restaurants
- Wi-Fi
- parking lot

5 Look at the Critical Thinking Skill box. Which of your questions from Exercise 4 are essential? Which are useful but not essential? Discuss with a partner.

CRITICAL THINKING SKILL
Prioritizing

Hajer asks the most important questions first. He asks about dates, then whether his friend can share his room. When arranging somewhere to stay, usually dates, costs, and arrival information are the most important. Information about local walks or room cleaning are useful, but not essential.

6 Think about a trip you would like to take. Make notes about…
1 why you are going and what you are going to do.
2 what kind of accommodations you are looking for.
3 when you are going and for how long.
4 what you need to know about your accommodations.

WRITING TASK

7 WRITE Follow the steps below.
1 Using Hajer's messages as a model, write to a vacation rental host. Introduce the reason for your trip, the dates, and the number of guests. Ask about the local area.
2 Exchange messages with another student. Write a reply as a host. Tell them your home is available and answer their questions.
3 Read the reply from your host. Write another message. Ask for arrival information, what is included in the price, and what you need to bring.

8 CHECK Use the checklist. Your messages…
☐ introduce the reason for your trip.
☐ give essential information about dates, etc.
☐ ask for useful information about the local area.
☐ answer the guest's questions.
☐ ask about essential arrival information.

9 REVIEW Read your partner's messages again. Did they include at least three things from the checklist? Are there any questions or answers you think they should add? Tell them.

Go to page 156 for the Reflect and review.

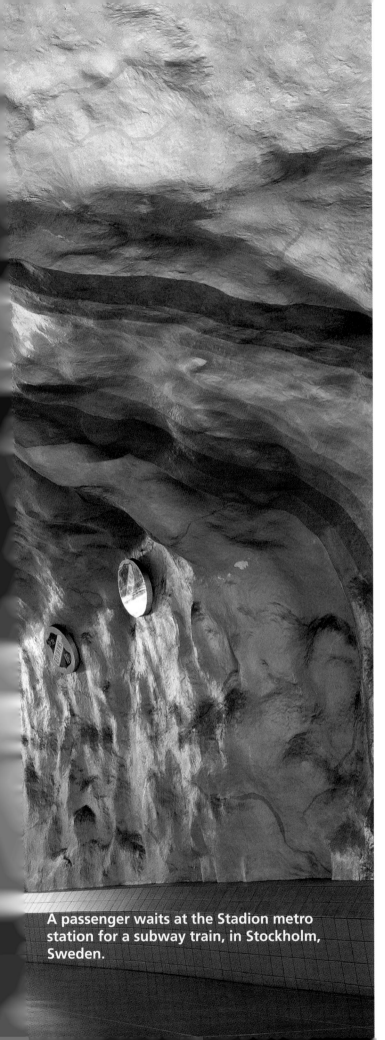

A passenger waits at the Stadion metro station for a subway train, in Stockholm, Sweden.

6

Journeys

GOALS

- Understand pronouns and determiners
- Talk about travel experiences
- Practice words related to air travel
- Use information you already know to help you understand a talk
- Practice ways to understand other English speakers
- Write an email asking for information

1 **Work in pairs. Discuss the questions.**

1 Look at the photo. What kind of trip do you think the person is taking?

2 How do you usually feel at the start of a trip?

WATCH ▶

2 ▶ 6.1 Watch the video. How does Salome answer the questions? Discuss in pairs.

NATIONAL GEOGRAPHIC EXPLORER

SALOME BUGLASS

1 How do you plan your trips?
2 How do you stay safe?
3 How do you communicate with the people you meet?

3 **Make connections. How would you answer the questions in Exercise 2? Tell a partner.**

I usually look online for the cheapest flights and I never travel alone at night.

6A
Daily trips

LESSON GOALS
- Understand pronouns and determiners
- Learn how to choose the best option
- Talk about the best forms of transportation

READING

1 Work in pairs. Discuss the questions.

1 How do you travel to work or study?

2 How long does your trip take? Do you enjoy it?

3 Do you know any stories of people who travel to class or work in an unusual way?

2 Complete the definitions with these words from the article on page 73.

goggles	helmet	lifejacket	wetsuit

1 You wear a _____ to stay warm in cold water.

2 You wear a _____ to keep your head safe.

3 You wear _____ to keep your eyes safe.

4 You wear a _____ to keep you safe if you fall in the water.

3 Read the article. Why does each person choose this way to travel? Discuss with a partner.

4 Look at the Reading Skill box. What do the pronouns and determiners (1–10) in the article refer to? Underline the nouns they are replacing.

READING SKILL
Understanding reference (2): pronouns and determiners

The writer uses pronouns and determiners to avoid repeating the same noun or phrase. Subject and object pronouns, (*he / him, she / her, they / them,* etc.) replace nouns. Determiners (*this, these, their,* etc.) show what thing you are talking about.

Look for nouns in the text to help you understand what the pronoun or determiner refers to. They may be in the same sentence, or in the one before or after.

5 Look at the Critical Thinking Skill box then read the article again. In your notebook, answer questions 1–5. Give reasons.

CRITICAL THINKING SKILL
Choosing the best option

When deciding if something is a good choice, it can help to look closely at all the options and compare them. For example, when choosing how to travel, think about the differences in cost, time, safety, how easy it is, what you need, and how enjoyable and healthy it is.

1 Which trip do you think saves the person the most time or money?

2 Which trip is the easiest and the most complicated?

3 Which trip do you think would be the most (and least) enjoyable?

4 Which trip do you think is the healthiest?

5 Who do you think has chosen the best option for their daily commute?

SPEAKING

6 Work in pairs. Find out about each other's daily trips. Make a note of the things listed below. Would either of you like to change or improve your daily commute?
- transportation
- reason for commute
- special clothes
- commute time
- what they like and dislike
- cost
- things to carry
- how healthy it is

7 Work with another pair. Tell them three facts about your partner's commute. Which person in your group has the best commute? Give reasons for your answer.

8 Work in pairs. Read the information on page 180 and do the task.

A better way to get to work

The average time it takes people to get to work around the world ranges from 39 minutes in Japan to 97 minutes in Israel. [1]**That** means many people spend between 3.5 and 8 hours per week on trains, buses, the subway, or in their cars. Some people are finding different and creative ways to get to work in the morning. [2]**These** people decided to use their travel time to do something they love!

Swim!

Benjamin David found it stressful traveling to work by car, so he swims to work instead. He puts his laptop, suit, and shoes in a waterproof bag to keep [3]**them** dry and swims 2 kilometers (fifteen to thirty minutes) to work down the Isar River in Munich, Germany! He says that [4]**it**'s faster and more relaxing than driving and keeps him fit. He wears swimming trunks in summer and a wetsuit in winter, and he always wears special plastic shoes to protect his feet from glass and old bicycles.

Snowboard!

Lucy Carter is a nanny in Tignes, France. [5]**She** loves snowboarding to work and seeing the sun coming up over the mountains. The trip downhill takes about fifteen minutes. She wears a warm snowboarding jacket, pants, and gloves and, for safety, a helmet. She carries the toys she needs in her bag, but says she lost some of [6]**them** one day when she fell over!

Paddleboard!

Liu Fucao works in an office in Chongqing, China. He paddleboards across the Yangtze River to get to work. Going by car takes more than an hour, but paddleboarding takes just six minutes. He wears his work shirt and pants on the board, but puts [7]**his** laptop, jacket, socks, and shoes in a special bag to keep them dry. Fucao is training for a career as a paddleboarder. He has won competitions in [8]**this** sport, but he still wears a lifejacket and ties himself and his bag to the board in case he falls in.

Fly!

František Hadrava works in a factory in Zdíkov, Czech Republic. He decided driving for fourteen minutes to work was too long, so he built a wooden plane and now flies to work! The flight takes seven minutes. He wears his work clothes, goggles, and a helmet, and lands in a field next to his work. He then pulls the plane across the road and parks [9]**it** at his work. It takes up four car-parking spaces. The plane cost [10]**him** around 3700 euros to build, but he says it's still cheaper than driving.

EXPLORE MORE!

Watch videos of Fucao, František, and Benjamin online. Search for "Video + full name + travel to work."

The most memorable journey I've ever made

LESSON GOAL
- Understand an interview about a memorable journey
- Use the present perfect to talk about experiences
- Say long and short vowel sounds

LISTENING AND GRAMMAR

1 Work in pairs. Look at the photos and discuss the questions.

1 Would you like to take a journey there?
2 What do you think would be the best transportation?

NATIONAL GEOGRAPHIC EXPLORER

2 ∩ 6.1 Listen to an interview with Salome Buglass. Why was Salome's journey memorable? Discuss with a partner.

Salome Buglass in Peru

3 ∩ 6.1 Listen to the interview again. Answer the questions.

1 What did Salome and her friends want to do on their trip?

_____

2 Why did they have to change their plan?

_____

3 What did they decide to do instead?

_____

4 What travel advice did the local people give?

_____

5 Why didn't they take the local people's advice?

_____

6 How long did their journey take?

_____

A winding road leading up to the mountain pass, Abra de Malaga, Peru

4 Read the Grammar box. Look at the examples in 1–3. What tense is used in each sentence? What's the difference in meaning between a and b? Discuss with a partner.

> **GRAMMAR** Present perfect (+ *ever* / *never*)
>
> Use the present perfect to ask and talk about experiences without saying when these things happened. Use *ever* to ask if something happened and *never* to say something didn't happen at any time before now. See page 27 for uses of the simple past.
> ***Have*** you **ever had** a bad travel experience?
> **I've never** had any terrible travel experiences, but **I've had** some pretty difficult ones.

Go to page 171 for the Grammar reference.

1 a What's the worst journey you'**ve ever had**?
  b What's the worst trip you **had** on your journey?
2 a I **haven't had** any terrible travel experiences.
  b I **didn't have** any terrible experiences on vacation.
3 a I'**ve never traveled** without a guidebook!
  b I **didn't travel** with a guidebook in Paris.

5 Complete the conversation with the verbs. Use the present perfect or simple past.

A: What's the most uncomfortable journey you ¹_____ (ever / make)?

B: I ²_____ (travel) on some very uncomfortable buses, but the worst was a train. There were no seats, it was very hot and then it ³_____ (break) down!

A: Oh no! ⁴_____ (you / ever / miss) a plane?

B: No, I ⁵_____ (have / not), but a month ago I ⁶_____ (miss) my train. ⁷_____ (you / ever / reserve) a ticket for the wrong day? I ⁸_____ (do) that once!

A: No! I ⁹_____ (never / do) that! I ¹⁰_____ (arrive) to stay with a friend on the wrong day once though. She ¹¹_____ (be) surprised to see me!

6 Work in pairs. Make questions using the present perfect with *ever*. Then ask and answer.
1 Have / travel by electric car or bus?
2 Have / miss your bus, train, or plane?
3 Have / be travel sick?
4 What's / most uncomfortable form of transportation / take?

PRONUNCIATION

7 🎧 6.2 Look at the Clear Voice box. Listen and repeat.

> **CLEAR VOICE**
> **Saying long and short sounds (2):** /ʌ/, /æ/, and /ɑː/
>
> English has several sounds that are very similar. To be understood, it's important to get the length of the vowel correct.
> /ʌ/ is a short sound (e.g., *bus*).
> /æ/ is a little longer (e.g., *plan*).
> /ɑː/ is a long sound (e.g., *start*).
> If you haven't got these sounds in your language, use a similar sound, but change the length.

8 🎧 6.3 Listen to the words. Circle the one you hear. Listen again and repeat.
1 cat   cut   2 cart cut   3 bag bug
4 duck dark   5 park pack   6 fun fan

SPEAKING

9 Work in pairs. Choose from the situations below or your own ideas. Make questions using the present perfect about them. Then ask and answer with your partner. Ask for more information using simple past questions.
- making a ticket reservation for the wrong day
- getting lost
- a very long walk or cycle ride
- traveling somewhere in an unusual way
- the best or worst journey ever

A: Have you ever reserved a ticket for the wrong day?

B: Yes, I have! I reserved a plane ticket for August, but the wrong year!

6C
Flying free with no luggage

LESSON GOALS
- Use information you already know to help understand a talk
- Talk about travel and flying
- Use verb patterns to talk about travel

READING

1 Work in pairs. Look at the infographic below. Write the names of the birds in order, from the longest to the shortest journey, in your notebook.

LISTENING

2 Work in pairs. You are going to listen to a bird expert talking about bird journeys. Look at the Listening Skill box. Then discuss the questions (1 and 2).

LISTENING SKILL
Using information you already know

You listen better when you know a little about the topic. Talking to a partner about what you already know about a topic and thinking about what words you expect to hear can help you understand. For example, if you know the topic is about bird journeys, you might hear words like *wings* and *fly*.

1 What other words do you expect to hear?
2 What information about bird journeys do you expect to hear? Use the infographic to help you.

BIRD JOURNEYS

Some birds stay in the same place all their lives, but many all around the world travel long distances every year. They sometimes fly thousands of kilometers to arrive at the best places at the best time of year to find a mate and breed.

- **The Arctic tern** has the longest journey of all birds. It flies 96,000 km per year between the Arctic and the Antarctic, and spends more time in daylight than any other bird.

- **The sooty shearwater** travels 64,000 km from the summer in New Zealand or Chile to the summer off the coasts of Japan, Russia, Alaska, or Canada.

- The tiny (18 g) **barn swallow** follows the spring, traveling 10,000 km from Northern Europe to Southern Africa.

- **Adélie penguins** live along the Antarctic coast. In winter, they walk north where the weather is warmer. In the summer, they walk south again to find land to build their nests. They travel about 13,000 km every year.

- **The northern wheatear** weighs just 25 g but flies 29,000 km from Alaska to East Africa, or 15,000 km from Canada to West Africa.

**Bird expert
Tim Dee**

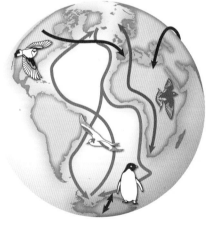
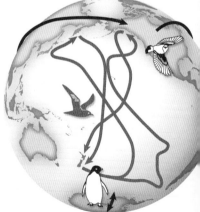

EXPLORE MORE!

Look online for information about the journeys of other birds and animals. Search for "animal journeys" or the name of your favorite bird or animal + "journey."

3 🎧 **6.4** Listen to Tim Dee talk about bird journeys. Did he mention any of the ideas you had in Exercise 2? Discuss with a partner.

4 🎧 **6.4** Listen again. Take notes on the differences Tim mentions between human flight and bird flight for each of these things.

- food
- luggage
- documents
- cost
- time
- maps

food: humans: airline food; birds: flies

VOCABULARY

5 Match these words with the definitions.

a abroad	b board	c check in	d gate
e land	f security	g take off	

1 arrive at an airport and show your ticket _____
2 leave the ground and start flying _____
3 airport check for dangerous items _____
4 stop flying and touch the ground _____
5 get on the plane and take your seat _____
6 the place at an airport where you get on the plane _____
7 to, or in, another country _____

Go to page 162 for the Vocabulary reference.

6 🎧 **6.5** Complete each sentence using the correct form of a word from Exercise 5. Then listen to check.

1 We had to wait in a long line of people to _____ at the airport.
2 I got my bag searched at _____ because I forgot to take out my water bottle.
3 Could all passengers for flight ZF564 please go to _____ number 2?
4 I like to travel _____ to see other countries and cultures.
5 She gets nervous when she _____ and _____.
6 Can we _____ the plane yet?

GRAMMAR

7 Read the Grammar box. Complete the sentences using -ing or to + base verb.

> **GRAMMAR** Verb patterns: -ing and to + base verb
>
> Some verbs are followed by -ing and some are followed by to with the base verb. When you learn a verb, you need to learn which form to use. Some verbs take both forms.
>
> **-ing**
> likes and dislikes e.g., *can't stand, don't mind, enjoy*
> Also: *avoid, feel like, finish, involve, keep, miss, practice, recommend, stop*
> I **miss seeing** the swallows.
>
> **to + base verb**
> *afford, agree, arrange, ask, continue, decide, fail, hope, intend, manage, need, offer, persuade, plan, promise, refuse, want, would like*
> They don't **need to ask** for directions.
>
> **Both -ing and to + base verb**
> *hate, like, love, prefer, try*

Go to page 172 for the Grammar reference.

I love [1]_____ (spend) time on my bike. It's good for you and you don't need [2]_____ (buy) a plane ticket! Next year, I want [3]_____ (ride) my bike through Brazil. I have persuaded my daughter [4]_____ (come) with me. I tried [5]_____ (get) my son [6]_____ (join) us, but he says he can't afford [7]_____ (take) time off work. I prefer [8]_____ (ride) my bike to [9]_____ (go) by plane or car because you see so much more. I'm 72, and I think it's important to keep [10]_____ (do) interesting things. I intend [11]_____ (stay) active until I'm at least 102!

SPEAKING

8 Complete the sentences about yourself. Use as many of the verbs in the Grammar box as possible. Discuss with a partner.

1 When I fly / go on a long trip / am abroad...
2 The next time I go on vacation...
3 I would most like to travel to... because...

6D
Understanding other English speakers

LESSON GOALS
• Understanding other English speakers
• Check understanding
• Notice difficult consonant sounds

SPEAKING

1 Look at the cartoon. What is happening? Discuss with a partner.

2 🎧 6.6 Listen to two short conversations. Write *conversation 1* or *conversation 2* beside the communication problem. More than one option is possible.

- speaking too fast _____
- speaking too slowly _____
- using difficult words _____
- the accent _____

3 Work in pairs. Discuss the questions.

1 What communication problems do you have a) when you speak English, b) when you listen to other people speak English?
2 How do you feel when you can't understand someone or they can't understand you?

MY VOICE ▶

4 ▶ 6.2 Watch the video. Does it mention any of the things that you talked about in Exercise 3? Discuss with a partner.

5 ▶ 6.2 Watch again. Check (✓) the advice the expert gives.

1 Ask for people to repeat things you don't understand. ☐
2 Talk to people from different countries. ☐
3 Pronounce words as clearly as you can. ☐
4 Try to change your accent. ☐
5 Use simple words with everyone. ☐
6 Speak as slowly as possible all the time. ☐
7 Repeat things using different words. ☐
8 Find a different way to communicate. ☐

6 Look at the Communication Skill box. Work in pairs and discuss questions 1–2.

COMMUNICATION SKILL
Understanding each other

If you and another person have problems understanding each other, you could:
- take a moment to **think** and ask yourself why and what you could do.
- ask questions to **check** you understood.
- ask someone to **repeat** or to say something in a different way.
- tell them briefly what you think they said, or ask them to **summarize** for you.
- find a **different way to communicate**: smile, nod, act, draw, or write it down.
- **be positive:** you can ask the other person to try to be positive, too.

1 Who do you usually speak to in English?
2 What is the first language of most of the people you speak English to?
3 What techniques from the box do you already use? Which will you use in the future?

PRONUNCIATION

7 Look at the Clear Voice box. Which words or sounds do you find difficult pronounce in English?

8 🎧 **6.7** Listen to three conversations. Which consonants do the speakers find difficult in each conversation (1–3)? Do you find any of these sounds difficult to make? Discuss with a partner.

1 _____

2 _____

3 _____

9 Look at the Useful Language box. Practice saying any words with sounds that are difficult for you to pronounce. Can you think of any other ways to say these things? Discuss with a partner.

SPEAKING

10 **OWN IT!** Work in pairs. Roleplay the situation. Follow the stages below. Use the tips from the Communication Skill box and the Useful Language to help you. Then change roles.

Student A: You are checking in at a hotel.

Student B: You are the hotel receptionist. You quickly tell Student A that their room number is 428 and that breakfast starts at 8:30.

Student A: You are not sure if Student B said room 428 or 438 and you're not sure if they said breakfast starts or stops at 8:30. Ask questions to check.

Student B: Answer Student A's questions. Then tell Student A that the Wi-Fi password is "welcome123." Ask Student A a question to check that they understood.

Student A: Answer Student B's question. Then ask Student B for a wake-up call at 7:30.

Student B: You are not sure if Student A said 7 or 7:30 for the wake-up call. Ask Student A a question to check.

A: Your room number is 428.

B: Let me check that I've understood. It's Room 428, not 438?

A: Yes, that's correct.

6E

What time does it leave?

LESSON GOALS
• Choose informal or more formal language
• Write questions to find out information
• Write an email to a travel company asking for information

SPEAKING

1 Look at these topics. What information might you need when planning a trip? Write a list of questions in pairs.

accommodations	costs	food
luggage	schedule	transportation

1 _____
2 _____
3 _____
4 _____
5 _____
6 _____

READING FOR WRITING

2 Read the emails. Underline the questions. Which questions are similar to the ones on your list?

3 Look at the Writing Skill box. Which email is more informal? Which is more formal? Circle the parts that helped you decide.

WRITING SKILL
Choosing informal or more formal language

Use informal language to write people you know well and more formal language for people you don't know well. Informal emails usually use:
• first names
• contractions (*I'm*)
• language to show feelings (*I'd love to*)
• shorter words and sentences
More formal emails often use:
• family names (*Mr. Moulton*)
• long forms (*I am*)
• factual language (*We arrive at 7 p.m.*)
• longer words and sentences
Subject lines should be short and say what the email is about. Informal subjects can be personal, funny, or use exclamation points, while formal subjects will be more factual and serious.

New Message

Subject: Joining a tour!

Hi Hardeep,

How're things? Your sister told me that you started a business taking people on roller-skating tours of the city. What a great idea!

Tan and I have never tried roller-skating, but we'd love to come on one of your tours. When and where do they start and how much do they cost?

I hope we can join you soon.

Love,
Daliah

New Message

Subject: Antwerp to Amsterdam tour reservation

Dear Mr. Sandhu,

I saw your ad online and would like to reserve a place on the two-day roller-skating tour from Antwerp to Amsterdam. I am a confident skater.

Could you tell me what dates are available and where we will stay? I would be happy with a bunk bed in a hostel to reduce the cost.

What should I bring with me? Do I need to carry all my water and food?

Also, what time will we leave? I would like to take the train from Brussels in the morning, if possible.

It says online that the cost for the tour is 180 euros, including skate rental. Is there a discount for those who have their own skates?

Sincerely,
Harry

4 Look at the Writing Skill box again. Work in pairs. Are these suitable subject lines for an email? Could Harry and Daliah use them for their emails? Why or why not?

Roller-skating tour	New business
Old friend	Train to Brussels
Discounts	2-day roller-skating tour
City tour	Carrying food and water

5 Look at the Useful Language box. Then look at 1–4 and circle formal (F) or informal (I).

Useful Language Using informal and more formal language in emails

INFORMAL	MORE FORMAL
Hi Hardeep, / Hey Hardeep,	Dear Mr. Sandhu, / Hello Hardeep,
What's up?/ How are you?	I hope this email finds you well.
We'd love to come with you.	I would like to reserve a place.
When can we join you?	Could you tell me what dates are available?
Thanks, / Love, / Take it easy,	Sincerely, / Sincerely yours, / Yours truly, / Best regards,

1 I would like to join one of your tours. Is it possible to make a reservation online?   F   I

2 I'm excited! How much do I owe you?   F   I

3 I am interested in the boat tours. Could you send me the schedule, please?   F   I

4 This sounds awesome! Where do we meet?   F   I

6 Read the ads on this page for adventure tours. Work in pairs. Choose an ad. Write questions to ask for more information about:

- accommodation
- transportation
- food
- schedules
- luggage, and
- cost.

WRITING TASK

7 **WRITE** Using Harry's email as a model, write a formal email to the tour company to ask for more information.

8 **CHECK** Use the checklist. Your email...
☐ has an appropriate subject.
☐ avoids informal language.
☐ asks at least four questions.
☐ says what kind of accommodations, transportation, food, and schedule you prefer.
☐ says how much experience you have.

9 **REVIEW** Exchange emails with another student. Did they include at least three things from the checklist? Note one thing on the email that your partner could improve.

Go to page 156 for the Reflect and review.

Enjoy the towns and countryside of Java by bike! Join one of our bike tours. Email info@solobikes.com for more information.

Explore the beautiful Tigre River in Argentina. Choose your date and time. Competitive prices. Email TigreBoats@TigreTours.com for more info.

A boy walks through "Strawpocalypse," an artwork made from 168,000 drinking straws from the streets of Ho Chi Minh City, Vietnam.

© Benjamin Von Wong | www.vonwong.com | Strawpocalypse

7

Inspiration for change

GOALS

- Use definitions to understand short texts
- Use relative clauses to define people and things
- Talk about the environment
- Predict the content when listening to a story
- Persuade others to use your ideas
- Write about someone who inspires you

1 Work in pairs. Discuss the questions.

1 Look at the photo. What does it show?

2 What do you think the artist is trying to say about the future?

WATCH ▶

2 ▶ 7.1 Watch the video. Answer the questions.

NATIONAL GEOGRAPHIC EXPLORER

IMOGEN NAPPER

1 Who or what inspired Imogen to be a scientist?

2 What kind of science does she do?

3 What example does Imogen give for how we can change the world?

3 Make connections. What has inspired you to do what you do (or want to do)? How do you think we can change the world?

Life-changing inventions

LESSON GOALS
• Use definitions to find meaning in a text
• Find connections between pieces of information
• Talk about inventions

READING

1 Work in pairs. Look at photos A–E on page 85. What does each invention do? Where do you think each inventor got their idea?

2 Match these words from the texts on page 85 with the definitions.

1 clean or dry a surface by moving something over it ○   ○ a accidentally

2 a sticky material that holds things together ○   ○ b create

3 make (something) ○   ○ c glue

4 by mistake ○   ○ d weak

5 not strong ○   ○ e wipe

3 Quickly read about each invention. Match the photos (A–E) to the paragraphs (1–5).

4 Read the texts again. Work in pairs. Which inventor…

1 designed a digital home helper?
2 used Spencer Silver's invention to help him when he was reading?
3 improved the design for windshield wipers?
4 wanted to help people get on trains?
5 made a material used for safety clothing?

5 Look at the Reading Skill box. Then underline the definitions of *windshield*, *Alexa, tactile paving, Kevlar,* and *adhesive* in the texts.

READING SKILL
Finding meaning (2): using definitions

To help you with new words and phrases in a text, look for definitions. Sometimes punctuation, such as: commas **,…,**; parentheses **( )**; quotation marks **"…"**; and dashes **—** can show us where the definition or a synonym is.

People used to erase—or rub out—pencil marks… Or the definition might be in the sentence before or after the word or phrase.

6 Look at the Critical Thinking skill box. Then work in pairs to answer questions 1–5.

CRITICAL THINKING SKILL
Finding connections

Finding connections between pieces of information helps us think about how things are similar or different. You can read different stories and compare…

• when each story happened and what the exact facts of the story are.
• how and why things happened.

Which inventions…
1 happened around the same time?
2 happened over a hundred years apart?
3 were discovered accidentally?
4 were improved by someone else?
5 keep people safe?

7 Read the texts again. Can you find any other similarities or differences? Discuss your ideas with a partner.

SPEAKING

8 Work in pairs. You are going to look at some other inventions.
Student A: Go to page 180.
Student B: Go to page 182.

9 Work in pairs. Look again at the inventions in Exercises 1 and 8. Which do you think is the most important? How do you think these products might be changed or improved in the future?

10 Think of some everyday problems. What invention could help solve them?

My friend uses a wheelchair. Some subway stations have no elevator. It would be amazing to invent a wheelchair that climbs stairs.

EXPLORE MORE!

Are there any other inventions you want to know more about? Look online and share the information with the class.

A Post-it® Notes

B Kevlar

C Alexa

D tactile paving

How did they think of that!?

³ Seiichi Miyake's tactile paving was first used in 1967. After one of his friends lost their sight, Miyake wanted to help blind and visually impaired people to walk along the street and get onto trains easily. Thirty years later, many countries made it law to have Miyake's raised yellow paving blocks at all train stations and crosswalks.

¹ In 1902, Mary Anderson was traveling by streetcar in the snow. The driver had to stop, get out of the streetcar, and wipe the snow off the windshield. Its front window was covered in snow again in seconds. Anderson had the idea to make a wiper to clean the windshield that the driver could control from inside the vehicle. In 1913, Charlotte Bridgwood improved the design and made it electric.

⁴ In 1968, Spencer Silver was trying to make a really strong glue for the airplane industry. Instead, the adhesive he made was a very weak one, but it could hold paper together and didn't make a mess. Nine years later, Silver's co-worker, Arthur Fry, used the glue to stick small pieces of paper into his book so he could easily find the correct page. In 1980, 3M, the company where Fry and Silver worked, started selling these Post-it Notes.

² In 1965, research scientist Stephanie Kwolek was trying to improve tires, when she accidentally created Kevlar—a very light plastic material, which is five times stronger than the strongest metal and doesn't catch fire. We now use Kevlar in products like vehicles, sports equipment, and cell phones. It's also in clothing that saves lives, such as hard hats, boots, and protective vests for police officers.

⁵ Rohit Prasad is the engineer who created Amazon's Alexa, which was first sold in 2014. Alexa is one of many home assistants, such as Apple's Homepod and Google Home, which help people to turn on music, find information, and buy things online. A popular 1960s TV show called *Star Trek* inspired these inventions. The main characters in the show live on a spaceship in the future and have conversations with the ship's computer.

E windshield wipers

85

7B
Something that inspires me

LESSON GOALS
• Understand people talking about things that inspire them
• Use defining relative clauses to describe a person, place, or thing
• Understand different accents

A man reads in a library created by trash collectors in Ankara, Turkey.

LISTENING AND GRAMMAR

1 🎧 7.1 Read and listen to the words of three people: Alem, Beatriz, and Zena. Who or what inspires each of them?

2 Read the Grammar box. Are sentences 1–3 about people, places, or things? Circle the relative pronouns.

> **GRAMMAR** Defining relative clauses
>
> A clause is part of a sentence. Use defining relative clauses to give important information about a person, place, or thing. Use relative pronouns *who / that* for people, *which / that* for things, and *where* for places.
> *A person **who** inspires me is Edwina Brocklesby.*
> *I've just finished the book **that** she wrote.*
> *The place **where** I feel inspired is Lake Falkner.*

Go to page 172 for the Grammar reference.

1 The books that are in the library are all from trash cans.
2 The beach where Beatriz likes to enjoy the view is on the shores of Lake Falkner.
3 Edwina is the woman who did a triathlon.

"A story that inspired me was one I read about some Turkish trash collectors who opened a library with books that they found in trash cans. They first shared the books with friends and family, but soon they had 6,000 books, so decided to share them with the local community. They think it's wonderful."

Alem

"The place where I feel inspired is Lake Falkner in Argentina. It's absolutely beautiful and very peaceful. I go there to hike, and my favorite place to stop and look at the view is the beach which runs alongside the lake."

Beatriz

"A person who inspires me is Edwina Brocklesby. She started running at 50 and did an Ironman triathlon at the age of 74. Imagine swimming 3.8 km, cycling 180 km, and then running 42 km! She's amazing! I've just finished the book that she wrote."

Zena

EXPLORE MORE!

Find out more about the library in Turkey. Search for "Turkish + trash collectors + library."

3 Circle the correct option to complete the sentences.

1 The thing *who / which* reminds me of camping is walking on grass with no shoes on.

2 She is the person *who / which* inspired me to volunteer.

3 I saw a blog post on social media *which / who* gave me the idea to walk across China.

4 The person *that / where* makes me want to travel to India is my friend Arminder.

5 Something *where / which* relaxes me is the sound of rain.

4 Change the two sentences in 1–4 into one sentence, using a relative clause. Complete each sentence to make it true for you.

1 _____ is an amazing person. She taught me so much.

My aunt is an amazing person. She who taught me so much.

2 _____ is a book. I think you should read it. _____

3 _____ is a place. I like to go and relax there. _____

4 _____ is a food. I eat it every day.

_____

5 Look at the Useful Language box. Then complete sentences 1–3 about yourself using *who*, *where*, *which*, or *that*.

> **Useful Language** Talking about things that inspire you
>
> **Things that give you ideas**
> It inspired me to (learn to play the guitar).
> It gave me the idea to (start my own business).
>
> **Things that make you feel emotions**
> It makes me want to (party / laugh).
> It makes me feel (happy / like singing).
>
> **Things that make you remember the past**
> It reminds me of (my childhood / visiting Japan).
> It makes me think of (winter mornings / being ten).

1 A song _____ makes me think of _____ is _____ because _____.

*A song **that** makes me think of **my sister** is "I need U" by BTS because **it always makes her want to sing**!*

2 A person _____ helped me _____ is _____ because _____.

3 A place _____ I feel _____ is _____ because _____.

PRONUNCIATION

6 Look at the Clear Voice box. Which accents do you find difficult to understand? Tell a partner.

> **CLEAR VOICE**
> **Understanding different accents**
>
> Most English speakers did not grow up in an English-speaking country. There are many ways to speak English. It can help your understanding of English to listen to lots of different accents.

7 🎧 7.2 Listen to the sentence below said in four different accents. Can you hear the differences? Which is the most similar to your accent? Discuss with a partner.

The place where I feel inspired is the lake near my house.

SPEAKING

8 Copy the headings into your notebook and complete them with one or two words linked to the headings about people, places, and things that inspire you.

(People) (Places) (Things)

9 Work in pairs. Ask and answer questions about why you wrote each word. Use defining relative clauses and the Useful Language.

A: Why did you write "Joe's cafe?"

*B: Joe's café is a place **where** I go to relax. It reminds me of a little café in my home town.*

7C
An inspiring story

LESSON GOALS
• Predict the content of a conversation
• Talk about protecting the environment
• Understand elision
• Talk about past habits

SPEAKING

1 Work in pairs. Discuss what items you think are thrown away in huge quantities around the world. What plastic do you throw away most?

LISTENING

2 🎧 7.3 Look at the Listening Skill box. Then look at the photo. What is the man doing? What might be the connection between the photo and the topic of plastic waste? Discuss with a partner. Then listen and check.

LISTENING SKILL
Predicting the content

Listening is easier when you have an idea of what it might be about. You can look at the pictures, headings, and captions around a listening task to think about what it might be about. Talking with someone about the things that you already know about a topic can help too.

3 🎧 7.3 Listen again. Answer the questions in pairs.
1 What is Musa upset about?
2 Who worked for no money at the beach?
3 What does Musa think people need to do to stop plastic pollution on the river?
4 What do Musa and Marjan do to use less plastic?
5 What does the story inspire them to do?

Afroz Shah, Versova Beach, Mumbai, India

VOCABULARY

4 ⌂ **7.4** Complete the sentences with these words from the conversation in Exercise 3. Then listen and check.

care about	environment	planet
pollution	recycle	reuse (v)

1 In my local area, we can _____ paper, plastic, metal, and glass.

2 I planted some trees last week because I want to help the _____ _____.

3 Air _____ in my area is really bad. There are too many cars, buses, and factories.

4 My sister doesn't _____ how much plastic she uses—and she uses a lot!

5 I always _____ water bottles, bags, and gift paper.

6 We only have one _____. I think it's important that we look after it.

Go to page 163 for the Vocabulary reference.

5 Work in pairs. Discuss which sentences from Exercise 4 you agree with or have had a similar experience to.

GRAMMAR

6 Read the Grammar box. Underline the sentence (a or b) that means the same as sentences 1 and 2.

> **GRAMMAR** *used to*
>
> Use *used to* + verb and *didn't use to* + verb to talk about habits you had in the past or things that were true in the past, but have changed.
> *I **used to** buy plastic toothbrushes, but I buy wooden ones now.*
> *There **didn't use to** be so much plastic pollution.*
> *What **did** you **use to** care about when you were a child?*

Go to page 172 for the Grammar reference.

1 I used to eat my lunch with a plastic fork.
  a In the past I ate my lunch with a plastic fork.
  b I usually eat my lunch with a plastic fork.

2 I didn't use to care about the environment.
  a I will care in the future, but I don't now.
  b I care now, but I didn't in the past.

7 Find the mistakes in 1–5 and correct them.

1 I didn't ~~used~~ *use* to care about my local area, but now I volunteer every week.

2 She used to throwing potato chip bags out of the car window.

3 Did you used to drive everywhere?

4 He use to fly somewhere every month.

5 What did you use eat for lunch as a child?

PRONUNCIATION AND SPEAKING

8 ⌂ **7.5** Read the Clear Voice box. Listen to the examples. Can you hear any difference?

> **CLEAR VOICE**
> **Understanding elision (1): *used to***
>
> Sometimes, when speakers say words quickly, some letters disappear. For example they can make *used to* and *use to* sound the same, because the *d* sound disappears.
> *It use**d** to be full of trash.*
> *I didn't use to have a water bottle.*

9 ⌂ **7.6** Listen and complete the three sentences you hear. Then, in your notebook write two true sentences and one false sentence about you. Use *use to* / *didn't use to*.

1 I _____ swim in the river.

2 How did _____ get to school?

3 I _____ reuse my bags.

10 Work in pairs. Read your sentences from Exercise 9 to your partner. Ask and answer follow-up questions to find out more. Then guess which of your partner's sentences are true.

Why did you use to care about it?
Did you use to...?

EXPLORE MORE!

Find out more about the Mumbai beach cleanup. Search for "Mumbai + beach + cleanup."

7D
Persuading people

LESSON GOALS
• Understand different ways to persuade people
• Choose the best way to persuade someone
• Practice persuading someone

SPEAKING

1 Work in pairs. Discuss the questions.

1 You want to go out, but your friend wants to stay in and watch a movie. Who usually chooses in the end? Why?

2 How do you persuade others to follow your ideas?

MY VOICE ▶

2 ▶ 7.2 Watch the video about ways to persuade people. Match pictures a–e with the persuading styles 1–5 below.

1 to insist ○ ○ a

2 to reason ○ ○ b

3 to discuss ○ ○ c

4 to connect ○ ○ d

5 to inspire ○ ○ e

3 ▶ 7.2 Watch the video again and take notes on the different styles in Exercise 2. Work in pairs. Who might you use each style with? Why?

4 Read the Communication Skill box then look at examples of persuading styles 1–10. Match the examples with the persuading style from the box. There are two examples for each style.

COMMUNICATION SKILL
Persuading people

Five common ways to persuade people to agree with your idea are to:

1 **insist**: tell people what you think the best idea is

2 **reason**: tell people why something is a good idea

3 **connect**: identify ideas and values you share to win someone's support

4 **discuss**: talk about possible ideas so that everyone gets something they want

5 **inspire**: encourage someone to see how great an idea is

Most people prefer one style, but it may be helpful to change your technique for different people, situations, and places. In some situations, you may need more than one style to get what you want.

a Share your excitement about something with others. _____

b Find an idea that keeps most people happy. _____

c Explain the benefits of your ideas. _____

d Get people to imagine the effect of your ideas. _____

e Discuss ideas to find one that involves what you prefer *and* helping the other person. _____

f Argue with others until they change their mind. _____

g Show you understand what's important to others. _____

h Give information, facts, and figures to show why people should do something. _____

i Present your ideas and tell people to use them. _____

j Ask what someone values and show how your idea supports that. _____

SPEAKING

5 Work in pairs. Discuss the questions.

1 Which persuading style is the most common in your country or in other countries you know well?

2 Which is more important to you:
   a persuading someone to do something
   b keeping someone happy by doing what <u>they</u> want?

6 Look at the Useful Language box. Then decide what persuading styles are used in each part of the conversation (1–5).

Useful Language Persuading people

Insist
I have a great idea! Let's…
I think it's a lot better if we…

Reason
I read an article and it's important that we…
The fact is…

Discuss
I'm happy to do (X) if you don't mind doing (Y).
What do you think about (going together)?

Inspire
Wouldn't it be great to…?
I heard this amazing story about…

Connect
I know that you believe…, so I think this idea will…
I think you would really enjoy…

A: I read this incredible story about kayaking in Norway. Wouldn't it be amazing to go kayaking? [1]_____ I also saw this TV show about how relaxing kayaking is. In fact, it's great for your health. [2]_____

B: I want to go to the beach and relax. You can go kayaking by yourself! [3]_____

A: It's important we do something we both enjoy. We both like sports, and you like hot weather, so… [4]_____

B: I want to go on vacation with you too. If we go somewhere hot, I might kayak on one of the days. [5]_____

7 Work in pairs. Practice the conversation in Exercise 6.

8 **OWN IT!** Make notes on the situations and people. Which persuading style would you use? What language would you use?

1 You want your boss to provide free healthy snacks at work.

2 You want a neighbor to stop parking their car outside your house.

3 You want a close friend to join a running group that you are in.

4 You want a classmate to help you prepare food for a class lunch.

5 You want your young child to put their jacket on and come home with you.

9 Work in pairs. Choose three situations in Exercise 8. Roleplay the situations, using different persuading styles and the Useful Language. Change roles.

7E
My role model

LESSON GOALS
- Use paragraphs and topic sentences
- Practice introducing topics
- Write about an inspiring role model

SPEAKING

1 Work in pairs. Discuss the questions.

1 Are you interested in the natural world? Why or why not?

2 Do you know what a role model is? Do you have one?

3 What, if anything, do you know about David Attenborough?

READING FOR WRITING

NATIONAL GEOGRAPHIC EXPLORER

2 Read Imogen Napper's blog post about someone who inspires her. Why does Imogen think David Attenborough is inspiring?

3 Look at the Writing Skill box. Which paragraphs do topics A–D describe? Write 1–4.

WRITING SKILL
Using paragraphs and topic sentences

Imogen uses four paragraphs to separate the different subjects she mentions in her writing. Paragraphs usually present one topic and have a line space between them. They help organize pieces of writing and make things clearer and easier to read. Imogen uses topic sentences to introduce each new paragraph. These tell us what the paragraph will be about.

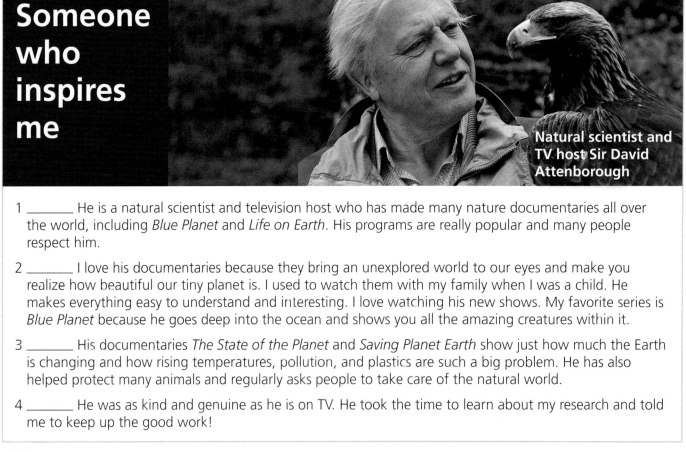

Someone who inspires me

Natural scientist and TV host Sir David Attenborough

1 _____ He is a natural scientist and television host who has made many nature documentaries all over the world, including *Blue Planet* and *Life on Earth*. His programs are really popular and many people respect him.

2 _____ I love his documentaries because they bring an unexplored world to our eyes and make you realize how beautiful our tiny planet is. I used to watch them with my family when I was a child. He makes everything easy to understand and interesting. I love watching his new shows. My favorite series is *Blue Planet* because he goes deep into the ocean and shows you all the amazing creatures within it.

3 _____ His documentaries *The State of the Planet* and *Saving Planet Earth* show just how much the Earth is changing and how rising temperatures, pollution, and plastics are such a big problem. He has also helped protect many animals and regularly asks people to take care of the natural world.

4 _____ He was as kind and genuine as he is on TV. He took the time to learn about my research and told me to keep up the good work!

A meeting David Attenborough ____

B introduction to David Attenborough ____

C David Attenborough's environmental work ____

D why she likes David Attenborough ____

4 Complete paragraphs 1–4 in the blog post with topic sentences a–d.

   a I think David Attenborough is inspiring because he has done so much to help the climate crisis.

   b I was delighted because I got to meet him recently at the Natural History Museum in London.

   c One person who I really admire is David Attenborough.

   d I admire David Attenborough because he has taught millions of people about animals, plants, and birds.

5 Choose four topics. Write the name of one person who inspires you in each of these four areas. Discuss your ideas with a partner.

environment   education   arts and entertainment   business

sports   health   fashion   internet

6 Look at the Useful Language box. Copy the sentences in your notebook and complete them with information about the people you wrote about in Exercise 5.

Useful Language Introducing topics

One person who I really admire is (David Attenborough).

Someone who really inspires me is (my grandmother).

I think (David Attenborough) is inspiring because (he educates people about nature).

I love (Imogen Napper's) work because (it helps protect the environment).

One of the things I respect the most about (my sister) is (that she doesn't let anything stop her).

7 Make notes on the answers to the questions. Use one of the people you wrote about in Exercises 5 and 6. Work in pairs and ask and answer the questions.

   1 Who do you think is inspiring?

   2 What do they do?

   3 Why do you think they are inspiring?

   4 In what ways have they changed the world?

   5 Have you ever met them or would you like to?

8 Use your notes from Exercise 7 to plan four paragraphs. Write a topic sentence for each.

WRITING TASK

9 **WRITE** Using Imogen's text as a model and the other information you've talked about and written, write a blog post about someone who inspires you.

10 **CHECK** Use the checklist. Your blog post...

☐ has a heading.

☐ has four paragraphs.

☐ has a topic sentence for each paragraph.

☐ answers the questions in Exercise 7.

☐ uses language to introduce topics.

11 **REVIEW** Exchange posts with another student. Did they include at least three things from the checklist? Ask and answer more questions about the person. Then make suggestions for how your partner might include the new information.

It has a heading. You used four paragraphs.

Go to page 157 for the Reflect and review.

EXPLORE MORE!

Do you want to watch David Attenborough in action? Watch one of his documentaries online.

8

The world of work

GOALS
- Understand cause and effect in an article
- Use the present perfect to talk about something that is unfinished
- Talk about jobs
- Use mind maps to help understand an interview
- Give a good impression at an interview
- Write a résumé

1 Work in pairs. Discuss the questions.
1 Look at the photo. Describe what you see.
2 What are the best and most difficult things about your job or studies?

WATCH ▶

2 ▶ 8.1 Watch the video. With a partner, answer the questions.

NATIONAL GEOGRAPHIC EXPLORERS

| RUBÉN SALGADO ESCUDERO | ANNE JUNGBLUT |

1 What do Rubén and Anne do?
2 What has been their favorite project at work?
3 What world problems do they want to tell people about?

3 Make connections. Discuss the questions. What do you have in common with Rubén and Anne? How are you different?

Two men work by solar lights in their motorcycle shop in Nbeeda, Uganda. A photo by Rubén Salgado Escudero.

95

8A
Is your job safe?

LESSON GOALS
- Understand cause and effect in an article
- Combine information from different sources
- Talk about how the world of work is changing

READING

1 Look at the photos. Discuss the questions.

1 Have you heard of the jobs in the photos? Do you know what they involve?

2 Can you think of other jobs that were once common that have changed or disappeared? In what ways have they changed and why?

2 Look at the Critical Thinking Skill box. Then skim the article and the infographic on page 97. What are the main messages? Are they similar or different? Tell a partner.

CRITICAL THINKING SKILL
Combining information from different sources

Using information from two or more sources helps us to think critically about a topic. You can compare each source and decide on your opinion. Think about how new information you read relates to the other sources and how this connects to, or changes, your own ideas.

3 Read the article and infographic again. In your notebook write what information they give us about topics 1–4.

1 three jobs of the future

2 three jobs that will disappear

3 the effect of technology on jobs

4 the effect of the environment on jobs

4 Work in pairs. Can you find this information in the article (A), the infographic (I), or in both (B)?

1 changes to workplaces and habits _____

2 reasons for changes to certain jobs _____

3 predictions about jobs in the future _____

4 advice for protecting your own job _____

5 numbers and percentages of people in jobs _____

5 Look at the Reading Skill box. Complete the table with the causes and effects using information from the article.

READING SKILL
Understanding cause and effect

A cause is the reason why something happened and the effect is what happened. The text gives lots of reasons why changes have happened in the world of work. Look for words such as *because, therefore, as,* and *so* or other ways of explaining, such as *digital storage* **means** *less paper.*

CAUSE	EFFECT
[1] *Improved technology*	working from home, flexible work hours
the arrival of cars, electricity, and computers	[2]
[3]	fewer jobs for people dealing with the public
robots can't care for people	[4]
people live until 80+	[5]
[6]	more environmental jobs
[7]	more bike and electric car mechanics
stay flexible and learn new skills	[8]

SPEAKING

6 Work in pairs. Discuss these questions. Have you noticed the changes in the article and infographic? Do you know anyone who does any of these jobs? Which ones? In what ways might your job or a job you want change in the future?

7 Work in pairs. Look at these jobs. Do you think they will still be around in ten years' time? Why or why not?

delivery driver   dental nurse   lawyer
parking attendant   website designer

EXPLORE MORE!

Search online to find two jobs that will be common in the future and two that might disappear. Search for "jobs of the future" or "disappearing jobs."

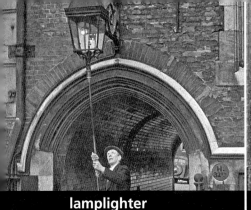
lamplighter

switchboard operator

carriage driver

The changing world of work

The world of work is changing fast. People used to travel to work and work regular hours, but improved technology means more and more people work at home and choose their working hours. Offices have also changed. Many offices now have comfortable sitting areas, free gym classes, and social events for staff.

Technology has killed or changed many jobs over the last 100 years. Carriage drivers, lamplighters, and switchboard operators lost their jobs because of cars, electricity, and computers. Now machines are taking over jobs such as supermarket cashiers, ticket sellers at stations, and check-in staff at airports. While many jobs are dying because of technology, we now need more people to fix and develop that technology. Good news for computer programmers and engineers!

Most healthcare jobs are also safe because everyone needs their services and, so far, no one has invented a robot that can listen and really care for someone. In addition, people are living longer, so in the future there will be more need for doctors, nurses, and healthcare workers.

Other areas of work are growing; because of climate change, we need more people to help companies make their businesses and buildings greener. There is also more need for people who can repair bikes and electric cars.

In the future everyone may have several different jobs and jobs may change often. It's a good idea to be confident with technology, to stay flexible and gain as many skills as possible so that you can always find work.

JOBS OF THE PAST AND JOBS OF THE FUTURE

DISAPPEARING JOBS

Postal worker

Factory worker

Vegetable picker

Bank teller

SAFE JOBS

Computer programmer

Engineer

Healthcare worker

Recycling worker

Teacher

JOBS AND THE FUTURE

 Machines could replace **14%** of jobs.

32% of jobs could change a lot because of technology.

A growing population means we will need **600 million** new jobs by 2030.

GREEN JOBS

 11 million people worked in green energy in 2018. This will grow.

 1.2 million wind power jobs

3.2 million biofuel power jobs

 3.6 million solar power jobs

 2.1 million hydropower jobs

97

8B
A different way to work

LESSON GOALS
• Understand an article about living without money
• Use the present perfect to talk about past experiences
• Practice saying /n/ at the end of a word

READING AND GRAMMAR

1 Work in pairs. Discuss the questions.
  1 What do you spend money on daily, weekly, and monthly? Make a list for each.
  2 What are <u>not</u> good ways to spend money?
  3 Do you think you could live without money? Why or why not?

2 Look at the photo. Mark Boyle lived without money for three years. How and why do you think he did it?

3 Match these words with the definitions.

a camper	b community	c economics
d exchange	e organic	f tire

  1 the people who live in an area _____
  2 the black rubber part of a wheel _____
  3 not using chemicals (of farming) _____
  4 giving one thing and receiving another _____
  5 the study of finance and money _____
  6 a small house on wheels _____

Living without **money**

Mark Boyle lived without money for three years between 2008 and 2011, and has lived without electronic technology since 2016.

He grew up in Ireland and studied business and economics at college. When he finished his degree he moved to the U.K. and managed an organic food company.

Mark has always been interested in alternative ways of living. In 2007, he decided to live without money for a year. He bought a cheap, old camper and started living on an organic farm. He exchanged three days' work on the farm for his rent and somewhere to grow his own vegetables.

Born in 1979, Mark has written four books. He uses the money from his books to help people live in a *freeconomic* community. *Freeconomists* exchange services and skills instead of working for money to buy things they need. For example, Mark needed new tires for his bike, so he wrote a blog post about eco-friendly tires for a company. The company gave him free tires.

People have had different reactions to Mark's unusual life. Some think his ideas are crazy, but his experience has motivated others to use less money themselves. They argue that the lifestyle Mark has chosen doesn't have a negative impact on other people or the environment. Personally, I admire Mark, but I love hot showers and the internet too much to live like him!

Mark Boyle outside his camper

4 Read the Grammar box. Look at the first sentence of the article. Why do we use *lived* in the first part of the sentence and *has lived* in the second? Discuss in pairs.

GRAMMAR Present perfect and simple past

Present perfect
Use the present perfect (*have / has* + past participle) for:
- actions or experiences that happened in the past (but we don't know or say when).
  *Mark **has written** four books.*
- an action or state that started in the past and is continuing or still true in the present.
  *Mark **has always** been interested in alternative ways of living.*

Simple past
Use the simple past for finished actions in the past with a known time.
*He **grew up** in Ireland.*

Use *for* with the simple past and present perfect to talk about periods of time (e.g., *for five years*). Use *since* with the present perfect to talk about dates or times (e.g., *since 2002, since 3 p.m.*).

Go to page 173 for the Grammar reference.

---

5 Read the article again. Circle all the examples of the present perfect and underline the examples of the simple past.

6 Complete the text with the present perfect or the simple past.

Like Mark Boyle, Kim Dinan ¹_____ (completely / change) her life in the last few years. In 2012, she and her husband ²_____ (leave) their good jobs and nice house and ³_____ (sell) all their possessions to travel the world. Since then, she ⁴_____ (go) to over 25 countries on five continents. Thanks to her job at *Backpacker* magazine, she ⁵_____ (also / climb) some of the highest mountains and ⁶_____ (have) many other adventures. A few years ago, she even ⁷_____ (walk) across Spain alone. So far she ⁸_____ (write) two books about her experiences.

PRONUNCIATION AND SPEAKING

7 🔊 **8.1** Look at the Clear Voice box. Listen and repeat.

CLEAR VOICE
Saying the final /n/ sound

Many past participles end with the spelling *en* (e.g., *taken*). When you make the sound /n/, put your tongue to the top of your mouth. The air should come out of your nose, not your mouth. Your throat should vibrate.
taken, been, spoken, given, written, done

---

8 Make full questions using the present perfect.
1 (you / ever / live) without something for a while?
   Have you ever lived without something for a while?

2 Do you know anyone who (earn money) in an unusual way?
   _____

3 (you / ever / make) a big decision to change your life?
   _____

4 (anyone / do) anything kind for you recently?
   _____

5 How long (you / be) studying English?
   _____

6 Do you know any books or movies about people who (give up their jobs) for a new life?
   _____

9 Work in pairs. Ask and answer the questions in Exercise 8. Ask a follow-up question in the simple past.
A: *Yes. I have. I lived without a car for a year because I wanted to save money.*
B: *How did you get around?*

10 Work with another pair and describe your partner's experiences.

8C
Dream jobs

LESSON GOALS
• Talk about jobs
• Make a mind map to help understand an interview
• Use *yet*, *just*, and *already* with the present perfect

VOCABULARY

1 Work in pairs. Look at the "dream jobs" in the photos. Discuss the questions.

1 Would you like to do any of the jobs?
2 What is your dream job?

2 🎧 8.2 Complete the definitions with these jobs. Then listen to check.

accountant	biologist	hairdresser	instructor
politician	reporter	researcher	

1 A(n) _____ cuts people's hair.

2 A(n) _____ records financial information for a person or company.

3 A(n) _____ is a scientist who studies living things.

4 A(n) _____ reports the news for a newspaper, website, or TV channel.

5 A(n) _____ teaches a skill such as yoga, fitness, or driving.

6 A(n) _____ works in politics and leads a region or a country.

7 A(n) _____ studies a subject in detail or tries to find information about a subject.

Go to page 163 for the Vocabulary reference.

3 Work in pairs. Discuss the questions.

1 What word endings do the jobs in Exercises 1 and 2 have?
2 Can you think of other jobs with these endings?
3 Which word endings are the most common?

LISTENING

NATIONAL GEOGRAPHIC EXPLORER

4 🎧 8.3 Listen to Anne Jungblut. What jobs does she mention?

_____

_____

5 🎧 8.3 Look at the Listening Skill box. Copy Anne's mind map on page 101 into your notebook. Listen again to Anne and complete her mind map by making notes on each topic.

LISTENING SKILL
Making mind maps 🎧

A good way to help you understand what someone says is to create a mind map: a diagram with the main idea in the middle and other ideas around it. This can help you understand, organize, and summarize information.

an astronaut

a musician

an author

6 Draw a mind map about yourself, using Anne's to help you. Discuss your mind maps in pairs.

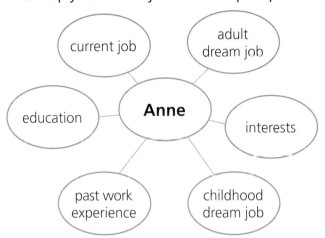

- current job
- adult dream job
- education
- **Anne**
- interests
- past work experience
- childhood dream job

GRAMMAR AND SPEAKING

7 Read the Grammar box. What's the difference in meaning between sentences 1, 2, and 3?

> **GRAMMAR** *Yet, just,* and *already*
>
> Anne uses *yet, just,* and *already* with the present perfect to say when something happened.
> She uses *yet* at the end of negative statements to say that something hasn't happened, but it might.
> *I haven't been there **yet!***
> Also use *yet* at the end of questions to find out if something has happened.
> She uses *already* to say something happened before the time of speaking.
> *I've **already** got my dream job.*
> She uses *just* to say something happened very recently.
> *I've **just** got back from a trip to the Arctic.*

Go to page 173 for the Grammar reference.

1 Have you done your homework yet?
2 I've just finished my homework.
3 I've already finished my homework.

8 Complete the sentences with *yet, just,* or *already.*

1 I haven't started college _____.
2 My sister has _____ moved to Oman to work. She went last week.
3 He's only 29, but he's _____ worked in many different places.
4 Have you finished your report _____ or do you need more time?
5 I have _____ turned the computer off. It's time to relax!
6 I've _____ asked my boss twice about taking vacation time. Still waiting for an answer!

9 Work in pairs. Discuss the questions about your own experience. Try to use *yet, just,* and *already* in your answers.

1 Do you have a full-time job?
2 Have you had an opportunity to practice your English outside class?
3 Have you learned anything interesting recently?
4 Do you know anyone who is doing their dream job?
5 Do you have work or study plans?
6 Have you recently moved or have you lived there for a while?

a photographer

a video game tester

a movie director

101

Making a good impression at an interview

LESSON GOALS
- Practice making a good impression at an interview
- Use positive language
- Understand linking sounds

A face-to-face interview

An online interview

SPEAKING & READING

1 Work in pairs. Discuss the questions.

1 Look at the photos. Do you think it's easier to make a good impression at an online interview or in person? Why?

2 Have you ever been to an interview for anything? Discuss your experiences.

3 How can people prepare for a job interview?

4 How might job interviews be different depending on the job or college, the position, or the country?

2 Read the quotes about interview experiences. Work in pairs. How were the experiences different? What did each person think was surprising?

"I didn't get a job because I wore the wrong color shoes! In my country brown shoes are formal, but over there they have to be black, or gray, or dark blue."

"I applied for a job and it took months. First the résumé, then a phone interview, then a test, and, finally, a face-to-face interview. In the end, I didn't get the job because I was too informal. In my country we often chat for a while before talking about the job. That was a mistake."

"I went for an interview and they got me to roleplay customer service situations. I had to act out talking with an angry customer. It was really embarrassing."

"I applied for a job in another country, but they said my résumé was too long. They wanted one or two pages. I gave them five or six pages!"

"I think I was too formal at my last interview. In my previous job interview they used titles, like Mr., Ms., or Dr., but where I did the interview they wanted first names. I think that's too informal and a bit disrespectful. We sat on comfortable chairs—not even around a table—and everyone was wearing jeans, drinking coffee, and eating cookies. I got the job, but I think they thought I was too polite."

MY VOICE ▶

3 ▶ 8.2 Watch the video about making a good impression at an interview. What main advice does it give for interviews anywhere in the world? Discuss with a partner.

4 ▶ 8.2 Watch the video again. What advice does it give for problems 1–5? Discuss in pairs.
1 "I don't like saying how great I am."
2 "I don't know what the interviewer will ask me!"
3 "I am not a confident person."
4 "I don't know how to do that."
5 "Oh, no! I can't think of an answer to this question!"

5 Look at the Communication Skill box. Then rewrite sentences 1–5 to make them positive.

COMMUNICATION SKILL
Making a good impression at an interview

Job interviews can be very different depending on the country, the company, or the job.

Before an interview it's a good idea to research the company, find out how they interview, and prepare questions you think they might ask.

At the interview be confident, give examples, and be positive. Reword negative phrases. Talk about what you are good at and how you are improving.

1 I don't know much about this company.
I'm looking forward to learning more about this company.

2 I'm not very good at "selling myself."

3 I can't speak in public.

4 I don't have very good study skills.

5 I'm not an organized person.

6 Look at the Useful Language box. Make the sentences in the box true for you. Tell a partner.

Useful Language   Using positive language at an interview
I'm confident with (computers).
I'm really good at (customer service).
I have experience with / I'm currently learning more about (managing a team).
I am a hardworking / organized / reliable team member.
I have studied / worked / volunteered (in an office for three years).
I have excellent communication / problem-solving / team-work skills.

7 Think about a job, volunteering role, or course you are interested in. Write answers to the questions in your notebook. Add two more questions.
1 Why did you apply for this job / course?
2 Have you ever trained someone to do something?
3 Can you give me an example of a time when you improved something at work?
4 What skills and experience do you offer?
5 Tell me about your strengths and weaknesses.
6 Have you ever solved a problem at work?

PRONUNCIATION AND SPEAKING

8 🎧 8.4 Look at the Clear Voice box. Listen and notice how the sounds link.

CLEAR VOICE
Understanding linking sounds: /w/ and /j/

When two vowel sounds come together, some speakers add an extra sound such as /j/ or /w/. Knowing this can help you understand spoken English better.
We /j/ asked them to /w/ invite a special guest.

9 🎧 8.5 Listen to the interview questions in Exercise 7. Circle the linking sounds /w/ or /j/.

10 OWN IT! Work in pairs. Use your notes from Exercise 7. Change roles.
Student A: Ask interview questions, take notes, and give feedback.
Student B: Answer the questions. Listen to the feedback.

EXPLORE MORE!

Search online for advice on how to answer different types of interview questions.

8E
Looking great on your résumé

LESSON GOALS
- Practice proofreading and checking information
- Learn how to write about your skills and experience
- Write a résumé

READING FOR WRITING

1 Look at these categories. Which kinds of information would you include in a résumé in your country or in the kind of work you do? Which would you <u>not</u> include?

- contact information
- education history
- hobbies and interests
- languages
- photo
- profile
- references
- work experience

Rubén Salgado Escudero is a freelance photographer.

RÉSUMÉ

CONTACT INFORMATION

Name: Rubén Salgado Escudero

Tel: +52 013478xxx

Website: www.rubensalgado.com

Address: xx Calle del Sol, Mexico City

Email: Rubén@emailexample.com

PROFILE

Enthusiastic, outgoing, and curious photographer with a passion for travel. I have exhibited my photographs in twenty cities worldwide, published my work in *Time, GEO, El País, Der Spiegel,* and *National Geographic,* and presented at international conferences including TEDx events.

WORK EXPERIENCE

May 2013–present: Freelance Photographer

Freelance photographer with special interest in social and cultural issues around the world. Projects include "Solar Portraits" for National Geographic.

2003–2013 3D animation, Berlin

Worked as part of a team to design and develop video games. Organized and managed 3D animation projects. Trained new employees.

EDUCATION HISTORY

1999–2003, Savannah College of Art and Design, U.S.A.

Bachelor's degree in Fine / Studio Arts, General

LANGUAGES

I speak Spanish, English, German, and Portuguese. I have excellent intercultural communication skills.

HOBBIES AND INTERESTS

Traveling, cooking, yoga, reading, languages, live music

REFERENCES

Available on request

2 Work in pairs. Read Rubén Salgado Escudero's résumé. What skills, experience, and qualifications does Rubén have?

3 Look at the Writing Skill box. Then find four errors in the résumé excerpt for a design job below. Think about spelling, grammar, punctuation, and whether the information is in the correct place.

WRITING SKILL
Proofreading and checking information

Any official writing such as a résumé should have no errors. Résumés need to impress the employer, so check for any mistakes in spelling, punctuation, grammar, typing, or formatting. This is called proofreading. Ask someone to check it before you send it. Also only include information that is necessary for the job you want.

RÉSUMÉ

WORK EXPERIENCE

2011–present: Company Director, Sanford Design

I manage a small team of designers. I am visiting homes and advise clients on furniture and wall color's. My job involves marketing, acounting, and financial planning. I speak English and Hindi.

2010–2011: Chef, Happy Sun Restaurant

I prepared delicious meals in a 120-seat restaurant. I was responsible for cooking, buying ingredients, and hiring staff.

---

4 Read the résumé excerpt again. Is any information unnecessary for a design job?

5 Look at the Useful Language box. Work in pairs. Discuss other information you could put in the parentheses.

Useful Language Writing about your skills and experience

Worked as part of a team to (provide excellent customer service).
My special interest is (the environment).
Trained (new members of staff).
Presented my work (at international conferences).
Organized (events for customers and employees).
My skills include (intercultural communication, sales, and problem solving).

6 Circle three personality adjectives and three work-related verbs in Rubén's résumé. Can you think of three more personality adjectives and work-related verbs that you could use in your résumé? Discuss your ideas with a partner.

7 Use the Useful Language and the adjectives and verbs from Exercise 6 to make sentences about yourself under these headings:
- Education
- Hobbies
- Work
- Languages

WRITING TASK

8 WRITE Using Rubén's résumé as a model and the other information you've talked about in Exercises 5–7, write a résumé for a job you want.

9 CHECK Use the checklist. Your résumé includes...
- [ ] all the important headings.
- [ ] information under the correct headings.
- [ ] personality adjectives and work-related verbs.
- [ ] important information for the job you want.
- [ ] some of the Useful Language.
- [ ] no errors.

10 REVIEW Exchange résumés with another student. Did they include at least three things from the checklist? Suggest ways they might improve their résumé.

Go to page 157 for the Reflect and review.

EXPLORE MORE!

Look online for examples of résumés in the area you work in or would like to work in.

A single figure walks in the forest in Inverness, Scotland in the U.K.

Health and happiness

GOALS

- Identify supporting examples
- Use the second conditional to talk about imagined situations
- Talk about health
- Stay positive when you don't understand
- Learn to say "no" when you need to
- Write a journal about things you are grateful for

1 **Work in pairs. Discuss the questions.**
1 Look at the photo. What can you see?
2 How do you feel when you look at the photo?
3 What do you do when you want to relax?

WATCH ▶

2 ▶ 9.1 Watch the video. How does Federico answer the questions? Discuss with a partner.

NATIONAL GEOGRAPHIC EXPLORER

FEDERICO FANTI

1 What do you do to relax?
2 How do you stay calm in a stressful situation?
3 What helps you sleep well?

3 **Work in pairs. Make connections. Answer the questions in Exercise 2 about yourself.**

9A
Pain and positivity

LESSON GOALS
• Understand an article about experiencing no pain
• Identify supporting examples
• Reflect on how things make you feel

READING

1 Work in pairs. What do you think the advantages and disadvantages would be of not being able to experience pain?

2 Match these words with the definitions.

a anxiety	b extraordinary	c heal
d hip	e in a good mood	f operation
g painkiller	h suffer	i treat
j wound		

1 feel or experience pain _____
2 try to make someone better _____
3 the feeling of being very worried _____
4 happy or positive _____
5 a cut or damage to the skin _____
6 grow and become healthy again _____
7 medicine to reduce pain _____
8 very special and unusual _____
9 the top and side of each leg _____
10 act of cutting open a person's body to make it better _____

3 Look at the Reading Skill box. Then read the article. What examples does the article give to support statements 1–5? Tell a partner.

READING SKILL
Identifying supporting examples

Writers often use examples to support their argument. They can help you understand the argument and judge whether you agree. For example, just saying Jo Cameron was "extraordinary" would be an opinion. But the next sentence tells us why.

1 It was sometimes dangerous to feel no pain.
2 It made life easier to suffer no pain.
3 Jo Cameron does not worry.
4 She has no fear in dangerous situations.
5 Jo's condition may help other people in the future.

4 Look at the Critical Thinking Skill box. Work in pairs. Ask and answer questions 1–5.

CRITICAL THINKING SKILL
Reflecting on how things make us feel

When we reflect on a text, we take time to think about what it means to us and our reactions to it. We can think about whether we agree or disagree with the ideas in the text, what our emotional reactions to it are, and why.

1 Is it surprising that Jo didn't realize she had the condition until she was in her 60s?
2 How would you feel if you discovered you had a rare condition like Jo's?
3 Do you think it would change your life? How?
4 Did the article make you feel there were more advantages or disadvantages to Jo's condition? Why?
5 How would you feel about scientists studying you to help treat other people's problems?

5 Work in groups. Do you feel differently about the idea of living with no pain after reading the article? Why or why not? What might be the advantages and disadvantages of living with no fear?

SPEAKING

6 Work in pairs. Which have you suffered from? Which of these types of pain do you think is the worst?

- a headache
- a toothache
- a stomachache
- a cut
- a burn
- an insect sting

7 Do you know of any ways to treat the kinds of pain in Exercise 6 without using medicine?

My grandmother used to put honey on bee stings.

Jo Cameron feels no pain.

What it means to live without pain

Jo Cameron says she is ordinary, but in reality she is extraordinary. Because of a very rare condition (only one other person in the world has it), she feels no pain and suffers no anxiety or fear.

Now in her 70s, Jo was in her 60s before she realized she was unusual. Until then, she just thought of herself as a very happy and healthy person.

When a problem with her hip became so bad that she could hardly walk, the doctors finally agreed to operate on it. Until then, because she wasn't suffering pain, no one realized how serious it was. After the operation, the doctors couldn't believe that she needed no painkillers. She had some tests and the results began to explain a lot of things about Jo's life.

Although Jo says she is happy with the way she is, she understands now that pain can let you know when there is danger or when the body has a problem. She has burned herself many times while cooking or ironing because she didn't get the warning signals. Sometimes she knows she's burning herself only because she smells it. On the other hand, she has had other operations and has given birth to two children with no need for painkillers at all. Another benefit of her condition is that when she cuts herself, her wounds heal very quickly.

She also feels no fear, thanks to large amounts of a chemical called anandamide in her body. When she had a small car accident, the other driver was shaking and upset, while she was completely calm. She says she isn't brave, she just doesn't feel frightened. It also means she's always in a good mood and, in tests for depression and anxiety, she scored zero. However, her condition means she is more forgetful.

Scientists believe they will be able to learn a lot about pain and ways to treat it from Jo. There is hope that in the future this will help produce better painkillers and treatments for anxiety, post-traumatic stress disorder, and wounds.

EXPLORE MORE!

Search online for more information on Jo Cameron or other people who don't experience pain.

9B

If I had more time, I would do less

LESSON GOALS
- Understand the main points of a blog post
- Use second conditionals for imagined or unreal situations
- Talk about what you would do in imagined situations

READING AND GRAMMAR

1 Look at the photo below. Work in pairs. Discuss the questions.

1 How often do you spend time at home doing nothing? Do you enjoy it?

2 Are you good at doing nothing?

The **art** of doing nothing

If I had a dollar for every time someone said "I can't relax," I'd be rich! For many of us, doing nothing is a skill we need to learn. But once you learn it, you'll love it!

The Dutch agree with me. They have a concept called *niksen*. And it's all about not doing anything or not doing anything with a *purpose*. People used to be negative about the idea of doing nothing, but as the world becomes more stressful, we begin to see how important this is. If I didn't slow down sometimes, I'd get sick!

However, when the Dutch talk about doing nothing, they don't really mean doing absolutely nothing. I'd be bored, if I just sat around all day! The art of doing nothing is more about learning to *be* and not trying to be useful all the time. Everyone has different ways to do this. In fact, Manoush Zomorodi has written a great book about how boredom actually makes you more creative: I wouldn't have so many ideas for my blog posts if I wasn't bored at times.

So how do I do nothing? Well, firstly, I make time for it. If I didn't schedule "me time," I'd probably start *doing* something. Sometimes I stay in bed and read, then have a good breakfast. Or I have my own little concert—play my music really loudly and sing and dance along.

I'll be honest, in the past I used to get stressed if I wasted time, but now I know that doing nothing feels great, helps me relax and makes me more creative.

What about you? Tell me how you do nothing!

110

2 Read the blog post. Find at least three answers for each category

1 Advantages of doing nothing.

_____

_____

_____

2 Things to do when "doing nothing."

_____

_____

_____

3 Work in pairs. Look at your answers in Exercise 3. Answer the questions.

1 What do you think is the main advantage of "me time?"

2 What do you do when you have time to "do nothing?"

3 How similar is the blogger's idea of "doing nothing" to yours?

4 Read the Grammar box. Underline the examples of second conditionals in the blog post. Then match them with the real situations 1–5.

> **GRAMMAR** Second conditionals
>
> The blogger uses the second conditional (if + simple past + would(n't) + base verb) to talk about imagined situations. She shortens would to 'd.
> *If I **didn't** slow down sometimes, **I'd** get sick.*
> Notice you can also put the if clause in the second half of the sentence.
> *I **wouldn't have** so many ideas for my blog posts if I **wasn't** bored at times!*

Go to page 174 for the Grammar reference.

1 The blogger doesn't get a dollar every time someone says "I can't relax."

If I had a dollar for every time someone says "I can't relax..."

2 She doesn't get sick from stress.

_____

_____

3 She doesn't sit and do nothing for 24 hours.

_____

_____

4 She sometimes feels bored.

_____

_____

5 She plans time for herself.

_____

_____

5 Complete the conditional sentences with the verbs in parentheses.

1 If she _____ (worry) less, she _____ (sleep) better.

2 If I _____ (not / have) exams soon, I _____ (have) more time to see you.

3 They _____ (see) their family more if they _____ (move) to Delhi.

4 If you _____ (not / go) out every night, you _____ (have) a lot more money.

5 We _____ (sail) every weekend if we _____ (have) our own boat.

6 If I _____ (live) by the beach, I _____ (swim) all the time.

7 I _____ (not / rent) a top-floor apartment if it _____ (not / have) an elevator.

SPEAKING

6 Complete the second conditional sentences about your lifestyle. Discuss with a partner.

1 I think I'd _____, if I spent more time doing nothing.

2 If I played video games all day, I _____.

3 If _____, I would speak English really well.

4 If I moved to another country, I wouldn't _____.

5 If I ate less _____, I _____.

6 I wouldn't feel _____ if _____.

7 Work in pairs. Ask and answer questions. Student A begins.

Student A: Go to page 181.

Student B: Go to page 182.

EXPLORE MORE!

Find out more about Manoush Zomorodi's ideas. Search for "Manoush Zomorodi + bored."

9C
Staying healthy

LESSON GOALS
- Use words and phrases to talk about health
- Stay positive and follow the main points of a monologue
- Use *must, have to,* and *should* to talk about rules and advice
- Pronounce long and short sounds

SPEAKING AND READING

1 Work in pairs. Look at the health infographic and answer the questions.

1 What advice does it give for eating and drinking?

2 Which of the advice mentioned in the infographic do you follow?

LISTENING

NATIONAL GEOGRAPHIC EXPLORER

2 [9.1] Look at the Listening Skill box. Listen to Federico Fanti. What things from the infographic does he mention?

LISTENING SKILL
Staying positive when you don't understand

Sometimes it's not possible to understand everything people say. It's important to stay positive, try to relax, and keep listening. Try to…

- get the main idea. Don't worry if you don't understand all the words.
- use the words you do know to help you.
- write keywords.
- look at and circle information as you listen.

The more you listen, the better you will become.

Federico Fanti

3 [9.1] Listen again. Are the sentences about Federico true (T) or false (F)? Give reasons for your answers.

1	He thinks he's quite healthy.	T	F
2	He isn't very careful about his sleep and diet.	T	F
3	He's never been to the hospital.	T	F
4	He has interesting ways to make his children take medicine.	T	F
5	He thinks it's important to eat when you are hungry.	T	F
6	He believes exercise has to be difficult.	T	F
7	He's been lucky with wild animals.	T	F

Staying healthy at work or study

Move Get some exercise. Walk or cycle. Climb the stairs. Take a walk at break time. Stand up and talk to others instead of sending emails.

Relax You must take breaks regularly. Switch off your screen, leave your desk, and take 5-10 minutes to think about your breathing.

Eat To stay healthy you should eat healthy food. Bring your own lunch from home—it's cheaper and healthier than eating out.

Drink Bring a reusable bottle of water to work. Try to refill your water bottle 3 or 4 times a day.

Socialize Talking to colleagues is a great way to relax and find out about new opportunities.

Sit Your eyes should face your computer screen and your feet should rest comfortably on the floor (with your knees level to your hips).

VOCABULARY

4 🎧 **9.2** Work in pairs. Match the verbs to the words in 1–6 to make collocations. Discuss any words in 1–6 you don't know the meaning of. Then listen to check.

feel	get	have	prevent	stay	take

1 _____ sunstroke / sick / better

2 _____ a serious accident / bad cold / high fever

3 _____ well / sick / very tired

4 _____ healthy / in good shape / young

5 _____ a cold / illness / putting on weight

6 _____ a break / your medicine

5 Work in pairs. Discuss the questions.

1 When was the last time you got sick?

2 Have you ever had a high fever or gotten sunstroke?

3 Have you ever had an accident and gone to the hospital?

4 What can people do to prevent illness?

5 How do you stay healthy and in good shape?

Go to page 164 for the Vocabulary reference.

GRAMMAR

6 Read the Grammar box. Rewrite the sentences with positive or negative forms of *must*, *have to*, or *should*. Start each sentence with *You*.

> **GRAMMAR** *must, have to, and should*
>
> Federico uses *have to / must / mustn't* + base verb to talk about rules and things that are necessary.
> *...you **must** eat when it is time.*
> *I **have to** mix their tablets with jam.*
> He uses *don't have to* for things that aren't necessary.
> *You **don't have to** think of it as "hard work."*
> He uses *should* and *shouldn't* to give advice.
> *You **should** drink lots of water if it's hot.*

Go to page 174 for the Grammar reference.

1 It's a good idea to wear a raincoat.
   You should wear a raincoat.

2 It's not necessary to go to the doctor. Just rest.
   _____

3 It's very important to wash your hands.
   _____

4 My advice is not to go to bed late.
   _____

5 Don't call an ambulance if it's not an emergency!
   _____

PRONUNCIATION

7 🎧 **9.3** Look at the Clear Voice box. Listen and repeat.

> **CLEAR VOICE**
> **Saying long and short sounds (3): /ɔː/ and /ɒ/**
>
> It is easy to confuse the short /ɒ/ sound (*hot*) and the long /ɔː/ sound (*water*). The difference in length between the two vowels is important.
> You can spell the sounds in different ways, especially the long /ɔː/ sound.
> *It was h**o**t. I was exh**au**sted.*

8 🎧 **9.4** Check (✓) the correct sound. Then listen, check, and repeat.

	/ɒ/	/ɔː/			/ɒ/	/ɔː/
1 abroad	☐	☐	5 w**a**nt		☐	☐
2 st**o**p	☐	☐	6 b**o**dy		☐	☐
3 s**aw**	☐	☐	7 th**ough**t		☐	☐
4 t**a**lk	☐	☐	8 bl**o**g		☐	☐

SPEAKING

9 Work in pairs. Choose a situation from the list or use your own ideas. Give six pieces of advice or information to a friend about what to do and not do.

- they say they are always tired
- they have moved to a new place and are lonely
- they have started attending your school but don't know the rules

9D
Saying "no" when you need to

LESSON GOALS

- Say "no" when you need to
- Choose how to say "no" in different situations
- Understand negative auxiliaries in speech

SPEAKING

1 Work in pairs. Discuss the questions.

1 How often do you say "yes" to things you don't want to do and why?
2 How do you feel when you say "no" to someone or they say "no" to you?
3 How do you usually say "no" to things?
4 Are there any situations where it might be rude to say "no" in your country?

MY VOICE ▶

2 ▶ 9.2 Watch the video about how you can say "no." Answer the questions in pairs.

1 Why do people say "yes" to things they don't want to do?
2 What can be the disadvantages of saying "yes?"
3 What can be the advantage of saying "no" at the beginning?
4 What can you do if you can't decide whether to say "yes" or "no?"
5 What are the advantages of giving reasons?
6 What problems can there be with giving reasons?

3 Look at the Communication Skill box. Then look at reasons 1–6 for saying "no." Work in pairs. Discuss which you have used in the past. Which would you think are good reasons?

COMMUNICATION SKILL
Saying "no" when you need to

It's OK to say "no" to things that you don't want to do, or don't have time to do. If you're not sure, you can ask the person to wait until you've decided. It can be helpful to give reasons. This shows that you aren't able to help, rather than that you don't want to. It's important to choose the right reason for the situation. You'll give different reasons to your family than you would with your work.

1 I have to study.
2 I have an appointment.
3 I am waiting for a delivery.
4 I have to help my family.
5 I have to clean my kitchen cupboard.
6 I am very busy with work at the moment.

114

4 What reasons for saying "no" might you give in these situations?

- Your friend asks you to water the plants in their apartment every day while they're on vacation.
- A family member wants to video call at 8 p.m.
- Your teacher needs your help to prepare for the end of year party.

5 Look at the Useful Language box. How do you say "no" politely in your language?

> **Useful Language**   Saying "no" politely
>
> **Giving reasons**
> I'm sorry, I really don't have time right now.
> I'd be happy to help next time, but I'm sorry I'm too busy right now.
> I'd love to help you, but I have to (study).
>
> **Asking for more time**
> Can I get back to you in a few days? I need to check my calendar.
> If you can wait until (May), I could do it.
> I won't be able to help you this week. Would (next week) work for you?
>
> **Suggesting another solution**
> Maybe you should ask my brother. He's really good at (math).
> I can't help you, but you could try (my friend).

PRONUNCIATION

6   🎧 9.5   Look at the Clear Voice box. Listen to the examples and notice how the speakers say *don't*, *won't*, and *can't*. Can you hear the final /t/ sound?

> **CLEAR VOICE**
> **Understanding elision (2): negative auxiliaries**
>
> Sometimes speakers don't stress the final /t/ in *can't, don't,* and *won't.* The final /t/ sound in negative auxiliaries can often be difficult to hear. This can make it hard to understand what a speaker is saying.
>
> *I'm sorry, I really **don't** have the time at the moment.*
> *I **won't** be able to help you this week. Could you wait a few days?*
> *I'm sorry I **can't** help you, but you could try my friend.*

7   🎧 9.6   Listen to five sentences. Are the speakers saying "yes" or "no?" Tell a partner.

SPEAKING

8 **OWN IT!** Work in pairs. Roleplay two of the situations. Take turns being Student A and B. Can you reach an agreement?

Situation 1

Student A:	Student B:
You need some help with some English that you don't understand. Ask Student B for help. If they say "no," you're worried you're going to fail your exam tomorrow.	You are going to the movies with a friend tonight. You are busy tomorrow morning. Politely say "no" to Student A. Give reasons.

Situation 2

Student A:	Student B:
You want to paint your apartment on Saturday and need help. It's the only day you can do it. Ask Student B.	You can't help on Saturday because you have band practice, but you know that your sister has no plans. Say "no" to Student B politely. Suggest your sister can help.

Situation 3

Student A:	Student B:
You need to borrow a bike for a charity ride on Saturday. Ask Student B if you can borrow theirs.	You've just bought an expensive new bike. You wanted to use the bike on Saturday. The last time a friend borrowed something from you, it was broken when they returned it. Say "no" to Student A. Give reasons.

9 Think of something you need help with. Walk around the classroom and ask your classmates for help. Say a polite "no" to everything your classmates ask you to do.

9E
I am so grateful for this!

LESSON GOALS
- Keep readers interested
- Find the positive in negative situations
- Write a gratitude journal

SPEAKING

1 Work in pairs. Discuss the questions.

1 Do you know people who you think are very positive? How do they stay positive?

2 What do you do to make yourself feel more positive?

3 How is positive thinking good for you?

2 Think about a time you felt stressed or unhappy. Did any of these (or other) things help? If not, which could be helpful? Discuss with a partner.

- writing down your thoughts
- getting more sleep
- phoning a friend
- using social media
- thinking positively
- doing exercise
- listening to a happy song
- spending time outdoors

READING FOR WRITING

3 Read the online diary. Check (✓) what Malina is grateful for.

1 a person	☐	5 a place	☐
2 a skill	☐	6 an object	☐
3 a life change	☐	7 a routine	☐
4 a hobby	☐	8 entertainment	☐

4 Look at the Writing Skill box on page 117. Find examples of how Malina keeps the reader interested in the online journal. With a partner find an example in each post.

Malina's gratitude journal

What am I grateful for today?
This online gratitude journal is helping me look at life in a positive way, even when things feel difficult! I feel happier and more confident now and I think I sleep better and feel less stressed too!

Week 3!

Monday
Today I'm feeling very grateful for this little guy! Two years old today! 😊 He's my nephew and he makes me remember how important it is to not be too serious! I love his laugh!

Tuesday
I am so glad that I can play the piano because it stops me from worrying. Today I practiced "Happy" by Pharrell Williams. I always feel, well, happy…when I play it!

Wednesday
My favorite moment of the day! That first sip in the morning just tastes so good. And I love just sitting with the hot cup in my hands and breathing in the smell.

Thursday
I feel lucky to have a garden. It reminds me how incredible nature is. I always think vegetables from the garden taste better. Today I planted a jasmine bush. It will smell incredible in summer.

Friday
I'm very thankful for yoga. I feel so relaxed after my yoga session this afternoon—I fell asleep at the end! If I didn't do yoga, I would be much less calm.

WRITING SKILL
Keeping the reader interested

Malina keeps the reader interested by…

- choosing nice photos and adding interesting details.
- keeping her posts short.
- sharing her feelings and giving reasons for how she is feeling using *as* or *because* or adding another sentence to say why.
- writing about her senses—things she can see, touch, smell, taste, and hear.

5 Look at the Critical Thinking Skill box. How would Malina see situations 1–4 in Exercise 6 more positively? Discuss with a partner.

CRITICAL THINKING SKILL
Finding positives in negative situations

Malina says that writing her gratitude journal made her more positive about difficult situations. It can be helpful to think about negative situations positively.

6 Change these negative situations to make them positive.

1 I can't leave the house because I'm sick.

_____

_____

2 Since it's raining we can't have a picnic.

_____

_____

3 I lost my job.

_____

_____

4 I was in a traffic jam for two hours.

_____

_____

5 I can't afford to go abroad this year.

_____

_____

7 Work in pairs. Discuss the questions.

1 Have you ever kept a journal similar to Malina's?

2 How do you feel about keeping a journal of things that you are grateful for?

8 Complete the sentences to describe what you feel grateful for. Think about the ideas in Exercises 3 and 4.

1 I am grateful for my _____ because it makes me feel _____.

2 When I hear _____ I feel _____.

3 I am so glad I can _____ as _____.

4 I love the taste of _____.

5 I feel thankful for _____ as _____.

6 _____ helps me relax.

7 The smell of _____ reminds me of _____.

8 I feel lucky to _____. I _____.

WRITING TASK

9 **WRITE** Using Malina's journal as a model and your answers from Exercise 8, write five short posts in journal form about things you were grateful for this week.

10 **CHECK** Use the checklist. Your journal has…

☐ an introduction in the first paragraph.

☐ at least five posts.

☐ what you are grateful for in each post.

☐ a reason why you are grateful using *as* or *because* in each post.

☐ positive thoughts in each post.

☐ reference to the senses and feelings, and interesting details.

11 **REVIEW** Exchange journal posts with another student. Did they include at least three things from the checklist? Were any posts similar to your own? Ask for more information about each post.

It has five things you are grateful for.

You used as, because, and since well.

You say the smell of chocolate makes you feel happy.

Go to page 158 for the Reflect and review.

Mucca Pazza, a 30-piece band from Chicago, performs at Globalfest in New York City, U.S.A.

10

Entertainment

GOALS

- Understand sequence in a story
- Talk about what happened before another past event
- Talk about movies and TV shows
- Listen for general meaning in an interview
- Show you value people
- Write a review of a show

1 **Work in pairs. Discuss the questions.**

   1 Look at the photo. What can you see?

   2 How do you think the people in the photo feel?

   3 What other types of entertainment might you see in a public place?

WATCH ▶

2 ▶ 10.1 **Watch the video. Answer the questions.**

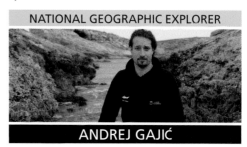

NATIONAL GEOGRAPHIC EXPLORER

ANDREJ GAJIĆ

   1 What type of music does Andrej like?

   2 How often does his band play together?

   3 How did the band get its name?

3 **Make connections. What kind of music do you like? What do you enjoy about playing or listening to music?**

I'm in a band too. I play the keyboard. I like it because it's relaxing.

10A
Stories from around the world

LESSON GOALS
- Read two traditional stories
- Understand sequence in a story
- Identify the moral of a story

READING

1 Look at the pictures. Discuss the questions.

1 What can you see in the pictures?
2 What do you think each story might be about?

2 Match these words with the definitions.

a folk	b greedy	c hide
d jealous	e jewelry	f realize

1 traditional (stories, art, etc.)   _____
2 wanting more than you need   _____
3 things people wear for decoration   _____
4 wanting something someone else has   _____
5 put something in a secret place   _____
6 know and understand something
   suddenly   _____

3 Read the stories on page 121. Are sentences 1–6 true for the story of Bawang (BW), Anansi (A), or both (B)?

1 It has two characters with
   opposite personalities.   _____
2 One character helped another
   character.   _____
3 The main characters are animals.   _____
4 One character decided not to
   be greedy.   _____
5 Two characters got punished
   for being greedy.   _____
6 One character gave good advice
   to another.   _____

4 Look at the Reading Skill box. Circle the time expressions in the stories on page 121.

READING SKILL
Understanding sequence in a story

Every story has a beginning, a middle, and an end. The writer uses different phrases (e.g., *as soon as*, *one day*, *after a while*) to show the relationship between events and the order in which they happened. Time expressions can make the story more interesting and avoid repetition of *and* or *then*.

5 Complete the tiger story with these time expressions.

after a while	a long time ago	as soon as
finally	first	next
the next day	when	

How the tiger got its stripes

[1]_____, when tigers had no stripes, a tiger needed help on his farm. He said he would give the other animals a cow if they helped him. [2]_____, he asked a monkey, but it was lazy. [3]_____, he asked a goat, but it ate everything. [4]_____, a hardworking rabbit came to help. [5]_____, the rabbit asked for its pay and the tiger gave him a cow. [6]_____ the rabbit got home, the tiger arrived. The rabbit offered to share the cow, but the greedy tiger ate most of it. [7]_____, the rabbit built a cage and said danger was coming. The tiger wanted one too, so rabbit built a cage around him. [8]_____ the tiger realized he couldn't get out, he started to fight his way out. To this day, the tiger has stripes from the cuts he got when he broke out of his cage.

6 Look at the Critical Thinking Skill box. Match morals 1–3 with the three stories of Bawang (B), Anansi (A), and Tiger (T).

CRITICAL THINKING SKILL
Identifying the moral

Traditional stories often have a "moral" or life lesson. Think about the personalities of the main characters, what they do, what they say, and how the story ends for them. Ask yourself, "What is the story trying to teach us?"

1 Don't give something then take it away. _____
2 It's better to share knowledge. _____
3 Choose kindness, not greed. _____

SPEAKING

7 Work in pairs. Do you know any similar stories? Go to page 181. Tell a story using the pictures. Then tell your stories to another pair.

Two Folktales

Storytelling may be one of the oldest forms of entertainment. Here are two popular folktales from different parts of the world.

Bawang Merah and Bawang Putih

INDONESIA AND MALAYSIA

Bawang Merah and Bawang Putih were very different half-sisters. Bawang Merah was greedy and lazy while Bawang Putih was kind and hardworking.

One day, Bawang Putih was washing clothes in the river when her favorite scarf washed downstream. She walked along the river until she met an old woman who had the scarf. The woman said "I will give it to you if you help clean my house." Bawang Putih worked hard until the house was cleaner than it had ever been. The old woman returned her scarf and offered her a choice of two pumpkins— one big and one small. Knowing the old woman was poor, Bawang Putih took the small pumpkin. When she got home, she cut it open and discovered it was full of gold and silver jewelry.

Bawang Merah and her mother were very jealous, so they went to the river and threw in their scarves. After a while, they found the old woman and cleaned for her. When the woman offered them a pumpkin, they took the big one. As soon as they arrived home, they cut it open, but found it was full of snakes.

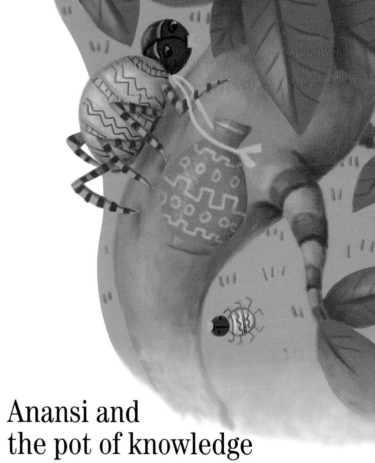

Anansi and the pot of knowledge

WEST AFRICA

Once upon a time, there was a very clever spider called Anansi who wanted to know everything about the world. He took an enormous clay pot and traveled around collecting knowledge.

When he had filled his pot, he decided that he wanted to keep all the knowledge for himself, so he tied the pot around his neck and started to climb a tall tree so he could hide it. The pot was heavy around his neck and made it difficult to climb.

After some time, his son noticed and said "Father, why don't you tie the pot to your back? Then you can climb the tree more easily." Anansi did this and was able to climb the tree easily.

He saw that his son had found a solution even without the pot of knowledge. Anansi had thought he knew everything about the world, but, in the end, he realized it wasn't true. He decided to hold the pot up so the wind could blow the information all over the world.

EXPLORE MORE!

Look for common folktales online. Search for "folktales + [name of country]." Think about the moral of the story.

10B
I hadn't made a sound!

LESSON GOALS
- Understand people talking about performing
- Use the past perfect to talk about things that happened before another past event
- Understand past perfect forms

LISTENING AND GRAMMAR

1 Work in pairs. Look at these activities, then discuss questions 1 and 2.

act	dance	play music
read a poem	sing a song	tell a joke or story

1 Have you ever done any of the activities in the box or anything else to entertain others?
2 How much did you enjoy the experience?

2 🎧 10.1 Read and listen to people talking about their experiences of performing. Which of the things from Exercise 1 did they talk about? Discuss with a partner.

3 🎧 10.1 Listen again. Correct the sentences. Write the correct versions in your notebook.
1 Malee hated telling jokes on stage.
2 Kofi had planned for his cousin's son to perform at his wedding.
3 Nam played very loudly.

"I remember my first comedy show well. I'd practiced for weeks, so I felt ready. But when I got on stage I couldn't remember anything. I'd forgotten all my jokes! I just stood there, staring at the audience for what felt like a long time! Thankfully, I'd written a few notes on my hand before I went on, so finally, I looked at them and started talking. Once everyone laughed at my first joke I relaxed and everything was OK. In fact, I loved it!"

Malee

"During the speeches at my wedding we noticed something moving under the table. It was my cousin's three-year-old son, Ebo. He had hidden under the table as part of a game with the other children! My wife picked him up and asked him to say a few words. As soon as he got the microphone, Ebo started singing "Happy Birthday!" He had obviously thought the big party was for our birthday. All the guests loved him and our family still tell this story about the surprise song at our wedding."

Kofi

"When I was at school, we had to put on a show and I had to play a few songs on my recorder with some other students in my class. The night before the show I felt very anxious because I hadn't learned the songs, but it was too late to learn them. So, the next day, I stood on stage and moved my fingers but didn't blow into the recorder. As soon as the concert had finished I went to find my mom. Luckily, she said nobody had noticed."

Nam

A boy plays the recorder in a music class.

122

4 Read the Grammar box. Complete the timeline with the phrases in bold from the example in the box.

> **GRAMMAR** Past perfect
>
> Use the past perfect to talk about something that happened before another past action and after phrases such as *when*, *after*, *until*, and *as soon as*.
> ***I'd practiced** for weeks, so **I felt ready**.*

Go to page 175 for the Grammar reference.

Past   *now*   *future*

1 _____   2 _____   **3 the show**

5 Look at the examples from the texts. In each sentence, underline the action that happened first.

1 I'd written a few notes on my hand before I went on.

2 We noticed something moving—Ebo had hidden under the table!

3 The night before the show I felt very anxious because I hadn't learned the songs.

4 As soon as the concert had finished I went to find my mom.

6 Match the sentence halves.

1 Once I'd finished telling the story about her…

2 When I finally got to the show…

3 I didn't know my teacher…

4 I had purple eye makeup on my nose, but…

5 He couldn't perform in the play because…

a I didn't notice until I came off stage. _____

b I realized she was standing right behind me! _____

c everyone had already gone home! _____

d had invited so many people. _____

e he had left his costume at home. _____

PRONUNCIATION

7 🔊 10.2 Read the Clear Voice box. Listen to the examples and notice the contractions.

> **CLEAR VOICE**
> **Understanding the past perfect**
>
> It can sometimes be difficult to hear the difference between the past perfect and the simple past. This is because many speakers contract **had** to **'d**.
> *No one **had** realized the children were hiding!*
> *They**'d** loved her.*

8 🔊 10.3 Listen to the past perfect sentences. Which is the easiest to understand—the contracted form or the full form?

1 I'd called my friends before the show.
   I had called my friends before the show.

2 He'd practiced the songs every day.
   He had practiced the songs every day.

3 They'd filmed everything.
   They had filmed everything.

SPEAKING

9 Complete the sentences in your own words. Use the past perfect. Work with a partner.

1 When I arrived at the theater, I realized that I…
   … I'd left the tickets at home.

2 I couldn't sing the song because I…

3 Everybody was surprised because the comedian…

4 My family were excited that I…

5 He had to sing without his guitar because…

10 Work in pairs. Look again at the kinds of performances in Exercise 1. Think of a time that you or someone you know entertained an audience in one of these ways. Make notes on:

• what the activity was and when it happened
• who the audience was
• what preparation you needed
• what went well or badly

11 Tell your partner the story. Use the past perfect where appropriate.

10C
It's so entertaining

LESSON GOALS
• Listen for general meaning in an interview
• Use movie and TV vocabulary to talk about your free time
• Practice using articles correctly

dancing

going to a concert

playing video games

going to the movies

watching movies and TV

reading fiction

watching a play

playing music

photography

LISTENING

1 Look at the photos. Work in pairs. Which of these things do you enjoy doing? What else do you do in your free time?

NATIONAL GEOGRAPHIC EXPLORER

2 🎧 10.4 Look at the Listening Skill box. Listen to the interview with Andrej Gajić. Check the photos showing the activities he usually does in his free time.

LISTENING SKILL
Listening for general meaning

When people talk, they often speak quickly and it's hard to understand, for example, the names or the titles of movies or books they mention. However, it isn't always necessary to get the exact names. Try to understand what they are saying about things or how they describe them to get the general meaning of the conversation.

3 🎧 10.4 Listen again to Andrej. What does he say about each topic? Discuss with a partner.

- *Only the Brave*
- *The Shawshank Redemption*
- *Lost*
- Stephen King
- *Under the Dome*
- books

VOCABULARY

4 🎧 10.5 Match these movie and TV words with the definitions. Which words can you also use to talk about a book? Listen and check.

a animation	b director	c drama	d mystery
e plot	f romantic comedy		g scene
h science fiction	i series	j star	

1 a story told with pictures, not actors _____
2 a story about people's lives and relationships _____
3 a story where something strange has happened _____
4 an imaginary story about space or the future _____
5 a funny story about love _____
6 a set of TV shows with the same characters, which usually runs for a long time _____
7 a section of a movie or TV show where the events happen in one place _____
8 the person who tells the actors what to do _____
9 a famous actor or singer, or the best performer in a show _____
10 events that happen in a movie or TV show _____

Go to page 164 for the Vocabulary reference.

5 Work in pairs. Discuss the questions.
1 What type of movies and TV shows do you like to watch?
2 What type of books do you like to read?
3 What is your favorite TV series?
4 Have you ever found a plot too difficult to follow?

GRAMMAR

6 Read the Grammar box. Why does Andrej use *a dome* and then *the dome* in this example?

"It's about a town that gets covered by a dome… The dome stops radio signal…getting to the town."

> **GRAMMAR** Articles
>
> Use *a* or *an* and *the* before most nouns.
> Use *a* or *an* to talk about what something is and to say what job someone has.
> *I'm a scientist.*
> Use *the* to talk about things there is only one of or something you and the listener know you're talking about.
> *The one where they get stuck on **the** desert island.*
> Use *a* or *an* to talk about something for the first time and *the* for the second time.
> Don't use an article with most place names or with uncountable nouns, plurals, people's names, and meals when talking in general.
> *I love listening to ~~the~~ music.*

Go to page 175 for the Grammar reference.

7 Complete the paragraph with *a* or *an*, *the*, or no article (–). Why did you choose each? Tell a partner.

In my [1]_____ free time, I like to read [2]_____ crime books. Once [3]_____ month, I go to [4]_____ book club. Last month, we read [5]_____ book called *The Number One Ladies Detective Agency* by Alexander McCall Smith. [6]_____ book is set in [7]_____ Botswana. [8]_____ main character, Precious, is [9]_____ private detective. It's one of [10]_____ best books I've ever read.

SPEAKING

8 Think of a movie, a TV series, a video game, or a book that you like. Think about the topics below and discuss with a partner.
- when you watched, read, or played it.
- where it's set, what it's about, and the plot.
- who the main characters are.
- why you enjoy(ed) it.

Showing you value people

LESSON GOALS
- Show you value people
- Use appropriate language to show a relationship is important to you
- Say words starting with /str/

SPEAKING

1 Work in pairs. Check that you understand these words and phrases. Then discuss questions 1–3.

good sense of humor	helpful	honest
intelligent	kind	respectful
shared interests	understanding	

1 Which of these characteristics do you look for in a friend?
2 Is there anything else you look for in a friend?
3 How would you describe the relationship in the photo?

2 How much do you agree or disagree with each sentence? Choose a number from 1 to 5. Discuss your answers with a partner.

disagree   agree
1 —— 2 —— 3 —— 4 —— 5

1 I am good at making new friends. ____
2 I am good at staying in touch with people. ____
3 I often arrange social events for others. ____
4 A few good friends are better than lots of friends. ____
5 I am confident with people I don't know well. ____

MY VOICE ▶

3 ▶ 10.2 Work in pairs. Discuss the questions. Watch the video about ways of showing you value people. How does the video answer each question?

1 What do strong relationships need?
2 What qualities do you think good friends have?
3 Why can it be difficult to make time for others?

4 Look at the Communication Skill box. Can you think of a time that these strategies were easy or difficult for you? Share your experiences in pairs.

COMMUNICATION SKILL
Showing you value people

Relationships grow and get stronger when you give them time and show you value them. You can use these four strategies to show warmth and positivity:

1 Share your feelings: Tell people what you like about them.
2 Keep up contact: Take time to call, message, or see people.
3 Show understanding: Be caring when people need you to be.
4 Say "thanks": Thank people for the things they do for you.

A group of friends in Auckland, New Zealand

5 Look at the Useful Language box. Then complete the conversation between Han and Shahadi below using the Useful Language.

> **Useful Language** Showing that a relationship is important
>
> **Show warmth**
> It's so good to see you!
> How are you doing?
> I missed you last night. I'm looking forward to seeing you next week.
>
> **Keep up contact**
> Sorry I haven't been in touch for a while. I'd love to catch up with you.
> Would you like to (get together)?
> I have tickets to (a comedy festival). Do you want to come?
>
> **Show understanding and support**
> That sounds really hard. I'm sorry to hear that.
> Oh, no! What happened? Are you OK?
> That's awful! What do you need?
> That's great news! Congratulations! I'm really happy for you.
>
> **Say "thanks"**
> That's really nice, thank you.
> Thanks for doing that. It was really helpful.

S: Hi! Han! It's so ¹_____ to see you! I haven't seen you in ages.

H: Oh! Shahadi! You look great! How are you ²_____?

S: I'm OK. I'm kind of stressed out! I'm trying to find Stratford Street. Do you know where it is?

H: Yeah. Go straight ahead. It's the next street on the left. Where are you going?

S: I'm trying out a new gym. Would you ³_____ come with me?

H: I'll walk with you, but I can't join you today.

S: Thanks for walking with me. That's really ⁴_____.

H: No problem. I have free tickets to a concert on Tuesday. Do you ⁵_____?

S: Sounds great. I'd love to ⁶_____ with you!

PRONUNCIATION

6 [🔊 106] Look at the Clear Voice box. Listen and repeat.

> **CLEAR VOICE**
> **Saying words starting with /str/**
>
> Words starting with two or more consonants can be difficult to say. Some speakers might add an extra vowel sound, for example, before the first consonant /estr/ or between the consonants /satr/, while others might miss one of the consonant sounds. If you want to be easy to understand, it's often better to say every consonant sound.
> /str/ **str**ong, **str**eam, **str**ict, **str**ange

7 Look at the excerpt from the conversation in Exercise 5. Underline the words with the /str/ sound. Work in pairs and practice the conversation.

S: I'm OK. I'm kind of stressed out! I'm trying to find Stratford Street. Do you know where it is?

H: Yeah. Go straight ahead. It's the next street on the left.

SPEAKING

8 **OWN IT!** Work in pairs. Take turns being Students A and B. Use the strategies from the Communication Skill box and the Useful Language. Make plans to meet.

Student A: You have been busy studying. You want to see your friend, but your only free time is Saturday evening. You will be going to the theater and have a spare ticket they can have for free.

Student B: You haven't seen your friend in a long time. You have been very busy at work, so you are tired in the evenings. You're worried about money. You are happy to help your friend study or to cook lunch for them one day this week.

9 Work in pairs. Think about a strong relationship you have. Answer the questions.

1 Why do you enjoy spending time with that person?

2 How often do you communicate? How?

3 What do you do when you are together?

4 What things do you do for each other?

5 Is there anything more you could do to show you value them?

10E

I totally recommend this show!

LESSON GOALS
- Give your opinion
- Describe a show
- Write a review of a show

SPEAKING

1 Work in pairs. Discuss the questions.

1 Do you ever go to the theater or to other live performances, e.g., concerts or dance?

2 Do you often read reviews before deciding to go?

3 What things do you write online reviews about?

READING FOR WRITING

2 Read the review. How did the reviewer feel about the show? Tell a partner.

3 Read the review again. Are the sentences true (T) or false (F)?

1 The reviewer didn't know the story.	T	F
2 The costumes were really good.	T	F
3 The story is set in the African grasslands.	T	F
4 The music in the show was the same as the movie.	T	F
5 The reviewer thought Simba and the monkey were amazing.	T	F

4 Look at the Writing Skill box. Underline all the opinions in the review. Which ways of giving opinions from the box do they use?

WRITING SKILL
Giving opinions

Reviews are an opportunity to share your opinion with lots of people. The reviewer can express their opinions in the following ways:

- using a range of adjectives as well as comparative and superlative forms
- using expressions like: *In my opinion, In my view, For me,* and *I thought*
- saying what they liked or disliked
- saying how they felt

5 Look at the Useful Language box. Find seven positive and two negative adjectives in the review. Can you think of any other adjectives to describe different types of entertainment?

Useful Language   Describing a show

Giving opinions
I thought / For me / In my view / In my opinion (the performers) were…
  amazing / fantastic / entertaining. (positive)
  terrible / awful / boring. (negative)
I loved / liked / disliked / hated the (star).
One thing I'd change is (the music).
My favorite (character / song / part) was…
The star of the show was (a young actor).

Describing the story
The story was (very sad). / It was set in the (forest).
It was about (a poor man who becomes rich). / It tells the story of (a young Russian girl).

Giving recommendations
I totally recommend this (show). / I wouldn't recommend this (show).

6 Think of a show (or other live performance) you have seen. Write six sentences giving your opinion of it. Discuss your ideas in pairs.

I saw Aladdin when I was at school. I thought it was amazing.

WRITING TASK

7 **WRITE** Using your notes and *The Lion King* review as a model, write a review of a show or performance you have seen.

8 **CHECK** Use the checklist. Your review...

☐ has a heading and a star rating.

☐ includes information about why you chose it.

☐ summarizes the plot, the people, and the place.

☐ includes opinions.

☐ gives a recommendation.

9 **REVIEW** Exchange reviews with another student. Did they include at least three things from the checklist? Ask questions to find out any missing information, then help your partner decide where to put it.

Go to page 158 for the Reflect and review.

THE LION KING

Rafiki in *The Lion King* in Singapore

★★★★★

I recently saw the musical *The Lion King* at the theater. I had watched Disney's classic animated movie many times when I was a child and I enjoyed the 2019 movie too, so it was really exciting to hear that the stage show was in town.

I loved it when the show started and all the animals danced down the aisle. There were giraffes, zebras, and a huge elephant, and their costumes were incredible. The elephant was so big it needed one dancer for each leg! It was amazing that they could still dance so well!

The story in the stage show is the same as the movies. Simba is a young lion in Africa whose father is the king of the grasslands. His uncle Scar is jealous that Simba will be king, so scares him away. However, when Simba grows up he returns to save the grasslands. The music in the stage show is a bit different to both movies but, in my view, it's still very powerful and at times I felt like singing along!

The performers were fantastic, especially Simba as a child. He had so much energy. But, for me, the star of the show was the woman who played the monkey, Rafiki. She had the most wonderful voice.

The one thing I didn't enjoy was the annoying person in front of me who chatted noisily with their friend throughout the whole show!

Overall, I totally recommend this show. It's perfect for all ages.

EXPLORE MORE!

Look for reviews of *The Lion King* stage show or movies online. Search for "Lion King stage show," "Lion King original movie," or "Lion King 2019 movie."

A waitress balances seven plates in a café in Hanoi, Vietnam.

130

11
Challenges

GOALS

- Recognize different genres and messages
- Report what someone says
- Use adjectives to describe emotions
- Listen for signposts in an interview
- Ask others to help you
- Write a report about classroom challenges

1 Work in pairs. Discuss the questions.

1 Look at the photo. What are the people doing? How do you think they feel?
2 What do you think could happen next?
3 What are the other challenges of working in a restaurant?

WATCH ▶

2 ▶ 11.1 Watch the video. Answer the questions in pairs.

NATIONAL GEOGRAPHIC EXPLORER
ANNE JUNGBLUT

1 What was challenging about Anne's postgraduate studies?
2 What does she find challenging about where she lives?
3 What solutions has she found?

3 Make connections. What's your biggest challenge at the moment? What challenges do you have every day? Discuss in pairs.

11A
Personal challenges

LESSON GOALS
- Recognize genre and message in a text
- Connect a topic to personal experience
- Discuss ideas for social media challenges

READING

1 Work in pairs. Look at the photo. Do you know anything about the ice bucket challenge? Do you know of other social media challenges?

2 Match these words and phrases from the texts with the definitions.

a donate	b go viral	c have access to
d raise	e tag	f waste

1 collect (e.g., money) for a particular purpose   _____

2 be shared widely on social media   _____

3 name someone else in a post   _____

4 use something valuable or important in an unhelpful way   _____

5 get the opportunity to use something that will help you   _____

6 give something (e.g., money or food) to charity   _____

3 Look at the Reading Skill box. Work in pairs. What features do social media posts often have?

READING SKILL
Recognizing genre and message

There are many different types—or genres—of texts: blogs, articles, emails, etc. Each genre has different features. For example, news articles have a headline and begin with a summary sentence, while blogs may have short paragraphs with links to other websites. Recognizing the genre can help you understand the message because different genres are written for different readers and reasons.

4 Skim texts 1–3 on page 133 and match them with genres a–c.

a blog post   _____

b email   _____

c news article   _____

5 Skim the texts on page 133 again and match them with the messages a–c.

a Facts about some popular online challenges   _____

b Reasons why online challenges are popular   _____

c Asking someone for advice   _____

6 Read the texts again. Are the sentences true (T) or false (F)?

1 The blogger thinks we only enjoy watching funny challenges.   T   F

2 The article claims the ice bucket challenge was popular in India.   T   F

3 Eva thinks a selfie challenge will show the council that the community cares.   T   F

7 Look at the Critical Thinking Skill box. Then answer questions 1–3.

CRITICAL THINKING SKILL
Connecting a topic to personal opinions and experiences

After you read, it can be helpful to think about how the information in a text relates to your own ideas, feelings, and experiences. Think about what you learned, how you feel, and what you might do.

1 How do you feel about each challenge mentioned?

2 Do you agree with the blogger's reasons for why social media challenges are popular?

3 Have you—or people you know—taken part in any social media challenges?

SPEAKING

8 Work in pairs. Think of a social media challenge that could go viral. Decide what you want to raise money for.

9 Work with another pair. Discuss your ideas from Exercise 8. Whose idea do you think might raise the most money?

What is it about social media challenges?

Almost every day someone I know shares a challenge to raise money for charity and asks people to join them. It could be posting ten photos in ten days, eating something disgusting, or sharing a no make-up selfie. Why are they so popular? Here are three reasons:

1 Human interest

People love seeing other people doing challenges. By watching friends do something difficult, silly, or funny we can share their experiences. We can enjoy their laughs—or their disappointments.

2 Videos and photos

Social media is perfect for video and photo sharing. It's more interesting than text and you can see your friends embarrass themselves. You can see celebrities do the same too!

3 Sharing

The best way to make online challenges go viral is for people to share posts and tag their friends. Someone shares an entertaining video of themselves and names three friends to do the same. Those three friends then challenge another three, and it's all over the internet in no time.

Online challenges are here to stay

In 2014, 17 million people around the world posted videos of themselves throwing buckets filled with ice and water over their heads. This simple challenge raised $115 million for the ALS Association, a charity that helps people with ALS, a disease which damages the brain and the body's muscle control.

The challenge inspired other ideas, such as the rice bucket challenge in India. There, many people don't have access to clean drinking water, so instead of wasting water, people gave buckets of rice to those in need or to food charities. In Lebanon and Venezuela some people made videos of themselves throwing empty buckets over their heads to show how important water is, while in the Ivory Coast people threw soapy water over themselves to communicate the importance of washing to prevent disease.

New Message

Subject: Social media challenge

Hi Juliana,

We had a meeting yesterday to talk about some ideas for raising money for an outdoor gym in the park. We all agreed that we should do something fun that could go viral online. Then the council can see that the community really wants it. We thought maybe people could post selfies of themselves looking really hot and red-faced after exercise. What do you think? Any better ideas?

Regards,
Eva

EXPLORE MORE!

Look online for examples of social media challenges. Search for "ice bucket challenge" or "social media challenge."

11B

Making the impossible possible

LESSON GOALS
- Understand an article about a personal challenge
- Report what other people have said
- Understand *told* in connected speech

READING AND GRAMMAR

1 Work in pairs. Discuss the questions.
1 Do you enjoy a difficult challenge? Why or why not?
2 What physical challenges have you done or have you heard about?

2 Read the magazine profile. What challenges has Ed faced? Discuss with a partner.

3 Read the profile again. Answer the questions about things people talked about. Look for words like *said* and *told* to help you. Underline the answers in the text.
1 What did doctors tell Ed and Nasser?
2 Who did Ed say he wanted to get better for?
3 What did Nasser tell Ed after half a year?
4 What does Ed say happens after he does a challenging climb?
5 How did Ed say he felt during the stair challenge?

Meet Ed Jackson:
a man who loves challenges

Ed Jackson was a professional rugby player, but in 2017 he had an accident diving into a swimming pool. Afterwards he couldn't move his body from the shoulders down.

Doctors told him that he'd probably never walk again, but Jackson didn't want to believe this. He had recently got engaged to the woman who is now his wife and he said that she was the main reason he wanted to recover. He spent six days staring at his toes and trying to make them move—and, finally, he succeeded! This was the start of a long journey.

While in hospital, Ed met Nasser, a man in his late thirties. Doctors had also told Nasser he would never walk again, but Ed encouraged him not to give up and six months later, Nasser told Ed he was walking with a stick.

Only a year after his accident, Ed climbed the highest mountain in Wales. Since then he has also climbed a 6,500-meter mountain in Nepal and he said that after each big climb he noticed his body could do new movements.

Two years later, 31-year-old Ed Jackson climbed 8,848 meters, the height of the world's highest mountain, by going up and down his parents' stairs 2,783 times. When he finished, he told a news reporter he had loved it despite it sometimes being "painful" and "boring." He also raised £46,000 for charity.

Jackson hopes his story can help people. That's why he started his own charity, M2M, which aims to support "people facing challenges in life."

4 Read the Grammar box. Complete sentences 1 and 2.

GRAMMAR Reported speech

The article uses *said* and *told* + pronoun or noun to report someone else's words. Sometimes the speakers add *that* before the reported speech. The speakers also change some pronouns.

"You'll probably never walk again." → *Doctors told him (that) he'd probably never walk again.*

"She's the main reason I want to recover." → *He said (that) she was the main reason he wanted to recover.*

"I am walking with a stick!" → *Nasser told Ed he was walking with a stick.*

"I loved it." → *He told a news reporter (that) he had loved it.*

Verb tenses change: simple present (*can*) → simple past (*could*), present progressive → past progressive, *will* → *would*, simple past + present perfect → past perfect

---

Go to page 176 for the Grammar reference.

1 Ed _____ that he wanted his charity to help other people facing big challenges.

2 Ed _____ Nasser to keep trying.

5 Choose the correct options.

1 "Ed Jackson was a professional rugby player."
The article *said* / *told* that Ed had been a professional rugby player.

2 "He has also climbed a 6,500-meter mountain in Nepal."
It told us that he *had also climbed* / *also climbed* a 6,500-meter mountain in Nepal.

3 "He'll never stop trying."
It said that *he'll* / *he'd* never stop trying.

4 "Jackson hopes his story can help people."
The article said that Jackson hoped his story *can* / *could* help people.

5 "The charity is raising money for a hospital in Nepal."
It said that the charity *was raising* / *raised* money for a hospital in Nepal.

6 "It hosts challenge events."
The article *told* / *said* that the charity hosted challenge events.

6 Rewrite the direct speech using reported speech.

1 "Everyone is so kind."
He said that _____ _____.

2 "He's feeling better."
He said _____.

3 "Your family will be proud!"
She told me _____.

4 "I am looking forward to next year."
She said _____.

PRONUNCIATION

7 🎧 **11.1** Look at the Clear Voice box. Listen to the examples and notice the two different pronunciations of *told*.

CLEAR VOICE
Understanding connected speech: *told*

In fast speech, some speakers drop the *d* in *told* if the next word begins with a consonant, e.g., *told me* → /təʊlmiː/.

Other speakers drop the /ð/ in *them* and the /h/ in *him* and *her*, e.g., *told her* → /təʊldə/.

/təʊldəm/ I **told them** it was for charity.

---

8 🎧 **11.2** Listen and complete the sentences. Which speaker is easier to understand?

1 I told _____ they could do anything.

2 I told _____ she might win.

3 I told _____ you'll call him later.

4 He told _____ I was awesome.

SPEAKING

9 Work in pairs. Talk about a challenge you have faced. Take notes on what your partner said.

Last month, I gave a presentation at work. It was the first time I had spoken in public and I felt really nervous!

10 Change partners and report what your partner from Exercise 9 said.

EXPLORE MORE!

Find out what M2M means and learn more about Ed Jackson. Search for "Ed Jackson + M2M."

LESSON GOALS
- Listen for signposts in an interview
- Describe emotions
- Talk about skills, permission, and possibility

What are the limits of the human body?

1  Humans can survive in water of **4.4°C** for **15–30 minutes**! Ice water divers wearing dry suits are able to stay safe for **30 minutes**. However, in 1999, Swedish Anne Bågenholm survived for **80 minutes** trapped under ice.

2 In cold temperatures we need to wear the right clothes to survive. The human body is usually **37°C**. Humans can't usually survive if their body temperature drops below **21°C**.

3  The average human is able to breathe until **4,572 meters** before needing oxygen. Only 200 people have climbed the world's tallest mountain, **8,848 meters** without oxygen.

4 Herbert Nitsch free-dived to **214 meters** in 2007. Most people can hold their breath for less than **2–3 minutes**. Herbert Nitsch is able to hold his for nine minutes.

5  Humans can generally survive without food for around **three weeks** and **3–7 days** without water. The longest anyone has gone without food is around **382 days** and water around **18 days**.

6 Most people can stay awake for no more than **24 hours** before they start to feel very tired, annoyed, or make poor decisions. However, Randy Gardner was able to stay awake for **11 days (264 hours)**

READING

1 Work in pairs. Read the infographic. What does it say about human limits for being…
1. somewhere very cold?
2. high in the mountains?
3. underwater without air?
4. without food?
5. without water?
6. without sleep?

LISTENING

NATIONAL GEOGRAPHIC EXPLORER

2 Look at the Listening Skill box. Then read the signposting phrases (1–6) from Anne Jungblut's talk about working in very cold places. Work in pairs. Decide what kind of information you think she might give next.

LISTENING SKILL
Listening for signposts

Signposts are words and phrases that tell you what kind of information is coming next. Here are some common signposts to…
- introduce a topic: *let's start by, first, to begin*
- give contrasting information: *on the other hand, although, but then again*
- give past, present, or future information: *a while ago, now, next year*
- give a reason: *because, since*
- give an example: *such as, like, for instance*

1. So I'll start by talking about…
   She's introducing a topic.
2. It's really different to our normal environment because of things like…
3. Although it's challenging to work in the freezing cold…
4. It can be five, six degrees plus in the Arctic. But then…
5. I'm able to work late since…
6. Before I go there…

3 🎧 **11.3** Listen to Anne's talk. How does she finish the sentences in Exercise 2? Tell a partner.

4 [🎧 11.3] Listen again. What challenges does Anne face? How does she solve them?

	Challenge	Solution
washing		
food		
water		
temperature	freezing -5°/-10°C	
work hours		
sleep		

5 Look at the infographic again. Which things does Anne mention? Tell a partner.

VOCABULARY

6 [🎧 11.4] Match the emotions 1–6 with definitions a–f. Listen and check.

a amazed	b anxious	c disappointed
d exhausted	e scared	f shocked

1 very tired _____
2 something wasn't as good as you'd hoped _____
3 surprised and upset about something bad _____
4 worried something bad might happen _____
5 afraid _____
6 extremely surprised _____

Go to page 165 for the Vocabulary reference.

7 Work in pairs. Use the adjectives in Exercise 6 to discuss how you might feel in these situations. More than one option is possible.

1 You got excellent results from an exam you thought you'd done really badly in.
2 You've just run 42 km.

3 You are sleeping in a tent in the forest. You wake up and there's a lion outside.
4 Your best friend lost their job.

GRAMMAR AND SPEAKING

8 Read the Grammar box. Complete 1–3 with *present, past,* or *future.*

> **GRAMMAR** *Can, could,* and *be able to*
>
> Use *can* and *be able to* to talk about things that you know how to do, that you're allowed to do, and that are possible.
> I **can** pack really well. (know how to)
> We **can't** take many things home with us. (not allowed to)
> We **can't** get normal food. (not possible)
> Use *could* and *couldn't* as the past tense of *can* and *can't.*
> I **couldn't** sleep because I was so cold.
> Use *will* or *won't + be able to* for future.
> We **won't be able to** take many things back.

Go to page 176 for the Grammar reference.

1 *can / can't + am / is / are (not) able to*
_____

2 *could / couldn't + was / were (not) able to*
_____

3 *will / won't + be able to*
_____

9 Read the infographic again. Complete the sentences with *can, can't, couldn't, able to,* and *not able to.*

1 The average person _____ survive for 40 minutes in water of 4 4°C.
2 Herbert Nitsch _____ hold his breath for nine minutes.
3 Humans are _____ survive without food for about three weeks.
4 Even Randy Gardner _____ stay awake for 12 days.

10 Do you have any unusual skills—or did you have any when you were a child? Make notes. Then tell a partner. Find out if they can or could do the same.

EXPLORE MORE!

Find out more about some of the people in the infographic. Search for "[the name] + human limits."

137

11D
Asking for help

LESSON GOALS
- Practice ways of asking for help
- Clearly pronounce voiced /tʃ/ and /dʒ/ at the end of words
- Practice asking for help

SPEAKING

1 Work in pairs. Discuss the questions.
 1 How often do you ask for help?
 2 In what situations would you ask for help?
 3 What are some reasons you <u>don't</u> ask for help?

MY VOICE ▶

2 ▶ 11.2 Watch the video about asking for help. What three stages does it advise when asking for help? Who should you ask for help?

3 Look at the Communication Skill box. Then read sentences 1–6. Which sentences give background information (B), explain goals (G), and describe challenges (C)?

COMMUNICATION SKILL
Asking for help

When you ask for help, find someone who has the time and skills to help you. Then:
1 Give them some background to what you need help with.
2 Tell them what you hope to achieve.
3 Explain what you are finding difficult and what you think they can help you with.

Asking for help using the right kind of question (for the situation and for the person you are asking) may also make the other person happier to help you.

You want to do a stand up comedy show.
1 People always say I'm (quite funny). _____
2 I'm finding it difficult as I (am quite shy). _____
3 I'm hoping to get better (at public speaking). _____
You want to run a marathon.
4 I've only ever (run 5 km before). _____
5 My aim is to (finish in less than four hours). _____
6 I'm training for (a marathon to raise money for charity). _____

4 Look at the Useful Language box. Work in pairs. How could you ask for help in the situations in Exercise 3? Would you prefer to use direct or indirect questions? Why?

Useful Language Asking for help

Direct
Can / Could you give me a hand with this?
Would you help me set the table?

Indirect
Would you mind (helping me move this fridge)?
Could you possibly help me out with (something important)?
I was wondering if you could help me (peel these oranges)?

5 Discuss the questions with your partner.
 1 What current challenges do you need help with? Explain the background and your goals.
 2 What help do you need and when?
 3 Who could you ask for help?
 4 Which phrases from the Useful Language box and Exercise 3 would you use?
 5 How would you apply the techniques from the Communication Skill box?

PRONUNCIATION

6 ∩ 11.5 Look at the Clear Voice box. Listen to the examples and notice the difference between the words with /tʃ/ and /dʒ/.

CLEAR VOICE
Saying /tʃ/ and /dʒ/

To make the sound /tʃ/ touch your tongue to the top of your mouth then move it down to let the air out. When you touch your throat you shouldn't feel a vibration because it is unvoiced.
/tʃ/ coa**ch**

To make the sound /dʒ/ touch your tongue to the top of your mouth then move it down to let the air out, this time try to make your throat vibrate.
/dʒ/ oran**ge**

7 🎧 11.6 Listen and repeat the sentences. Circle the /tʃ/ and /dʒ/ sounds. Work in pairs. Practice saying the sentences.

1 Could you switch on the flashlight? I need to change the light in the refrigerator.
2 You have a huge knowledge of languages. Could you coach me in German?
3 Would you judge our singing competition in March?
4 We don't know much about science. Do you know anyone who could teach us?
5 Could you please watch our things? We're doing a swimming challenge for charity.

SPEAKING

8 **OWN IT!** Work in pairs. Read the situations (1 and 2). Choose one situation or use your own idea. Decide who to ask for help. Make notes on background information, goals, and challenges. Ask other students in the class for help. Use the tips in the Communication Skill box, the Useful Language, the phrases in Exercise 3, and your notes from Exercise 7. Did anyone agree to help you?

1 You have moved into a new apartment with a shared yard. It's a mess. You don't want to annoy your new neighbors, but you'd love to make the yard look better and put a bench in that you can all use. You have an idea for how it could look and would like to share it and get people to each do something to help.

2 You want to put on a talent show to raise money for the local community. You need a big room for the show, some chairs, and someone to make food and drink for before and after the show. You also need people to sing, dance, act, tell stories, or play music. Your friend said they can make ads and help you sell tickets.

Volunteers working at a charity construction project in Argentina

A fun challenge

LESSON GOALS
Learn how to write factual information
Learn language for writing reports
Write a report about classroom challenges

SPEAKING

1 Work in pairs. Write the word *knowledge* in your notebook. How many words can you make using some of the letters in this word in any order?

READING FOR WRITING

2 Read the report about a class that did a similar challenge to the one in Exercise 1. Answer the questions.

1 What word did they use?

2 What were the rules of the challenge?

3 What information did the writer record?

4 What future challenges does the writer recommend?

3 Read the Writing Skill box. In your notebook rewrite the information below following the advice.

WRITING SKILL
Writing factual information

When writing a report, it is important to think about what the reader needs to know. Include information like number of people, times, and rules. Use clear, brief sentences to keep each fact separate and easy to understand. Avoid using informal language and personal pronouns like *I* and *me*.

1 My class has fifteen students and our challenge was to write lots of words beginning with B.

2 It was OK to write words like *big, bigger, biggest* and my teacher timed everyone using her phone.

CLASSROOM CHALLENGE REPORT

Introduction
The purpose of this report is to provide information on a classroom challenge. The class of six students completed a simple challenge and recorded the results.

The challenge
The challenge was to see how many new words the class could make using the letters in a long word. Students had one minute to write down their words. The teacher wrote the word "exhausted" on the board then started the timer. After one minute, everyone counted up the words. The words could use the letters in any order, but had to be three letters or more. They recorded results for how many and how long their words were.

Results
The average number of words was six. The highest number was eight (*eat, hat, sad, the, tea, heat, hate, shut*). Most words were three or four letters long, but one student wrote *seated* and another wrote *there*.

Conclusions
In summary, this was a fun challenge for the class. In future, it would be interesting to find out what students could do in ninety seconds.

Results: number of words students made			
Student	Number of words	Student	Number of words
Norbert	8	Norma	6
Jaewon	6	Matheus	5
Rafa	5	Anwar	6
Average 36 ÷ 6 = 6 words			

4 Look at the Useful Language box. Circle examples of each kind of language in the report.

Useful Language Writing reports

Introduction
The purpose of this report is to (present the results of a classroom challenge).
In order to prepare this report (the class...).

Ordering tasks
Before we started, (the class decided the rules).
First, we (talked about the rules).
Second, we (predicted our results).
After that, (we did the challenge).
Then, we (discussed the results).

Stating facts
The challenge for the class was to (say the alphabet backwards).
The average time was (ten seconds).
Each student had to (learn ten new words).
Most students thought (they could)...
Every student (in the class took part).
The results found that (most students)...

Conclusion
In conclusion / To conclude, (this challenge)...
In summary / To summarize, (this task)...

5 Match headings 1–4 with sentences A–D.

1 Introduction	2 The challenge
3 Results	4 Conclusions

A Everyone had to read as much of a text as possible in one minute. _____

B This report gives information about a classroom challenge. _____

C To summarize, it was a fun challenge, but more difficult than we thought it would be. _____

D The results showed that most people read about half of the text. _____

6 Read about the counting challenge and look at the table. Make sentences about the information in the table using the Useful Language. Share your ideas with a partner.

Most students did the challenge in less than a minute.

Counting challenge

How many seconds did it take for students to count to 30 changing between English and their first language? For example, one (English), *dos* (Spanish), three (English), *cuatro* (Spanish), etc.
Rule: If students make a mistake, they can correct it and continue.

Student	Results	Student	Results
Norbert	60 seconds	Norma	55 seconds
Jaewon	45 seconds	Matheus	63 seconds
Rafa	35 seconds	Anwar	80 seconds
Total:	Average = 58 seconds		

WRITING TASK

7 Work in groups of four.
1 Decide on an idea for a challenge. Use the idea on this page or your own.
2 Make a list of rules and information you need to record, e.g., time, quantity.
3 Do the challenge with the rest of your class. Take notes of the results.

8 WRITE Using the report on page 140 as a model, write a report about the classroom challenge from Exercise 7.

9 CHECK Use the checklist. Your report...
☐ uses appropriate headings.
☐ includes information about time, distance, quantity, etc.
☐ states factual information clearly.
☐ gives the results.
☐ uses formal language.
☐ gives ideas for more research.

10 REVIEW Compare your report with your group and give each other suggestions for how to improve. Exchange reports with a different student. Did they include at least three things from the checklist?

Go to page 159 for the Reflect and review.

EXPLORE MORE!

Look online for other challenges to do with friends.
Search for "fun challenges you should try with friends."

A racing driver remains calm and focused while driving at high speeds.

12

Technology

GOALS

- Recognize paraphrased information
- Use the passive voice
- Talk about technology
- Take notes when you listen
- Take turns on a group video call
- Complete an online returns form

1 Work in groups. Discuss the questions.

1 Look at the photo. What technology is in the photo that you can and can't see?

2 How might cars change in the future?

WATCH ▶

2 ▶ 12.1 Watch the video. Which kinds of technology does Isaí mention? Which does Paola mention? Write I, P, or B (both).

NATIONAL GEOGRAPHIC EXPLORERS

ISAÍ MADRIZ   PAOLA RODRÍGUEZ

1 batteries ____		5 microscope ____
2 boat ____		6 phone ____
3 camera ____		7 smartwatch ____
4 laptop ____		8 television ____

3 Make connections. Discuss the questions.

1 Do you agree that all of the examples from Exercise 2 are technology? Why or why not?

2 How often do you use each thing?

12A
The art of technology

LESSON GOALS
• Recognize paraphrased information
• Draw conclusions
• Talk about upcycling and recycling

READING

1 Look at the title of the article on page 145. It is a well-known expression. Work in groups. Discuss the questions.

1 What do you think the expression means?

2 Do you know any expressions with a similar meaning in your language?

2 Work in pairs. Complete the definitions with these words or phrases from the article.

devices	environmentally friendly	
get rid of	junk	materials
pleasure	sculpture	waste

1 _____ means stuff people do not want because it is old, broken, or useless.

2 _____ means the unwanted part that remains after you have used something.

3 _____ are small machines that people use, for example, to connect to the internet.

4 _____ are what we make other things from. Examples are plastic, wood, and metal.

5 A(n) _____ is a 3-D work of art, often made from wood, stone, or metal.

6 Something that is _____ does not damage our air, our water, or our planet.

7 To _____ something means to throw it away because you no longer want or need it.

8 To experience _____ means to feel enjoyment or happiness.

3 Work in groups. Follow the instructions and answer the questions.

1 Skim the article. How does it relate to the title?

2 Scan paragraph 1. What do you think *upcycling* is?

4 Look at the Reading Skill box. Then read the article. In which paragraph (1–3) can you find a paraphrase of a–c below?

READING SKILL
Recognizing paraphrase

Paraphrasing means giving the same information in a different way. It can be used to shorten, simplify, or combine ideas or to avoid repetition. Comprehension questions often paraphrase a text, so it is useful to recognize common paraphrasing methods, such as changing the grammar, word order, and some of the vocabulary.

a Old technology parts made the artist think about the natural world. _____

b Recycling and upcycling are two ways to deal with the problem of old technology. _____

c The artist used junk to make a prize-winning sculpture while still at school. _____

5 Look at the Critical Thinking skill box. Circle the correct options in 1–3. Underline the parts of the text that help you.

CRITICAL THINKING SKILL
Drawing conclusions

When reading a text, sometimes you can understand a point based on information the writer gives even though they don't mention this point directly. For example, if a friend writes: "Just dropped my phone! Time to buy a new one," you can draw the conclusion that the phone is broken.

1 Upcycling is *different from / the same as* recycling.

2 Dishaw loves *sneakers / reading novels*.

3 Chappell has been turning *junk / the natural world* into art for some years.

SPEAKING

6 Work in pairs. Have you ever upcycled a piece of furniture or an item of clothing? What do you do with your old devices?

EXPLORE MORE!

Search for more information about Gabriel Dishaw and Julie Alice Chappell. Whose work do you like more, and why?

One person's trash is another's treasure

1 Modern technology has improved our world, but there is a hidden cost to all the devices we now have, such as TVs, computers, and smartphones. People often get rid of old devices when they get a new one, creating up to 50 million tons of waste every year. Recycling old technology can solve part of the problem, but some artists have found a more creative solution by upcycling it instead. In other words, they turn it into art, which brings pleasure to themselves and to others.

2 When **Gabriel Dishaw** was a teenager, he did a school project on "Junk Art," using parts from old machines to make a sculpture of a woman riding a donkey. When his piece won first prize in a competition, Dishaw became more and more interested in working with old technology and giving it a new life in creative and environmentally friendly ways. He says that typewriters and adding machines have some of the most interesting parts. His sculptures explore things that he loves, such as characters from popular movies, comics, and video games. He has also made many sculptures of sneakers.

Sculpture from *Star Wars* series by Gabriel Dishaw

Dragonfly by Julie Alice Chappell

3 In her art, **Julie Alice Chappell** also wants to make people think about the environmental cost of throwing away our electronic technology. Her interest began when she found a box full of parts from old computers. The microchips looked like insects to her, so she took them home and enjoyed turning them into ants with her children. Some years later, when Chappell got some circuit boards from old computers and video games, the shapes and colors reminded her of nature. She cut pieces from the boards and combined them with other materials to produce the beautiful sculptures of butterflies, spiders, and other bugs that she makes and sells today.

12B
Who was it made by?

LESSON GOALS
- Listen to a talk about how technology has changed our world
- Understand and use the passive voice correctly
- Say -s sounds at the ends of words

a pizza

a letter

a house

a painting

LISTENING AND GRAMMAR

1 Work in groups. What do you think the things in the photos above all have in common?

2 🎧 12.1 Listen to a podcast about technology. Complete the sentences with the word or number you hear and decide what the word *one* refers to in each sentence. Tell a partner.

1 Picnic has created one that can make _____ pizzas every hour.

2 Bond has developed one that can hold a _____ and write letters.

3 ICON has produced one that can build a small _____ in less than a day.

4 In _____, one called CloudPainter won a painting competition.

3 Read the Grammar box. Underline all seven examples of passives in the box.

> ### GRAMMAR Passives
>
> Most sentences use the active voice to focus on the person or thing that does the action (the agent).
> *Technology is changing our world in many ways.*
> The passive voice is used instead when the speaker doesn't want to mention the agent or the agent isn't known. In passive sentences, the object of the sentence is turned into the subject. The passive can be formed from any tense.
> *Robots* **have been created** *that can deliver pizzas to customers.*
> Sometimes the agent is added after the passive verb using *by* and a noun.
> *Letters* **will be written** *by robots.*
>
> **Go to page 177 for the Grammar reference.**

4 ♫ 12.2 Work in pairs. Complete the sentences with the correct passive form of the verbs. Then listen to check your answers.

1 The earliest battery _____ (create) around 220 years ago in Italy.

2 The first modern photograph _____ (take) in France in 1826 or 1827.

3 Light bulbs _____ (invent) by two people in the year 1879.

4 Electric refrigerators _____ (use) to keep food fresh since the 1920s.

5 The first electric computer _____ (build) in the U.S. in the 1940s.

6 These days, smartphones _____ (carry) by over 3.5 billion people around the world.

7 It is likely that powerful new technologies _____ (develop) in the future.

8 Voices that sound human can now _____ (produce) by computers.

5 ♫ 12.2 Work in groups. Listen again. Discuss which of the sentences you think were spoken by a person and which were produced by a computer.

6 Work in pairs. Read about two inventions.
Student A: Go to page 181.
Student B: Go to page 182.
Make questions from prompts 1–4. Then ask the questions about your partner's two inventions. Take notes. Can you guess what your partner's inventions are?

1 Where / invented?   3 How / used?
2 When / invented?   4 Where / often found?

7 Think of an invention you know about or a product you use. Write a few sentences to describe it. Use the passive voice when possible. Work in groups. Take turns describing and guessing the inventions.

A: It's a material. It can be soft or hard. It can be made into many things. A lot of it is found in the oceans, unfortunately.

B: Plastic?

EXPLORE MORE!

In addition to making pizza, writing letters, building homes, and creating art, find out about other things that can be done by robots. Share what you learned.

PRONUNCIATION

8 ♫ 12.3 Look at the Clear Voice box. Listen and repeat.

CLEAR VOICE
Saying final -s sounds

There are three common pronunciations for words that end with -s:

• /s/ when the previous sound is /t/, /p/, /k/, or /f/
robots, backpacks, apps

• /z/ when the previous sound is a vowel or /b/, /d/, /g/, /l/, /m/, /n/, /ŋ/, /r/, /v/, or /w/
computers, smartphones, videos

• /əz/ when the previous sound is /ʃ/, /tʃ/, /s/,/z/, or /dʒ/
searches, pages, addresses

9 ♫ 12.4 Listen to six words. Write the word you hear and check (✓) the final -s sound. Then listen again and repeat.

	/s/	/z/	/əz/
1 _____	☐	☐	☐
2 _____	☐	☐	☐
3 _____	☐	☐	☐
4 _____	☐	☐	☐
5 _____	☐	☐	☐
6 _____	☐	☐	☐

SPEAKING

10 Work in groups. Discuss the questions. Give examples and try to give as much detail as possible.

1 In what ways could a robot help you in your daily life?

2 Is there anything you would never want a robot to do for you?

3 In what ways do you think robots could help all humans?

4 Are there any things you think people should never get robots to do?

12C
Tech-Oh no!-logy

LESSON GOALS
- Learn and use words and phrases related to technology
- Take notes when you listen to an interview
- Make predictions about the future

VOCABULARY

1 Work in groups. Look at the lesson title. Discuss what you think it means and how it relates to the photo.

2 🎧 12.5 Work in pairs. Complete the definitions by adding computer (C) or internet (I). Then listen to check.

1 **Electronic** devices use electricity and _____ chips to run.

2 Social media includes _____ sites and **apps** that let people share ideas and photos.

3 **Software** and apps are **programs** that people use on a / the _____, a smartphone, and so on.

4 To **download** something means to copy it from a / the _____ onto a / the _____ or other device.

5 To **install** something means to put it onto a / the _____'s **drive** or **memory** so that it can be used.

6 To **program** a / the _____ means to write instructions that let it perform useful actions.

Go to page 165 for the Vocabulary reference.

LISTENING

3 Work in groups. Look at the Listening Skill box. Discuss some other well-known abbreviations and symbols you know.

LISTENING SKILL
Taking notes when you listen

Taking notes when you listen can help you understand what you hear. Use these strategies to take notes quickly and effectively:

- Use abbreviations (short ways to write things) instead of full words. These can be well-known abbreviations, such as *tech* for *technology,* or they can be ones that you make up, such as *wthr* for *weather*.

- Use symbols instead of words, such as:
  & or **+** (and)
  / (or)
  → (becomes or causes)

- Write down only main ideas and important words, like nouns, verbs, and adjectives. For example, if a speaker says, "We experienced three serious problems during the second week...," your notes might be *2nd wk: 3 big probs*

People look at their smartphones in a café.

148

4 🎧 12.6 Work in pairs. Look at the notes. Discuss what you think each abbreviation and symbol means. Then listen to an interview with Isaí Madriz. Complete the notes with a word or abbreviation.

On trip:
Storm + ¹_____ → hole in tent
water → no power cos ²_____ damaged
charged devices w/ solar panel = slow!

Future?:
Batts: last longer w/ more ³_____
⁴_____: smaller + more memory, not cheaper

---

5 🎧 12.7 Listen to an interview. Take notes as you listen. Then exchange notes with a partner. Do you both have the main points?

6 Work in pairs. What problems have you had with technology? Do you agree with what Paola says about technology?

GRAMMAR

7 Read the Grammar box. Then find and underline any other examples of modals of prediction and possibility in the audioscripts for tracks 12.6 and 12.7 on page 192.

GRAMMAR Modals of prediction and possibility

To make a prediction, use *will* or *won't* + base verb.
I'll be able to understand how corals feel
To talk about things that will possibly happen, but you're not sure of, use *may, might,* or *could* + base verb. To talk about things that possibly won't happen, use *may not* or *might not*.
*Do you think these problems **might** get better?*
Use *will probably* to talk about very likely things or *probably won't* for very unlikely ones.
*Cameras **will probably** get smaller... They **probably won't** get cheaper, though.*

Go to page 177 for the Grammar reference.

8 Work in pairs. Put these phrases in the correct order to make some predictions. Then change the bold phrase or phrases in each sentence and make new predictions that you believe will happen.

1 become much smaller / but more powerful / **computers** / I think / **probably** / **will**
2 **at school** / children in the future / possibly / **have robot teachers** / will
3 on vacation / might / people / when they go / **take rockets, not planes**
4 but it / **ever live** / could happen / won't / probably / **on Mars** / people
5 if I have enough money, / **buy a new phone** / might / **in a few months** / I

PRONUNCIATION

9 🎧 12.8 Look at the Clear Voice box. Listen and repeat.

CLEAR VOICE
Saying final consonants: /g/ and /k/

The consonant sounds /g/ and /k/ are very similar, but /g/ is voiced and /k/ is not. This means that your throat should vibrate when you say the /g/ sound but not when you say the /k/ sound.
/g/ ba**g**, blo**g**, du**g**, pi**g**
/k/ ba**ck**, blo**ck**, du**ck**, pi**ck**

SPEAKING

10 Work in pairs.
1 In your notebooks each write one sentence about something you predict will or might happen in the future in each of the areas below.
2 Tell your partner your prediction.
3 Take notes on your partner's prediction.
4 Discuss how likely you think each other's predictions are. Give reasons.

---

education	food
sports	fashion
arts and entertainment	

12D
Making effective video calls

LESSON GOALS
- Learn how to take turns on a group video call
- Learn useful language for managing a group video call
- Practice having a group discussion

SPEAKING

1 Work in pairs. Make a list of reasons why people make video calls.

2 Work with another pair. Compare your list and discuss the questions.

1 What do you think are the most common reasons for making video calls?

2 How many people in your group make video calls? To whom? How often?

3 Do you think you'll make more or fewer video calls in the future? Why?

3 Work in pairs. Match reasons 1–6 with one person's advice (A–F) from the social media posts.

1 Everybody on the call will hear you better, and you will hear them more easily too. _____

2 Others on the call might get a negative feeling if things are messy. _____

3 It may be hard for the other people to see your face because it's too dark or bright. _____

4 The other people may feel sick or find it hard to focus if there is a lot of movement. _____

5 The expressions on your face will be easier for the other people to see and understand. _____

6 You will feel comfortable. _____

 Jeff

How can you look and sound good during video calls?

 Wendy

A Choose a room that's clean and tidy. If you can't change the room, move your device so the camera only shows a tidy area.

Junko

B Make sure the room isn't too dark. If possible, have a light in front of you, not one that shines directly into your face.

 Julio

C Sit close to your device so your face and the top part of your body fill most of the screen.

 Tyler

D Try not to move around too much during the call—especially if you are on your phone.

 Fatimeh

E In most cases, wear clothes that look good on you and that are not too formal or informal.

 Rahul

F If possible, either use headphones with a microphone or use headphones and a separate microphone in front of you.

4 Read the possible problems. Discuss if (or when) you think they are a problem and how you would deal with them. Add one other possible problem and think of a solution. Finally, discuss your ideas with another pair.

1 People eating or drinking during a video call.
2 Having a video call in a busy, noisy room.
3 _____

MY VOICE ▶

5 ▶12.2 Watch the video. Take notes on the different suggestions for making a point. Then compare your notes with a partner.

6 Look at the Communication Skill box. Then discuss questions 1–3 in pairs.

COMMUNICATION SKILL
Taking turns on a group video call

Turn taking means one person speaks while the other people listen and wait for a chance to share their opinions. There are different strategies you can use to signal that you want to speak on a video call.

1 Make a noise, such as *Um*, or say a word or phrase like *I'd like to add something*.
2 Use body language, such as leaning forward or raising or waving a hand.
3 Use one of the features of the app, such as the mute button or sending a chat message.

1 Which do you think is the best advice? Do you use any of these strategies already? Are there some things you would never do?
2 How easy or difficult is it for you to take your turn to speak in a group call?
3 What advice from the video might be useful for turn-taking in face-to-face conversations? Which would not?

7 Work in groups. Think about when you're on a video call. How did you let other people know when you wanted to speak? How successful was this method and why?

8 Look at the Useful Language box. Which heading would you put 1–3 under?

Useful Language Managing a group video call

Adding your point
Could I just add something?
I've got a couple of points I'd like to make.
A point I'd like to add is...

Dealing with an interruption
Thanks, [name of person interrupting]. Just to finish my point...
Sorry, could I just say...

Allowing and inviting others to speak
Sorry, I interrupted you. Please continue.
Have you finished, Tim?
Did you have something to add, Ali?
Is your hand up, Sam?
Can we hear from you, Kai?

1 Go ahead, please.
_____

2 Yes, I also think that...
_____

3 Sorry, if I can just finish...
_____

9 OWN IT! Work in groups of four. Choose one of the situations to discuss. Roleplay a group video call. Make sure everyone takes their turn to speak.

1 You all think that you use technology too much, especially for entertainment. Discuss three enjoyable things you can do with other people that don't need technology.
2 You have all heard that robots might take people's jobs in the future. Discuss three jobs that robots will probably never be able to do as well as humans.
3 You are all thinking about taking an online course in the future. Discuss either three advantages or three disadvantages of online learning.
4 You are all interested in making a science fiction movie about the future. Discuss three new kinds of technology that might appear in the next 25 years.

EXPLORE MORE!

Which video call apps are popular in your country? Which of those apps have you used? Which one do you like the most, and why?

12E

Return, replace, or refund

LESSON GOALS
- Give only necessary information when you write
- Describe a problem
- Complete an online returns form

SPEAKING

1 Interview your classmates. How many people answer "yes" to each question? Have you ever…

1 paid for some software or an app?
2 bought a digital device in a shop?
3 bought a second-hand piece of technology?
4 read reviews written by other customers before you bought any technology?
5 What are the advantages and disadvantages of buying technology online or in a store?

READING FOR WRITING

2 Read the online returns forms and label photos A–D with a word or phrase from the forms.

A _____

B _____

C _____

D _____

3 Read the online forms again. Match the customers in forms A and B with situations 1–4.

1 received an incomplete product _____
2 had a problem with delivery of an item _____
3 wants to get their money back _____
4 wants to receive two missing items _____

A

Return an item

Order Number

2343-5466-ABDS

Description of Problem

I'm writing about a problem with the tablet that I ordered last week on Tuesday at 11:17 a.m. The order number is 2343-5466-ABDS. The first problem is that I paid for next-day delivery, but the tablet wasn't delivered until yesterday. This was very disappointing. The second problem is that the battery runs out of power very quickly. It only lasts three or four hours, usually. This is really frustrating too. I checked online and I see that other people have the same problem, so I don't want a replacement tablet. Could you refund payment, please, including the extra money I paid for next-day delivery, and explain how to return the device? Thank you. I look forward to hearing from you soon.

Requested Action ⌄

Return the item for a refund

B

Return an item

Order Number

3435-9041-HGEW

Description of Problem

The description on the website says the keyboard comes with a cable to charge it, but there was no cable in the box. The description also says it comes with a free 32GB USB drive, but there was no USB drive in the box either.

Requested Action ⌄

Send a missing part or piece

4 Work in groups. Look at the Writing Skill box. Discuss whether or not the two online forms follow the advice in the box.

WRITING SKILL
Giving only necessary information

In general, clear, effective writing includes only the information that a reader needs to know in order to understand the situation. For example:

• If a specific piece of information is not important, there is no need to mention it at all.

• In non-personal forms of writing, mentioning your personal feelings is usually not helpful.

• Even if you are not happy about a situation, it is a good idea to be polite.

5 Work in pairs. How would you rewrite A to follow the advice in the Writing Skill box?

6 Look at the Useful Language box. Which of the problems have you had with a delivery?

Useful Language Describing a problem

The (box / packaging) was damaged.
The (screen / case) was (scratched / broken).
(A cable / The manual) was missing.
It said the (batteries / instructions) were included, but they weren't.
The device doesn't (turn on / work).
It was delivered late. / I didn't receive it.
I was sent the wrong (color / number of items).
The item didn't match the description.
The quality wasn't good.

7 Think about problems you have had when you bought some technology. These can be ones mentioned in the online return forms or other problems. Make notes about some of them. Use the Useful Language and your own ideas.

8 Work in groups. Discuss the problems you made notes about in Exercise 7. Talk about who experienced the worst problems, and why.

WRITING TASK

9 **WRITE** Look at your notes from Exercise 7 and choose one problem. Create a similar form to the ones in Exercise 3 and write the necessary information in each section.

10 **CHECK** Use the checklist. Your form…
☐ makes it clear what the item is.
☐ has a clear description of the problem(s).
☐ only includes necessary information in the description.
☐ includes a clear and appropriate requested action.
☐ has a polite and factual tone.

11 **REVIEW** Exchange forms with another student. Did they include at least three things from the checklist? Give each other feedback to help improve your writing.

Go to page 159 for the Reflect and review.

EXPLORE MORE!

What are the three most popular online shopping sites in your country now? How often do you use each one? Have you ever had problems when ordering something?

Reflect and review

1 All about me *Pages 10–21*

1 Look at the goals from Unit 1. How confident do you feel about them? Write the letters (a–f) in the table.
  a Skim an article about personality
  b Practice talking about daily habits
  c Talk about people's personalities
  d Listen for opinions in an interview
  e Learn strategies for talking to new people
  f Write a personal profile

I feel confident	I need more practice

2 Work in pairs. Discuss the questions.
  1 What are three things that you often do?
  2 What adjectives can you remember to describe people's personalities?
  3 What are three strategies you can use to talk to people you don't know?

3 Choose three ways you can practice the Unit 1 goals. Add one more idea. Then share your ideas with a partner.
  ☐ Find online articles and skim them
  ☐ Ask my friends and family about their daily habits
  ☐ Do some online personality quizzes
  ☐ Watch interviews online
  ☐ Practice talking to people I don't know well
  My idea: _____

2 Memory *Pages 22–33*

1 Look at the goals from Unit 2. Check (✓) the three goals you feel most confident about. Underline the three goals you would like to practice more.
  ☐ Recognize synonyms in a blog post
  ☐ Use the simple past to talk about memories
  ☐ Deal with unfamiliar vocabulary in an interview
  ☐ Talk about school subjects
  ☐ Show an interest when listening
  ☐ Give details and reasons in a story

2 Work in pairs. Discuss the questions.
  1 What new things did you learn in this unit? What did you enjoy learning?
  2 What are synonyms and why do we use them? Give an example.
  3 How can we show interest when other people are speaking?

3 Think about the three goals you underlined in Exercise 1. Choose three ways you can practice these goals. Then share your ideas with a partner.
  ☐ Keep a record of any important words I find and their synonyms
  ☐ Read and comment on blog posts
  ☐ Make records of irregular past verbs I want to use
  ☐ Make illustrated vocabulary cards for each school subject
  ☐ Listen to online interviews and write down useful vocabulary
  ☐ Watch videos of conversations to see how people show interest
  ☐ Write about my experience of learning English

3 Food for thought *Pages 34–45*

1 Look at the goals from Unit 3. How confident do you feel about them? Write a number between 1 (very confident) and 6 (not at all confident).

_____ Recognize indirect information in an article
_____ Talk about ongoing events in the past
_____ Practice words related to eating at a restaurant
_____ Listen for reasons in an interview
_____ Learn how to make your reasons clear
_____ Write clear instructions in a recipe

2 Think about the Unit 3 goals. Complete the sentences with your own ideas. Then compare your sentences with a partner.

1 I find it difficult to…
2 I really enjoy…
3 I need some help to improve…

3 Read these ideas for practicing the Unit 3 goals. Decide which three are the most useful for you.

Read articles about subjects that interest me and look for information that is expressed indirectly

Identify examples of the simple past and past progressive while I'm reading

Listen to podcasts and interviews online and listen for people giving reasons for what they do

Roleplay restaurant situations with my friends

Practice telling a partner why I like doing something

Find food recipes in English and try making them

Write instructions to a friend on how to do something

4 Goals and ambition *Pages 46–57*

1 Look at the goals from Unit 4. How confident do you feel about them? Write the letters (a–f) in the chart.

a Scan an article about achieving an ambition
b Talk about future plans
c Talk about goals and motivation
d Recognize fillers in a podcast
e Explore ways to give encouraging feedback
f Write comments on an online forum

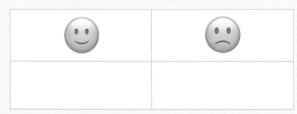

2 Write a short blog post about your future plans and goals for learning English. Explain how you are going to achieve your goals. Then share your blog post with a partner. Write a comment on your partner's blog post.

3 Think about the goals in Exercise 1 and how you are going to practice them. Complete the sentences with your own ideas. Then compare your ideas with a partner.

• To improve my scanning skills,…
• To practice talking about future plans,…
• To practice talking about goals and motivation,…
• To learn how to recognize fillers in a podcast,…
• To get experience in giving feedback,…
• To communicate with people in English online,…

Reflect and review

5 Home and away *Pages 58–69*

1 Look at the goals from Unit 5. Check (✓) the three that are the most important to you. Think about why they are important.

☐ Use context to find meaning in a review
☐ Use zero and first conditionals to talk about facts, suggestions, and consequences
☐ Use extreme adjectives
☐ Understand the key points of a conversation
☐ Learn strategies to show you can be flexible
☐ Write online messages about accommodations

2 Work in pairs. Discuss the questions.
1 Which goal is the easiest for you? Which are more difficult?
2 Which of the goals would you like to practice? Why?

3 Think about the Unit 5 goals that are the most important to you. Write some things you can do to practice them. Use some of these phrases or your own ideas. Then share your ideas with a partner.

Read reviews about things that interest me
Listen to podcasts and interviews
Make mind maps for new vocabulary
Find and complete online grammar practice exercises
Write comments on online blogs
Regularly use an online dictionary
Join online discussion groups
Read descriptions of different houses
Practice strategies for being a good guest and host

Things I am going to do are:

_____

_____

6 Journeys *Pages 70–81*

1 Look at the goals from Unit 6. How easy are they for you? Rank them from 1 (the easiest) to 6 (the most difficult).

_____ Understand pronouns and determiners
_____ Talk about travel experiences
_____ Practice words related to flying
_____ Use information you already know to help you understand a talk
_____ Practice ways to understand other English speakers
_____ Write an email asking for information

2 Work in pairs. Complete the sentences.
1 Some pronouns and determiners are…
2 Some words related to travel and flying are…
3 Things I can do to help me understand other English speakers better are…

3 Choose two of the goals from Exercise 1 that you would like to practice. Check (✓) the things you can do to practice. Add two more ideas of your own.

☐ Underline pronouns and determiners when I read
☐ Try to predict what I'm going to hear <u>before</u> I listen to something
☐ Keep a vocabulary notebook
☐ Read travel blogs
☐ Learn phrases for asking someone to say something again
☐ Practice asking questions to check information when I don't understand
☐ Practice writing formal emails and exchange them with friends

My ideas: _____

_____

7 Inspiration for change Pages 82–93

1 Look at the goals from Unit 7. How confident do you feel about them? Write a number between 1 (very confident) and 6 (not at all confident).

_____ Use definitions to understand short texts
_____ Use relative clauses to define people and things
_____ Talk about the environment
_____ Predict the content when listening to a story
_____ Persuade others to use your ideas
_____ Write about someone who inspires you

2 Work in pairs. Think about the Unit 7 goals. Discuss the questions.

1 Which goal is the easiest for you? Why do you think that is?
2 Which goal is the most difficult for you? What can you do to practice it?

3 Read these ideas to practice the Unit 7 goals. Choose the three ideas that are most useful and make notes about how you will do them. Then share your ideas with a partner.

☐ Read short texts in online magazines and on social media
☐ Practice writing my own definitions of new words using relative clauses
☐ Write descriptions of stories that inspire me and share them with other students
☐ Listen to parts of audio books or short stories and predict what I will hear next
☐ Listen to podcasts about the environment and make notes of useful vocabulary
☐ Think of something I feel strongly about and practice persuading others to agree with me
☐ Tell a partner about a friend who inspires me

8 The world of work Pages 94–105

1 Look at the goals from Unit 8. Check (✓) the three goals you feel most confident about.

☐ Understand cause and effect in an article
☐ Use the present perfect to talk about something to be finished
☐ Talk about jobs
☐ Use mind maps to help understand an interview
☐ Give a good impression at a job interview
☐ Write a résumé

2 Complete the sentences with your own ideas.

1 Three new words for jobs that I have studied in this unit are...
2 An example of a present perfect sentence is...
3 One way to make a good impression at a job interview is...

3 Think about the goals from Exercise 1 that you are least confident about. Which of the ideas below can help you work towards those goals? Add another idea of your own. Then share your ideas with a partner.

☐ Read articles and infographics and look for words that show cause and effect
☐ Make predictions about future changes and explain how they might happen
☐ Write about my own experiences, using the present perfect and the simple past
☐ Write questions with *Have you ever…?* and ask and answer them with a partner
☐ Roleplay a job interview with a friend
☐ Find and compare different examples of online résumés

My idea: _____
_____

Reflect and review

9 Health and happiness *Pages 106–117*

1 Look at the goals from Unit 9. Work in pairs. Use these words and phrases to say how confident you feel about them. You can use the words and phrases more than once.

achieve	confident	improve
more work	need some help	practice
very happy		

- Identify supporting examples
- Use the second conditional to talk about imagined situations
- Talk about health
- Stay positive when you don't understand
- Learn to say "no" when you need to
- Write a journal about things you are grateful for

2 Think about the Unit 9 goals. Complete the sentences with your own ideas. Then compare your sentences with a partner.
1 If my teacher gave me a difficult article to read, I would…
2 I would definitely go to the doctor if…
3 If I didn't agree with someone, I would…

3 Choose three of the Unit 9 goals. Work in pairs. Discuss one way to practice each goal.

To identify supporting examples, I can practice underlining words that show opinions in articles.

Then, I can look for examples that support those opinions in the following sentences.

10 Entertainment *Pages 118–129*

1 Look at the goals from Unit 10. How important are they for you to achieve? Rank them from 1 (very important) to 6 (not very important).
_____ Understand sequence in a story
_____ Talk about what happened before another past event
_____ Talk about movies and TV shows
_____ Listen for general meaning in an interview
_____ Show you value people
_____ Write a review of a show

2 Work in pairs. Complete the sentences.
1 Three words which can show sequence in a story are…
2 Three words related to TV and movies are…
3 Three ways to show I value people are…

3 Think about the two most important goals from Exercise 1. Choose two ways you can practice these goals. Add two more ideas. Then share your ideas with a partner.
- [ ] Read stories and underline phrases that show sequence
- [ ] Write about a past event using time expressions to show the sequence of events
- [ ] Ask people about the TV shows and movies that they enjoy
- [ ] Join online fan groups for TV shows and movies that I enjoy and write comments
- [ ] Watch videos of talk shows and interviews and try to understand the general meaning of what people say
- [ ] Practice showing understanding and warmth when I talk to my friends and family
- [ ] Read reviews of shows that I've seen recently

My ideas: _____ _____

11 Challenges *Pages 130–141*

1 Look at the goals from Unit 11. Work in pairs. Tell your partner if you agree or disagree with the statements and why.

After studying Unit 11, I can:
- recognize different genres and messages.
- report what someone says.
- use adjectives to describe emotions.
- listen for signposts in an interview.
- ask others to help me.
- write a report about classroom challenges.

2 Choose one of the topics (1–3) and make a mind map for it.

1 Ways to recognize different genres and messages
2 Adjectives to describe emotions
3 Ways to ask for help

3 Work in pairs. Ask your partner about the goals from Exercise 1 they would most like to practice. Use these ideas to give some advice. Then ask your partner for advice.

Read texts from a range of different genres
Make notes about the characteristics of different genres
Read news reports and find examples of reported speech
Talk with a partner and then write about your conversation, reporting what you both said
Write short dialogues about people who feel different emotions
Keep a list of different ways to ask for help
Practice writing reports about different challenges in life

----

12 Technology *Pages 142–153*

1 Look at the goals from Unit 12. How confident do you feel about them? Write the letters (a–f) in the table.

a Recognize paraphrased information
b Use the passive voice
c Talk about technology
d Take notes when you listen
e Take turns on a group video call
f Complete an online returns form

I feel confident	I need more practice

2 Work in pairs. Think about the Unit 12 goals. Discuss the questions.

1 Which goals did you feel most confident about? Why?
2 Which goals do you want to practice?
3 Which goals are the most useful? Why?

3 Look again at the goals you need to practice. Which of these ideas can help you? Compare your ideas with a partner.

  Watch videos about new technology
  Practice video calls in English with my friends
  Read articles about inventions and technology and underline any passive forms
  Listen to a podcast and take notes
  Review texts from this book and identify paraphrased information in the questions
  Imagine a problem with technology I own and practice describing it to a friend
  Write sentences about inventions and technology using the passive voice

Vocabulary reference

UNIT 1

confident (adj) /ˈkɒnfɪdənt/   *He is very confident and is always sure that he is right.*

creative (adj) /kriˈeɪtɪv/   *She's always making things—she's really creative.*

friendly (adj) /ˈfrendli/   *He is kind, helpful, and very friendly to everyone.*

honest (adj) /ˈɑnɪst/   *I can always believe what she says because she is honest.*

patient (adj) /ˈpeɪʃnt/   *It's important to be calm and patient when you work with children.*

professional (adj) /prəˈfeʃənl/   *He always works hard and is polite and professional.*

serious (adj) /ˈsɪəriəs/   *He's a quiet and serious person and doesn't often laugh.*

1 Circle the correct option to complete the sentences.

1 Richard is very *friendly / serious* and enjoys meeting new people.
2 I usually watch funny movies, but this movie is actually very *honest / serious*.
3 She knows that she's a good singer—she's very *confident / patient*.
4 You can be *patient / honest* with me and say what you think.
5 Ferdi isn't very *serious / creative*—he isn't good at thinking of new ideas.
6 She's a *patient / professional* mother and never gets angry with her children.
7 It's important to follow all the rules and be *professional / creative* in this job.

2 Work in pairs. Complete the sentences with personality adjectives and your own ideas.

1 I think it's important to be _____ because…
2 I would like to be more _____.
3 I think the adjective _____ describes me best.
4 I like people who are _____ and _____.

UNIT 2

art (n) /ɑrt/   *We use paint and brushes in our art class.*

biology (n) /baɪˈɑlədʒi/   *In yesterday's biology lesson we studied how the heart works.*

chemistry (n) /ˈkemɪstri/   *The students looked at different kinds of metals in their chemistry lesson.*

drama (n) /ˈdrɑmə/   *We're studying a Shakespeare play in our drama class.*

geography (n) /dʒiˈɑgrəfi/   *My favorite subject is geography—I love learning about mountains and rivers.*

gym (n) /dʒɪm/   *Last week we played soccer in gym class.*

history (n) /ˈhɪstri/   *You need to remember lots of names and dates for history.*

IT (n) /ˌaɪ ˈtiː/   *Our IT class was about how to make simple computer games.*

math (n) /mæθ/   *I'm not very good at math because I can't remember the multiplication tables.*

physics (n) /ˈfɪzɪks/   *In today's physics class, we're learning about light and color.*

1 Look at the quotes from teachers (1–10). Write the correct school subject for each quote.

1 "Look carefully at your painting." _____
2 "I want you to do this work without using your calculators." _____
3 "Add the salt to the water and heat the water again. What do you notice?" _____
4 "How do we make electricity?" _____
5 "Please get into groups of four and get a ball out of storage." _____
6 "Romeo and Juliet are two characters in this play." _____
7 "What is the capital of Brazil?" _____
8 "How do we know that a spider is not an insect?" _____
9 "Turn on your computer and open a new document." _____
10 "What are the dates of the First World War?" _____

2 Work in pairs. Discuss the questions.
1 What was your favorite subject at school?
2 What school subject were you best at?
3 What subject did you find most difficult?

UNIT 3

delicious (adj) /dɪˈlɪʃəs/ *This cake is delicious.*

dish (n) /dɪʃ/ *The best dish on the menu is the lasagne.*

prepare (v) /prɪˈpær/ *Do you want me to prepare dinner tonight?*

raw (adj) /rɔ/ *Did you cook this chicken enough? It looks raw.*

serve (v) /sɜrv/ *I usually serve salmon with potatoes and broccoli.*

vegan (n) /ˈvigən/ *I don't eat anything that comes from animals because I'm a vegan.*

vegetarian (n) /ˌvɛdʒəˈtɛriən/ *She's a vegetarian, so she doesn't eat meat or fish.*

1 Complete the text with words from the word list. Two words are not needed.

It was my sister's birthday yesterday, so she invited some friends around for lunch. I offered to ¹_____ the meal. At first, I wanted to make my sister's favorite ²_____: vegetable lasagna. But then I remembered that her friend, Amy, is a ³_____. So I had to think of something with no cheese, milk, or any other animal products. I found a great recipe for pasta with tomatoes and pine nuts, but I didn't know that Amy's brother, Tom, has a nut allergy! Anyway, it was fine, because I decided to ⁴_____ the pasta with salad, so Tom had the salad and everyone said the food was ⁵_____!

2 Complete the sentences with your own ideas. Then compare with a partner.
1 The most delicious food is…
2 My favorite vegetarian dish is…
3 Some people want to be vegan because…
4 The last time I prepared food was…

UNIT 4

challenge (n) /ˈtʃæləndʒ/ *I like the challenge of learning a new language.*

encourage (v) /ɛnˈkɜrɪdʒ/ *She's a very good teacher and always encourages her students when they face something difficult.*

praise (n) /preɪz/ *He received a lot of praise for his essay.*

prize (n) /praɪz/ *The prize for this competition is a round trip flight to New York.*

punish (v) /ˈpʌnɪʃ/ *When my father wanted to punish us, he sent us to bed early.*

reward (n) /rɪˈwɔrd/ *Police will give a reward for any information about the crime.*

1 Match the beginnings of the sentences (1–5) with the endings (a–e).
1 I answered the question correctly _____
2 There is a big reward _____
3 The coach encouraged the players _____
4 I don't punish my children, but I always _____
5 Running a marathon will be a challenge, _____

a to play well and improve.
b give them praise when they do well.
c but I'm looking forward to it.
d and I won a $500 prize.
e for anyone who can help us.

2 Work in pairs. Say if you agree or disagree with the sentences and why.
1 We need challenges in our lives.
2 Sometimes you can give people too much praise.
3 Children should get a reward when they do something good.

Vocabulary reference

UNIT 5

amazing (adj) /əˈmeɪzɪŋ/   *This book is amazing—it's really funny and clever.*

disgusting (adj) /dɪsˈɡʌstɪŋ/   *The food at the restaurant last night was disgusting!*

enormous (adj) /iˈnɔrməs/   *He lives in an enormous house with eight bedrooms and a swimming pool.*

filthy (adj) /ˈfɪlθi/   *Please clean the bathroom—it's filthy!*

freezing (adj) /ˈfrizɪŋ/   *It's freezing outside and I think it might snow later.*

spectacular (adj) /spɛkˈtækjələr/   *The views from the top of the mountain are spectacular.*

terrible (adj) /ˈterəbəl/   *Our vacation accommodations were terrible, so we left early and moved into a hotel.*

tiny (adj) /ˈtaɪni/   *My bedroom is tiny, but I have my own bathroom.*

1 Circle the correct option to complete the sentences.

1 The cake looked delicious, but it tasted *filthy / disgusting*.
2 My friend thought the movie was very bad, but I thought it was *amazing / terrible*.
3 Please clean the kitchen. It's *enormous / filthy*.
4 Our old car was big, but our new one is *tiny / amazing*.
5 Yesterday it was very warm, but today it's *freezing / tiny*.
6 His house is quite boring, but his garden is *spectacular / disgusting*.
7 We have a very small cat, but our neighbor's cat is *freezing / enormous*.
8 I hated the book. It was *spectacular / terrible*.

2 Think about these topics. Then compare your ideas with a partner.
* two types of food that you think are disgusting
* two terrible movies
* two amazing books
* a tiny animal
* an enormous animal
* a spectacular place

UNIT 6

abroad (adv) /əˈbrɔd/   *We lived abroad for three years when I was a child.*

board (v) /bɔrd/   *It's time to board the plane now.*

check in (v) /tʃek ˈɪn/   *We need to check in at least two hours before our plane leaves.*

gate (n) /ɡeɪt/   *The flight departs from gate number 3.*

land (v) /lænd/   *What time does the plane land?*

security (n) /sɪˈkjʊrəti/   *Please check your bags at security.*

take off (phr v) /teɪk ˈɔf/   *I like looking out of the window while the plane is taking off.*

1 Complete the email with the correct form of the words and phrases from the word list.

Hi Tara,

We're having an amazing time in Egypt, but our journey here was terrible! First of all, we wanted to leave early for the airport, but our taxi didn't arrive on time. When we got to the airport, there was a long line of people all waiting to ¹_____. Then at ²_____, I took my laptop out of my hand luggage and dropped it! We finally got to the ³_____ just a few minutes before the departure time. We ⁴_____ the plane and then…nothing happened! The plane just waited on the ground for two hours! When the plane finally ⁵_____, everyone on the plane was happy. But the weather during the flight was terrible and the plane ⁶_____ in Cairo in the evening— three hours late! Maybe next year we won't go ⁷_____ for our vacation—we'll stay home!

See you soon,

Amber

2 Work in pairs. Discuss the questions.
1 Do you always leave on time when you travel?
2 What's the longest period of time you've ever spent in line?
3 Do you prefer going on vacation abroad or in your own country? Why?

UNIT 7

care about (phr v) /kɛr ə'baʊl/ *I care about making the world cleaner and greener.*

environment (n) /ɛn'vaɪrənmənt/ *Cutting down trees is very bad for the environment.*

planet (n) /'plænɪt/ *There are plenty of ways that we can help to look after our planet.*

pollution (n) /pə'luʃən/ *We want to find better ways to fight pollution in our cities.*

recycle (v) /ri'saɪkəl/ *We recycle plastic, glass, and paper at our school.*

reuse (v) /ri'juz/ *You don't have to throw plastic bags away—you can reuse them.*

1 Complete the text with words from the word list.
Everyone should ¹_____ the world we live in. We only have one ²_____. That's why we should all think about the ³_____ in our daily lives. There are lots of ways that we can look after our rivers, trees, and green spaces. We can plant flowers in our gardens to encourage insects, birds, and animals to visit. Planting trees is also a good way to reduce the amount of air ⁴_____. We should think about our trash before putting it in the trash can. Sometimes we can ⁵_____ something several times before throwing it away and we can ⁶_____ most items that are made of plastic, glass, paper, or cardboard.

2 Work in pairs. Complete the sentences with your own ideas.
1 Three items that I recycle regularly are…
2 Three items that I reused for a different purpose are…
3 Three ways to reduce water or air pollution are…

UNIT 8

accountant (n) /ə'kaʊntənt/ *My accountant calculates my tax payments.*

biologist (n) /bai'ɑlədʒɪst/ *As a biologist, she looks at how some plants can grow in the desert.*

hairdresser (n) /'hɛr,drɛsər/ *My hair is too long—I need to make an appointment with my hairdresser.*

instructor (n) /ɪn'stɹʌktər/ *I love driving, so I think I might train to become a driving instructor.*

politician (n) /,pɑlə'tɪʃən/ *Our politicians want to introduce laws to protect the environment.*

reporter (n) /rɪ'pɔrtər/ *My sister works as a reporter for a local newspaper.*

researcher (n) /rɪ's3:rtʃər/ *When I wrote a novel, I paid a researcher to check information for me.*

1 Read the sentences and match them with the jobs from the word list.

1 "Do you want to try a shorter style this time?" _____

2 "I'm writing an article about the future of IT." _____

3 "We promise to spend more money on health and education." _____

4 "Last year your company spent more than $15,000 on training." _____

5 "For this project, I have to find out information about the music industry." _____

6 "Now move your arms slowly above your head and breathe out." _____

7 "Most animals only have one heart, but the octopus actually has three." _____ _____

2 Work in pairs. Discuss the questions. Give reasons for your answers.
Which of the jobs from the word list:
• has the best salary?
• has the best working hours?
• is the most interesting?
• is the most difficult?
• involves a lot of travel?
• do you need to study for the most?

Vocabulary reference

UNIT 9

feel sick /fil ˈsɪk/, feel very tired /fil ˈveri ˈtaɪrd/   *I ate something bad and now I feel sick.*

get better /get ˈbetər/, get sick /get ˈsɪk/, get sunstroke /get ˈsʌnstrəʊk/   *I'm not well and I hope I get better soon.*

have a serious accident /həv ə ˈsɪərɪəs ˈæksɪdənt/, have a bad cold /həv ə bæd ˈkəʊld/, have a high fever /həv ə haɪ ˈfivər/   *My brother had an accident on his way to school.*

prevent a cold /prɪˈvent ə ˈkəʊld/, prevent illness /prɪˈvent ˈɪlnɪs/, prevent putting on weight /prɪˈvent ˈpʊtɪŋ ɒn ˈweɪt/   *Not eating late at night is one way to prevent putting on weight.*

stay healthy /steɪ ˈhelθi/, stay in good shape /steɪ ɪn gʊd ˈʃeɪp/, stay young /steɪ ˈjʌŋ/   *You can stay young by doing things you enjoy and looking after your body.*

take a break /teɪk ə ˈbreɪk/, take your medicine /teɪk jər ˈmedɪsɪn/ *I'm tired so I'll take a quick break from my work.*

1 Complete the sentences with the correct form of the verbs from the word list.

　1 Taking vitamins and washing your hands regularly are two ways to _____ a cold.

　2 The doctor gave me this medicine which I have to _____ three times a day.

　3 I _____ a fever, so I can't go to work today.

　4 I'm _____ sick today, so I'm going to bed early.

　5 I want to _____ healthy, so I exercise every day.

　6 He stayed too long in the sun yesterday and he _____ sunstroke.

2 Write some advice in your notebook for young people on how to stay fit and healthy. Use the verbs from the word list and some of these words and phrases.

a bad cold	exercise	healthy	sick
illness	in shape	tired	

UNIT 10

animation (n) /ˌænɪˈmeɪʃn/   *The movie was a mix of animation and real actors.*

director (n) /dɪˈrɛktər/   *The director will tell the actors what to do.*

drama (n) /ˈdrɑmə/   *I like watching dramas about people's relationships.*

mystery (n) /ˈmɪstəri/   *The story is a mystery about a child who hears strange noises at night.*

plot (n) /plɑt/   *The acting in the movie was excellent, but the plot was silly.*

romantic comedy (n) /rəʊˈmæntɪk ˈkɑmədi/   *In this romantic comedy, two young people fall in love and decide to buy a zoo.*

scene (n) /sin/   *The best scene in the movie was the ending.*

science fiction (n) /ˌsaɪəns ˈfɪkʃən/   *People from the future travel back in time in this science fiction movie.*

series (n) /ˈsɪriz/   *Are you going to watch that new series on TV tonight?*

star (n) /stɑr/   *The star of the show is the family's pet cat, Tigger.*

1 Choose the correct option to complete the sentences.

　1 It can take hundreds of hours to produce just a few minutes of *animation / drama*. A two-minute *plot / scene* can take around six months to create.

　2 The *star / series* of this movie has never been in a serious *drama / romantic comedy* before, although he's famous from the popular *science fiction / mystery* TV *scene / series* about a family that moves to the planet Mars.

　3 The *star / plot* of this movie was difficult to understand and, although I usually enjoy *animations / mysteries* and stories about strange events, I didn't really understand the ending.

　4 She's a successful writer and *director / drama*. Her movies include several very funny *plots / romantic comedies* from the 1990s.

2 Work in pairs. Complete the tasks.
　1 Give an example of an animation, a romantic comedy, and a science-fiction movie from the last ten years. Say why you liked or didn't like each movie.
　2 Describe one of your favorite scenes from a movie.

UNIT 11

amazed (adj) /əˈmeɪzd/   I'm amazed that your brother won the competition—I didn't even know he could sing!

anxious (adj) /ˈæŋkʃəs/   I'm feeling anxious about tomorrow's exam.

disappointed (adj) /ˌdɪsəˈpɔɪntɪd/   He's feeling disappointed because he wasn't able to finish the race.

exhausted (adj) /ɪgˈzɑːstɪd/   I've worked so hard today, I'm exhausted!

scared (adj) /skerd/   She's scared of spiders and snakes.

shocked (adj) /ʃɑːkt/   We were all shocked when we heard about your car accident.

1 How are these people feeling? Write an adjective from the word list for each person.

  1 "What? I can't believe it. How awful!"

    _____

  2 "Oh, no! I only got 45% in the test."

    _____

  3 "I'm worried about the party tonight. I might not know anyone there." _____

  4 "Help! There's a big spider in the kitchen!"

    _____

  5 "I'm so tired. I can't keep my eyes open."

    _____

  6 "I was surprised and really happy to find out that my grandfather wants to run a marathon."

    _____

2 Work in pairs. Think of something that made you feel one of the emotions from the word list. Tell your partner about what happened. Can they guess the correct emotion?

  A: I swam in the ocean for the first time when I was 12 years old.
  B: Were you anxious before you did it?
  A: No, but I was scared when I was in the ocean!

UNIT 12

app (n) /æp/   I've got a really good dictionary app on my phone.

download (v) /ˈdaʊnloʊd/   You can download the music from this website.

drive (n) /draɪv/   The photos are all saved on my drive.

electronic (adj) /iˌlekˈtrɑːnɪk/   You are not allowed to take electronic devices into the exam.

install (v) /ɪnˈstɑːl/   I tried to install the new printer, but it isn't working.

memory (n) /ˈmeməri/   My laptop hasn't got much memory, so it's very slow.

program (n) /ˈproʊɡræm/   I can create drawings on my computer with this free program.

program (v) /ˈproʊɡræm/   My sister learned how to program computers at college.

software (n) /ˈsɑːftwer/   With this software, you can translate texts into different languages.

1 Match the questions (1–5) with the answers (a–e).
  1 Where is the video of yesterday's lesson? _____
  2 What does this software do? _____
  3 Why doesn't my phone have much memory? _____
  4 How can I install this program? _____
  5 Which electronic device do you use most often? _____
  a It helps to protect your computer.
  b Just click that button there.
  c Probably my phone.
  d There are too many apps on it.
  e I saved it onto the shared drive.

2 Work in pairs. Answer the questions.
  1 Describe your favorite app. How often do you use it?
  2 Do you think we spend too long looking at electronic devices? Why or why not?
  3 What are some of the possible problems of downloading things for free?

Grammar reference

UNIT 1

1B   Adverbs of frequency

Indefinite adverbs of frequency

- Use indefinite adverbs of frequency to give a general idea of how often you do or feel something.

  always (100%)
  often
  usually
  sometimes
  occasionally
  rarely
  never (0%)

- Use *not* with *always*, *often*, and *usually* to make them negative.
  I do**n't usually** wake up early on the weekend.
  I'm **not often** late for work.

- Indefinite adverbs of frequency generally go before a verb.
  I **sometimes** play tennis.
  NOT I play sometimes tennis.
  But they go after *be*.
  He is **occasionally** late for work.
  NOT He occasionally is late for work.

- You can also put *often, occasionally, sometimes,* and *usually* at the beginning or the end of a sentence.
  Sometimes, I work from home.
  I work from home **sometimes**.

- You can use *a lot* to say you do something often. It goes at the end of the sentence.
  I play tennis **a lot**.

> **Remember!**
> Use adverbs of frequency on their own to give a short answer.
> A: Do you **sometimes** play video games?
> B: No, **never**.

- Use *How often…?* to ask about frequency.
  How often do you travel abroad?

- You can also use *Do you…?* with *always, often, usually,* and *sometimes.*
  Do you always ride your bike to work?

Definite adverbs of frequency

- Use definite adverbs of frequency to be more specific about how often something happens. You can use phrases with *every…* and *once / twice / three times a (day / month / year)*, etc.
  I go to the movies **once a month**.

> **Remember!**
> You don't say *one time* or *two times* (*a day / month*, etc.).

- Definite adverbs of frequency generally go at the end of the clause or sentence.
  He tries to exercise **every day**, but sometimes it's only **three or four times a week**.

1   Rewrite the sentences using the adverbs.

1   My teacher gives us homework on Fridays. (always)
_____

2   I am late for work. (never)
_____

3   I meet my friends on the weekend. (not often)
_____

4   We go to the theater. (about once or twice a year)
_____

5   We eat out. (a lot)
_____

6   I go to a café. (several times a week)
_____

1C   Simple present and present progressive

- Use the simple present to talk about things that last for a long time, e.g., facts, things that are always true, regular events, habits, and routines.
  I usually **arrive** at work at around 8:30.
  My brother **lives** in a big city.

- Use the present progressive to talk about something which is happening at the time of speaking or around the time of speaking. Use it for things that do not last for a long time.
  It **isn't raining** today.
  I**'m reading** a great book at the moment.

- Note the contrast in this sentence.
  She normally **works** in the office, but she**'s working** from home this week.

> **Remember!**
> There are some state verbs (e.g., *believe, know, remember, want*) that are not usually used in the progressive form.
> I **know** what you mean.
> NOT I am knowing what you mean.

2   Complete the sentences with the simple present or present progressive form of the verbs.

1   Please be quiet. I _____ (listen) to the radio.

2   What _____ (you / cook)? It smells great.

3   We rarely _____ (go) to the movie theater. We usually _____ (watch) movies at home.

4   I _____ (know) a great place for real Italian food. _____ (you / want) to go there?

5   Ava isn't here at the moment. She _____ (play) tennis with Esme. They _____ (play) every Saturday morning.

UNIT 2

2B Simple past

- Use the simple past to talk about something that happened and finished in the past. We often use it with a past time expression (*ten minutes ago, yesterday, last week, in 2020, when I was a child,* etc.).
- To form the simple past of regular verbs, add -*ed* to the base verb.
  play—I **played** *soccer this morning.*
  Note the following exceptions to this rule.

	Base verb	Simple past
For verbs that end in -*e*, add -*d*.	arrive	arrive**d**
For verbs that end in consonant + -*y*, change the -*y* to -*ied*.	study	stud**ied**
For one-syllable verbs that end in a consonant + vowel + consonant, double the final consonant and add -*ed*.	stop	stop**ped**
For verbs that end in a consonant + vowel + consonant and the stress is on the last syllable, double the final consonant and add -*ed*.	prefer	prefer**red**
For verbs that end in a consonant + vowel + consonant and the stress is <u>not</u> on the last syllable, add -*ed*.	open	open**ed**

- Some verbs have an irregular past form. The base form and the simple past form are different. For a full list, see page 178.
  I **went** *to a café yesterday.*
  I **had** *a very happy childhood.*
  Samir **bought** *a new phone last week.*
- To make a negative simple past sentence, use *didn't* + base verb.
  I **didn't like** *that movie.*
  He **didn't go** *to university.*
- The simple past of *be* is *I / she / he / it was* and *you / we / they were*. To form the negative of *be*, use *not* or -*n't*.
  There **was** *a park here when we* **were** *kids.*
  I **wasn't** *tired last night.*
  Zuzanna and Jan **weren't** *at work today.*

1 Complete the sentences with the correct simple past form of the verbs.

1 Last year, we [1]_____ (go) to Mexico on vacation. We [2]_____ (have) a good time and we [3]_____ (stay) in a big hotel. We [4]_____ (spend) hours at the hotel pool and that's where I [5]_____ (learn) to swim.

2 I [6]_____ (enjoy) my time at school, but I [7]_____ (not like) some subjects, like history and geography. Physics and math [8]_____ (be) my favorites. And I [9]_____ (not be) very good at sports, so I [10]_____ (not enjoy) gym much.

2C Making questions

Question word	Auxiliary	Subject	Base verb
	Are	**you** OK?	
	Were	**they** happy?	
	Do	**you**	**speak** English?
	Did	**you**	**finish** your homework?
What	**is**	**your email address**?	
Why	**are**	**you** sad?	
When	**does**	**the movie**	**start**?
Where	**did**	**your parents**	**go** to school?

- To form a question, use this order: Question word, Auxiliary verb, Subject, Base verb
- When the answer to the question is *yes / no*, do not use a question word.
  A: Do you like coffee? *B:* **Yes,** *I do.*
  A: Am I late? *B:* **No,** *you aren't.*
- To give a short answer to *yes / no* questions, use the correct form of the auxiliary verb *be* or *do*. Do not use the base verb.
  A: Are you hungry? *B: No, I'm* **not.**
  A: Do you like math? *B: Yes, I* **do.**
  NOT *Yes, I like. or Yes, I do like.*
- To make an open-ended question, use a question word (*what, when, where, which, who, why,* or *how*).
  What *is your name?*
  When *does the supermarket close?*
  Where *do you live?*
  Which *jacket is yours?*
  Who *do you like most in your family?*
  Why *were you late?*
  How *are you?*

Grammar reference

- For simple present questions, use the auxiliary verb *be* (*am / are / is*) when there is no base verb in the sentence. For simple past questions, use *was / were*.
  *What **is** your favorite subject?*
  ***Was** Mai in class today?*

- For simple present questions, use the auxiliary verb *do / does* when there is a base verb in the sentence. For simple past questions, use the auxiliary verb *did*.
  ***Do** you **play** a musical instrument?*
  *What movies **does** Juan **like**?*
  ***Did** you **have** a good weekend?*
  *What **did** the teacher **say** yesterday?*

- The form of the auxiliary verb *do* (not the base verb) shows that the question is about the past or the present.
  ***Did** you **speak** to Ranvir?*
  NOT ~~Did you speaked to Ranvir?~~

2 Find and correct the mistake in each question.

1 Where you are from?
  Where are you from?

2 Why that song do you like?
  _____

3 Did you enjoyed the food?
  _____

4 What your favorite subject at school was?
  _____

5 Where you went to college?
  _____

6 Where is you work now?
  _____

7 Your sister speaks well English?
  _____

8 How old your brother?
  _____

UNIT 3

3B   Simple past and past progressive

- Use the simple past to talk about something that happened and finished in the past.
  *I **saw** Olga yesterday.*

- Use the past progressive to talk about an action in progress at a specific time or over a period of time in the past.
  *They **were waiting** for a long time.*

- Form the past progressive with subject + *was / were* + *-ing* verb.

Subject	*was / were*	*-ing* verb
I / He / She / It	was	waiting.
You / We / They	were	studying.

- You can use the past progressive with the simple past when one action happens in the middle of, or interrupts, a longer action that started earlier. Use the past progressive for the longer action and the simple past for the action that interrupts.

- You can use *when, while,* or *and* to link the actions. Use *while* or *when* before the past progressive. Use *and* or *when* before the simple past.
  *I was making lunch **when / and** he called.*
  ***While / When** I was making lunch, he called.*

- You can put the past progressive first or second in the sentence. If the part of the sentence with *when / while* comes first, use a comma.

1 Complete the sentences using the simple past or past progressive form of the verbs.

1 I _____ (fall) asleep while I _____ (watch) TV.

2 I _____ (see) you last night. You _____ (wait) for the bus.

3 While we _____ (walk) to the park, it _____ (start) raining.

4 My parents _____ (meet) when they _____ (work) in the same school.

5 I _____ (read) my book in the café when Helen and George _____ (walk) in. It _____ (be) great to see them.

3D   Indefinite pronouns

- Use indefinite pronouns to talk about people or things in general. Use them as the subject or object in a sentence. Indefinite pronouns can start with *some-, any-, every-,* or *no-*. They can end with *-body, -one, -thing,* or *-where*.

Some- and **any-**
- You can use *some-* in positive statements and *any-* in negative statements.
  *I want to eat **something**. (= it's not important to say what I want to eat)*
  *I didn't eat **anything** this morning. (= I ate nothing)*

168

- You can use any- to mean "it doesn't matter which" in a positive statement.
  I don't mind where we eat. **Anywhere** *is OK.*
- Use *any-* for general questions when you don't know what the answer will be.
  Can **anyone** *help me?*
  Did you do **anything** *interesting at the weekend?*

> **Remember!**
> You can use *some-* to make offers.
> *Would you like* **something** *to eat?*
> *Do you want to eat* **somewhere** *else today?*

Every-

- Use *every-* in positive and negative statements and in questions. *Every* has a similar meaning to *all*. Use *every-* with a singular verb (*Everyone was...*, *Everything is...*).
  Thank you for a lovely meal. **Everything** *was delicious.*

No-

- Use *no-one, nobody, nothing,* and *nowhere* as alternatives to *not anyone, not anywhere,* etc.
  We saw **no one**. (= We did**n't** see **anyone**.)
  There's **nothing** *to drink.* (= There is**n't anything** to drink.)
- Don't use *not* with *nothing, no one, nowhere,* etc.
  I said **nothing**. / *I did**n't** say* **anything**.
  NOT ~~I didn't say nothing.~~

2 Complete the conversations with these words. There is one word you don't need.

anyone	anything	everything	no one
nothing	someone	something	somewhere

1 A: What shall I cook tonight—omelette, chilli, risotto?
  B: I'm happy to eat _____.
2 A: Thank you so much for dinner. _____ was delicious.
  B: You're welcome.
3 A: _____ phoned you earlier. It was a woman.
  B: Did she leave a message or give any information?
  A: No, _____. She didn't even say her name.
4 A: Do you know _____ who is vegan?
  B: No, _____.
5 A: Shall we go _____ for lunch?
  B: Yes, good idea. How about that new Mexican restaurant?

UNIT 4

4B Future plans

- Use *be + going to + base verb* for future intentions and plans. You have already made the decision before the time of speaking.
  I'm going to buy a new phone.
  She isn't going to work tomorrow.
  They're going to get married next year.
  What are you going to do in the summer?
- Use the present progressive for definite arrangements in the future (for something that is already fixed and is more than just an intention or a hope). You often need to mention a time, day, or date to make the meaning clear.
  I'm meeting Erica at 7 o'clock this evening.
  They're getting married on March 25.
- It is sometimes possible to use both *going to* or the present progressive with no difference in meaning. For example, both these sentences are about something that has been decided before the time of speaking.
  I'm going to watch soccer tonight. / I'm watching soccer tonight.

> **Remember!**
> When the verb after *going to* is *go*, you can leave it out.
> *I'm going to the supermarket.* (= I'm going to go to the supermarket.)

1 Choose the best options to complete the conversations.

1 A: You need a haircut!
  B: I know. [1]*I'm going to call / I'm calling* the hairdresser to make an appointment soon—maybe I can do it this afternoon.
2 A: [2]*I'm going to meet / I'm meeting* Kerry and Toni this evening for pizza. Do you want to come along?
  B: Which restaurant [3]*are you going to go to / are you going to*?
  A: We're not sure. [4]*We're going to decide / We're deciding* when we meet. Anyway, [5]*we're going to meet / we're meeting* downtown at 6.30.

4C will and won't for promises, offers, and spontaneous decisions

- Use *will* to make promises and offers.
  A: Can I tell you a secret? B: Sure. I **won't tell** *anyone.*
  A: I've got a lot of work. B: I'll help you.
- Use *will + base verb* to make a spontaneous decision (a decision you make at the time of speaking).
  A: It's cold in here. B: Yes, you're right. I'll close the window.

Grammar reference

2 Write a response to each situation. Use *will* or *won't* to make a decision, a promise, or an offer. Use the words in brackets.

1 There's a knock at the door. (get / it)
   I'll get it.

2 Your friend needs a ride to the station. (take / you)
   _____

3 Your car is in a "no parking" area. (move / it)
   _____

4 You need your friend to help you. (help / me)
   _____

5 There's no milk in the fridge. (go and buy / some)
   _____

6 It's important to be early for the meeting. (not be / late)
   _____

UNIT 5

5B Zero conditionals

- Use the zero conditional to talk about facts and situations that are always true, or when one thing always follows another.
  *If you **heat** water to 100°C, it **boils**.*
- Form the zero conditional with *if* + simple present + simple present.
- You can also use *when* instead of *if* in zero conditional sentences.
  *When you **heat** water to 100°C, it **boils**.*
- You can put the *if* / *when* clause first or the main clause first. When the *if* / *when* clause is first, use a comma.
  *The red light **flashes** if the power **is** low.*
  *If the power **is** low, the red light **flashes**.*

1 Complete the conversations with the correct form of the verbs.

1 A: What does orange light mean?
   B: If it [1]_____ (flash), it [2]_____ (mean) the power [3]_____ (be) low.

2 A: Did Lucia reply to your email?
   B: Yes. She always [4]_____ (answer) quickly when I [5]_____ (send) her an email.

5B First conditionals

- Use the first conditional to talk about possible future situations and their results.
  *If I **see** Dina, I'll **give** her your message.*
- Form the first conditional with *if* + simple present + *will* / *won't*.
- You can put the *if* clause first or the main clause first. When the *if* clause is first, use a comma.
  *If I **have** time, I'll **email** you the photos.*
  *I'll **email** you the photos if I **have** time.*
  *If I'm too tired, I **won't go** to the party.*
  *I **won't go** to the party if I'm too tired.*

2 Complete the conversations with the correct form of the verbs.

1 A: If we [1]_____ (not leave) now, we [2]_____ (miss) the bus.
   B: Don't worry. We [3]_____ (get) a taxi if we [4]_____ (miss) the bus.

2 A: Ola is taking her driving test next week.
   B: Well, if she [5]_____ (not pass), she [6]_____ (not be) happy.

5C Comparatives and superlatives

- Use comparative adjectives to compare different things.
  *The U.S. is **smaller** than Canada.*
- Use *the* + superlative adjective to compare one thing with other things in a group.
  *Russia is **the biggest** country in the world.*

	Adjective	Comparative	Superlative
For most one-syllable adjectives, add -er and -est.	small	small**er**	small**est**
For adjectives ending in -e, add -r and -st.	nice	nice**r**	nice**st**
For most adjectives ending with a vowel and a consonant, double the final letter and add -er and -est.	big	big**ger**	big**gest**

Do not double the final letter if it is -w, -x, or -y.	slow	slower	slowest
For one- and two syllable adjectives ending in -y, change the -y to -ier and -iest.	dry early healthy	dr**ier** earl**ier** health**ier**	dr**iest** earl**iest** health**iest**
For most adjectives with two or more syllables, use *more* or *the most*.	expensive	**more** expensive	**most** expensive

- There are a few irregular comparative forms.
  good —→ **better** —→ **best**
  bad —→ **worse** —→ **worst**
  far —→ **farther** / **further** —→ **farthest** / **furthest**
  *The weather is **better** today than yesterday.*
  *This is the **worst** day of my life.*
- Use *than* to compare two things.
  *The train is quicker **than** the bus.*
- Most extreme adjectives (*amazing, enormous, freezing,* etc.) are not used in the comparative or superlative form.
  *Russia is **bigger** than Japan.*
  NOT ~~Russia is more enormous than Japan.~~
  *Today is the **coldest** day of the year.*
  NOT ~~Today is the most freezing day of the year.~~
- *Less* is the opposite of *more. Least* is the opposite of *most.*
  *The place I live in is **less crowded** than downtown.*
  *It's not a good idea to buy the **least expensive** clothes.*

> **Remember!**
> We don't often use *less* or *least* with short or irregular adjectives.
> *This laptop is better than my old one.*
> NOT ~~This new laptop is less bad than my old one.~~
> *I'm the youngest person in my family.*
> NOT ~~I'm the least old person in our family.~~

3 Complete the conversation with the correct comparative or superlative form of the adjectives. Add *the* or *than* where necessary.

A: What's ¹_____ (good) way to see the city?

B: The subway is ²_____ (easy) and ³_____ (fast) the bus. That's ⁴_____ (bad) thing about the bus—it's slow. ⁵_____ (big) problem with the subway is that it's ⁶_____ (expensive) the bus. The bus is ⁷_____ (cheap) way to get around the city. The bus is usually ⁸_____ (crowd) the subway, so you can get a seat.

6B Present perfect (+ *ever* / *never*)

- Use the present perfect to talk and ask about experiences in someone's life without saying when these things happened. Use it to describe a single event or something that happened several times.
  *I **have been** to Russia twice.*
  *Sara **hasn't eaten** sushi.*
  ***Have** you **been** to Japan?*
- Form the present perfect with *have / has* + past participle. Use the contracted forms *'ve* and *'s* in informal situations. Some past participles are the same as the simple past form, but some are irregular. Use the irregular verbs list to help you (page 178).
- You can use *ever* in present perfect questions. It means "at any time in your life." It goes before the past participle.
  *Have you **ever** eaten Thai food?*
  *Has Salman **ever** been to the U.K.?*
- Use *never* with the present perfect. It means "at no time." It goes before the past participle.
  *I've **never** seen Star Wars.*

> **Remember!**
> We don't usually use *ever* with the present perfect in positive statements.
> *I have been to Mexico.*
> NOT ~~I have ever been to Mexico.~~
> But you can use *ever* in positive statements with superlatives.
> *This is **the best** food I have **ever** eaten.*

- You can use *What's the…you have ever…?* with superlative adjectives to ask about someone's best / worst experiences.
  ***What's the** best beach **you have ever** been to?*
- Use the present perfect to talk or ask about an experience in general. Use the simple past to give details about what happened at a specific time in the past.
  *A: **Have you ever been** skiing?*
  *B: Yes, I **have.** I **tried** it in California last year.*

1 Complete the conversations with the present perfect form of the verbs.

1 A: ¹_____ _____ (you / study) a lot of Shakespeare's plays?

B: No, ²_____ (I / never / read) any of his plays before now.

2 A: What's the most interesting country ³_____ (you / ever / go) to?

B: Well, ⁴_____ (I / go) to lots of great places and ⁵_____ (I / have) some amazing experiences. But I think India is the most interesting place ⁶_____ (I / ever / visit).

Grammar reference

6C Verb patterns: -ing and to + base verb

Verb + -ing

- Sometimes, two verbs appear together in a sentence. After many verbs, the second verb needs to be in the -ing form: *avoid, don't mind, enjoy, feel like, finish, involve, keep (on), practice, miss, recommend, stop,* etc.
  *She **practices singing** every day.*
  *I **finished working**.*
- An -ing form also follows many verbs which express likes and dislikes (*like, dislike, love, can't stand, hate,* etc.).
  *I **love traveling** by train.*
  *I **hate sitting** down all day.*

Verb + to + base verb

- After many other verbs, the second verb needs the form to + base verb: *(can) afford, agree, aim, arrange, ask, choose, decide, fail, hope, intend, manage, need, offer, persuade, plan, promise, refuse, try, want, would like,* etc.
  *We **need to leave** soon.*
  *We're **planning to go** to the beach.*
  ***Would** you **like to visit** the museum?*

> **Remember!**
> Use an object between verbs like *persuade* and the base verb.
> *He persuaded **me** to go with him.*
> With *ask* and *want*, you sometimes need to use an object before the base verb.
> *He asked **me** to help him.*

Both -ing and to + base verb

- A small number of verbs can go before both the -ing form or to + base verb with no or little difference in meaning. These include: *continue, hate, like, love, prefer,* and *start.*
  *I **started learning** / **to learn** English three years ago.*

2 Complete the email with the correct form of the verbs.

Hi Masha,

Hello from Peru! I meant ¹_____ (write) you sooner, but we've been really busy. We decided ²_____ (go) to Cuzco because we wanted ³_____ (see) Machu Picchu first. So, we managed ⁴_____ (get) a flight when we arrived here. Cuzco is great and I love ⁵_____ (walk) around the place. I really enjoy ⁶_____ (speak) Spanish! We're planning ⁷_____ (spend) four days here and then go back to Lima. I'm sure that when we get to Lima, we'll feel like ⁸_____ (do) nothing for a few days. OK, I need ⁹_____ (book) the train tickets to Machu Picchu now.

Speak to you later,
Natasha

UNIT 7

7B   Defining relative clauses

- A defining relative clause is part of a sentence. It gives important information about a person, place or thing. It says exactly what person, place, or thing we are talking about. A defining relative clause comes immediately after this person, place, or thing. The relative clause begins with a relative pronoun (*who, which, where, that,* etc.).
  *The movie **that I saw yesterday** was good.*
- Use *which* or *that* in defining relative clauses to talk about things.
  *I've found a book **which / that** helps me with English grammar.*
- Use *who* or *that* in defining relative clauses to talk about people.
  *The person **who / that** inspires me the most is my grandmother.*
- Use *where* to refer to places. Use *when* to refer to times.
  *Look, there's the hotel **where** we stayed last year.*
  *June is the month **when** I usually go on vacation.*

> **Remember!**
> The relative pronoun (*that, which, who,* etc.) replaces the subject or object. Do not also include the subject or object.
> *A person who ~~she~~ inspires me is Edwina Brocklesby.*
> *Have you read the book that I lent you ~~it~~?*

- You can leave out *who, which,* or *that* when it is the object of the relative clause.
  Have you read the book (that) I loaned you?

1 Rewrite the sentences using a defining relative clause.

1 I met someone yesterday. He says he knows you.
   I met someone yesterday who says he knows you.
2 _____
   Did you move the magazine? It was on the table.
   Did you move _____?
3 That's the person. She helped me.
   That's _____.
4 There's the restaurant. We ate there last week.
   There's _____.
5 Here's the book. You wanted to borrow it.
   Here's _____.

7C   used to

- Use *used to* to talk about habits or situations in the past which have changed.
  *I **used to go** to the movies every week, but now I don't.*

- Use *used to* + base verb
  *There **used to be** a park here.*
- To form the negative, use *didn't use to* + base verb.
  *Teresa **didn't use to have** long hair, but she does now.*
- To form a question, use *did* + subject + *use to* + base verb.
  *A: **Did** you **use to have** long hair? B: Yes, I **did**.*

2 Rewrite the sentences with the correct form of *used to* so the meaning is similar.

1 I ate meat in the past. But I don't eat meat now.
   I used to eat meat. _____

2 When I was a child, I rode my bike to school every day.
   When _____.

3 I drank more coffee in the past than I do now.
   I _____.

4 Was there a café here in the past?
   Did _____?

5 I usually recycle things now, but I didn't in the past.
   I _____.

UNIT 8

8B Present perfect and simple past

Present perfect

- Use the present perfect (*have / has* + past participle) to talk about something that happened at some point in the past. Use the present perfect when you don't know (or you don't say) when the event happened.
  *They**'ve bought** a new house.*
  ***Have** you **seen** Valeria recently?*
- You can also use the present perfect to talk about something that started at some point in the past and continues to the present.
  *I**'ve been** tired all day.*
  *She**'s worked** here for ten years.*

- The past participle of *go* can be both *been* or *gone*, but there is an important difference in meaning:
  *He has **gone** to Rome.*

(= He recently went to Rome, and he is there now.)
*He has **been** to Rome*
(= He went to Rome at some point in his life, but he is not there now.)

- Use *since* + a point in time (when the situation started) with the present perfect.
  *He has worked in IT **since 2015**.*
  *I've had this jacket **since I was a teenager**.*

Simple past

- Use the simple past to talk about something that happened and finished in the past.
  *I **grew up** in the north of England.*
  *She **moved** to Lima ten years ago.*
- Use *for* + a period of time (*ten years, six months, two weeks, a few minutes, a long time*, etc.) with the simple past or the present perfect.
  *I lived in Oxford **for five years**.*
  *She's worked here **for six months**.*
  *We have had this car **for a long time**.*

1 Complete the conversations with the present perfect or simple past form of the verbs.

1 A: [1]_____ (you / ever / be) to Spain?
   B: Yes, we [2]_____ (go) there a couple of years ago.

2 A: Elif [3]_____ (work) here since 2015.
   B: Yes, she [4]_____ (start) here just before me.

3 A: How long [5]_____ (they / be) married?
   B: About ten years. They [6]_____ (get) married just after university.

4 A: [7]_____ (you / see) Raphael yesterday? He [8]_____ (not come) into the office.
   B: No. I [9]_____ (not see) him for a long time. I last [10]_____ (see) him six months ago.

8C *Yet, just,* and *already*

- Use *yet* in negative statements with the present perfect to say that something has not happened. Use *yet* in questions with the present perfect to ask if something has happened. *Yet* usually goes at the end of the sentence.
  *I haven't finished my work **yet**.*
  *Have you spoken to Ash **yet**?*

  Note that *not yet* is a common and useful response to a present perfect question.
  *A: Have you been shopping? B: No, **not yet**.*

- Use *just* with the simple past to say something has happened very recently. *Just* usually goes before the main verb.
  *I **just** emailed my mother.*

173

Grammar reference

- Use *already* with the present perfect to say something has happened before the time of speaking (often sooner than expected). Use *already* in positive statements and questions. *Already* usually goes before the main verb or at the end of the sentence.
  *I've **already** had lunch. / I've had lunch **already**.*
  *Have they **already** left?*

2 Put the words in brackets into the correct position in the conversations.
  1 A: I've made some food. Do you want any? (just)
    B: No, thanks. I've eaten. (already)
  2 A: Have you had your interview? (already)
    B: No, I haven't had it. It's tomorrow. (yet)
  3 A: Have you finished the report? (yet)
    B: Yes. In fact, I've sent it to you. (just)

UNIT 9

9B Second conditionals

- Use the second conditional to talk about imagined, hypothetical, or unlikely situations in the present or future.
  *If I **didn't have** so much work, I'd go out tonight.*
  *If you **went** to bed earlier, you **wouldn't** be so tired.*
- Form the second conditional with *if* + past tense + *would*. You can contract *would* to *'d*, especially in speaking. The clauses can go in either order. When the *if* clause is first, use a comma.
  *If it **wasn't** cold, I'd go for a walk.*
  *I'd go for a walk if it **wasn't** cold.*
- You can say *If I / he / she / it were…* .
  *If I **were** very rich, I'd stop working.*
- You can use *If I were you, I'd…* to give advice.
  *You look tired. **If I were you, I'd** go to bed.*

> **Remember!**
> Do not use *would* in the *if* clause.

1 Rewrite the sentences using the second conditional.
  1 I don't live near a train station, so I need to drive a lot.
    If I lived near a train station, I wouldn't need to drive a lot.
  2 I don't have a coat, so I feel cold.

  3 It's raining, so I won't go for a walk.

  4 She wants to go out tonight, but she needs to work.

5 I'm not you, but I think you should look for a new job.

___

9C *must, have to,* and *should*

- Use *must* + base verb and *have to* + base verb to talk about rules and things that are necessary. *Have to* and *must* are similar in meaning. Use them in positive statements.
  *We **must / have to** leave now or we'll miss the bus.*
  *You **must / have to** wear a seatbelt when you drive.*
- *Can't* and *don't have to* have different meanings. Use *can't* + base verb to talk about things we are not allowed to do, or to say it is important <u>not</u> to do something.
  *You **can't** do that—it's dangerous.*
  *We **can't** be late.*
- Use *don't have to* + base verb to say something is not necessary.
  *I **don't have to** work tomorrow—it's the weekend.*
- You can use *should / shouldn't* + base verb to say what is the correct thing to do. You can use *should* or *shouldn't* to give or ask for advice.
  *You look tired. You **should** go to bed.*
  *You **shouldn't** eat so much fast food.*
  *What **should** I do?*
- Form *have to* and *don't have to* like normal verbs.
  *I **have to** go.*
  *She **has to** go.*
  *What **do** I **have to** do?*
  *We **don't have to** take a test.*
  *My sister **doesn't have to** wear a uniform at school.*
- To form questions with *must* or *should*, put the modal verb before the subject.
  *What time **must we** arrive?*
  *Where **should we** go?*

2 Choose the correct option to complete the conversations.
  1 A: You ¹*can't / don't have to* go to the meeting, but you can if you want to.
    B: OK, I won't go. I ²*should / don't have to* finish my report instead.
  3 A What time ³*do we have / must we* to be at the gym?
    B: The class starts at 6:30 and we ⁴*don't have to / shouldn't* be late.
  4 A: You ⁵*can't / don't have to* use your phone when you're driving.
    B: I know. It's against the law.
  5 A: Is there a sauna at the gym?
    B: Yes. But you ⁶*should / shouldn't* reserve a space in advance. It's always popular.

UNIT 10

10B   Past perfect

- Use the past perfect to make it clear that one past action happened before something else in the past.
  We left after we'd had breakfast.
- Use the simple past to talk about the main past action, and the past perfect to say what happened before that. You can often use time expressions (*by the time, when, after, as soon as, until*, etc.) to link the two parts of the sentence and make the time clear.

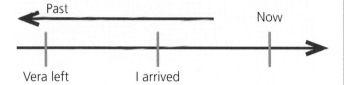

Vera left   I arrived

Vera had left when I arrived.

- The past perfect can be in the first or the second part of the sentence.
  When I arrived, Vera had left.
- You can use the past perfect with *already* and *just*.
  I didn't go to see the movie because I'd already seen it.
  The meeting had just started when I got to the office.
- Form the past perfect with *had* + past participle. Some past participles are the same as the simple past form, but some are irregular. Use the irregular verbs list to help you (see page 178). You can often use the contracted forms *'d* and *hadn't*, especially in speaking.
  I'd forgotten my keys.
  They hadn't seen the movie.
  Had you been there before?

1 Complete the sentences with the simple past or past perfect form of the verbs.

1 We _____ (have) a lot to talk about because we _____ (not see) each other for a long time.

2 The concert _____ (already start) when we _____ (arrive) at the theater.

3 The bus _____ (just leave) when I _____ (get) to the station.

4 Rachel _____ (already leave) by the time we _____ (get) to the party, so we _____ (not see) her.

10C   Articles

a / an

- Use *a* or *an* (indefinite article) to talk about what something or someone is.
  She's a teacher.
  That's an interesting story.

- Use *a / an* with singular nouns to talk about something which it is one of many.
  Is there a bank near here?
- We often use *a / an* when we talk about something for the first time.
  I saw an amazing movie last night with my friend. The movie had lots of good actors in it.

> **Remember!**
> Use *a* before a consonant sound and *an* before a vowel sound.
> *a university, an umbrella*
> *a house, an hour*

the

- Use *the* (definite article) to talk about something specific. This is when there is only one of something, you are talking about something for the second time, or it is obvious what you are talking about.
  Where's the TV remote control?
  I saw an amazing movie last night with my friend. The movie had lots of good actors in it.
- Use *the* with these things.

"plural" countries	*the* U.S., *the* U.K.
some geographical features and regions	*the* Equator, *the* Middle East, *the* Arctic
mountain ranges, rivers, canals, seas, oceans, deserts	*the* Pacific, *the* Danube, *the* Andes, *the* Sahara
the names of movie theaters, theaters, hotels, and museums	*I went to the British Museum.*

no article

- Use no article with plural or uncountable nouns to talk about things in general
  Children love playing games.
- Use no article with these things.

meals	*Breakfast is at 7:30.*
subjects	*Math is my favorite subject.*
sports	*I play basketball.*
continents, countries, states, cities, towns, and villages	*There are a lot of countries in Europe.* *She's from Turkey.*
mountains and lakes	*I flew over Kilimanjaro.* *How big is Lake Macquarie?*
streets, parks, squares, stations, airports	*I live on West Street.* *We flew to Narita Airport.*

Grammar reference

2 Complete the conversations with *a*, *an*, *the*, or no article (–).

1 A: Have you seen my [1]_____ glasses?
B: Yes, they're in [2]_____ kitchen. You left them there when you had [3]_____ lunch.

2 A: Did you see [4]_____ Italy v Germany game last night?
B: No, I didn't. What was [5]_____ score?
A: It was 2–0 in favor of [6]_____ Italy. It was [7]_____ great game.

3 A: What do you do?
B: I'm [8]_____ student. I'm studying [9]_____ music.
A: Cool! Do you play [10]_____ instrument?
B: Yes, I play in [11]_____ band, actually. We have [12]_____ concert tonight at [13]_____ Westside Theater, if you want to come. [14]_____ show starts at 8 o'clock.

UNIT 11

11B Reported speech

- You can use *say* and *tell* to report what someone says. Use an indirect object (*me*, *you*, *the teacher*, etc.) after *tell*. You can also use *that* when you are reporting.
  *He **said** (that) he was a doctor.*
  *He **told me** (that) he was a doctor.*
- When you report with *said* and *told*, you usually have to change the verb tense.

	Direct speech	Reported speech
simple present → simple past	*"I **work** in Ancona."*	*She said she **worked** in Ancona.*
present progressive → past progressive	*"It**'s snowing**."*	*He said it **was snowing**.*
simple past → past perfect	*"I **missed** the bus."*	*He told us he**'d missed** the bus.*
present perfect → past perfect	*"We**'ve** just **had** lunch."*	*He said they**'d** just **had** lunch.*
will → would	*"He**'ll** call you later."*	*She said he**'d** call me later.*

- It is possible to report what a person says without using *said* or *told*. It's also possible to summarize the information, rather than report all the words.
  "I'll probably be about 20 minutes late." → *Jim just called to say he might be late.*

1 Rewrite the direct speech using reported speech.

1 "I've always wanted to be a doctor."
  She said _____.

2 "There's a nice café in the park."
  He said _____.

3 "We'll contact you in a few days."
  They told _____.

4 "I'm planning to run a marathon next month."
  She told _____.

5 "I forgot to do my homework yesterday."
  He said _____.

11C *Can, could,* and *be able to*

- Use *can, could,* and *be able to* to talk about ability (things that you know how to do), possibility (things that are possible), and permission (things you are allowed to do).
- Use *can / can't* + base verb to refer to the present or the future.
  *Sara **can speak** three languages.*
  *We **can't park** here.*
  ***Can** you **help** me later?*
- Use *could / couldn't* + base verb as the past form of *can*.
  *I **could swim** when I was three.*
  *I **couldn't stay** outside for long—it was too cold.*
- Use *be able to* + base verb as an alternative to *can* or *could*.
  *Some people **are able to stay awake** for days.*
  *I **wasn't able to speak** English until I was fifteen years old.*
- *Be able to* is not a modal verb. We form the negative with *not* or *'nt* and we form questions by putting *be* before the subject.
  *I**'m not able to come** with you.*
  ***Were** you **able to fix** the problem?*
- You can also use *be able to* in other forms, for example with *will* and the present perfect.
  ***Will** you **be able to come** with us tomorrow?*
  *I**'ve been able to ski** since I was six.*
- Use *was / were able to*, not *could*, to talk about a situation in the past when the meaning is "managed to."
  *We got lost, but we **were able to** find our way home.*
  *(= we **managed to** find our way home.)*

2 Complete the sentences with the correct form of *can, could,* or *be able to* and the verbs. There is sometimes more than one possible answer.

Humans [1] _____ (use) and control fire for a very long time. As soon as humans [2] _____ (use) fire safely, they [3] _____ (cook) food and make tools. Today, thanks to fire, we [4] _____ (send) people into space and it is possible that one day in the future, and again because of fire, we [5] _____ (live) on another planet.

UNIT 12

12B Passives

- Use active sentences to focus on the person or thing that does the action (the agent).

  Johannes Gutenberg invented the printing press in the 1400s.

  (This sentence focuses on Johannes Gutenberg.)

- Use the passive when you do not want to focus on who does the action. This is usually because who does the action is not important, not obvious, or not known.

  *The printing press **was invented** in the 1400s.*

  (This sentence focuses on the printing press.)

  The object of the active sentence (e.g., *the printing press*) becomes the subject of the passive sentence.

- Form the passive with a form of *be* + past participle. You can also add modals (*will, can,* etc.) before *be* + past participle.

Subject	be	Past participle
These	are(n't)	**made** in Japan.
The first emails	were(n't)	**sent** in the 1970s.
My laptop	is(n't) being	**repaired**.
My car	was(n't) being	**serviced** this morning.
Our lives	have(n't) been	**transformed** by technology.
We	will / won't be	**served** by robots in shops.
The movie	can('t) be	**downloaded** for free.

- Form questions by putting the subject after the first auxiliary verb.

  *Where **are** most computers **made**?*

  ***Has** the room **been cleaned**?*

- Use the passive with *by* + noun to say who or what does the action (the agent).

  *The printing press was invented **by** Johannes Gutenberg.*

  *The new species was discovered **by** Australian scientists.*

1 Complete the sentences with the correct passive form of the verbs.

1 More than four million cell phones _____ (sell) every day around the world.

2 The first glass _____ (produce) around 4,000 years ago.

3 What new discoveries _____ (will / make) in the future?

4 Robots _____ (use) by humans since the 1950s.

5 The planet Venus _____ (can / see) in the night sky very easily.

12C Modals of prediction and possibility

- Use *will* or *won't* + base verb to make a prediction about the future. Use *will* or *won't* when you are sure about something.

  *In the future, most people **will work** from home. There **won't be** any offices.*

- Use *will probably* to talk about likely things or *probably won't* for unlikely ones.

  *The price of food **will probably** go up.*

  *We **probably won't** have robot teachers in the future.*

- Use *may, might,* or *could* + base verb to talk about things that are possible in the future, but not very likely. Use this language when you are not sure about something.

  *It **may / might / could** rain later, but I'm not sure.*

- Use *may not* or *might not* to talk about things that probably will not happen in the future. Do not use *could not* in this way.

  *English **may / might not be** the most important language in the future.*

  NOT *English could not be the most important language in the future.*

  Note that *may* is generally more common than *might* in formal situations, like writing.

2 Complete the sentences with a modal. Use the information in brackets to help you. There is sometimes more than one possible answer.

1 In the future, most humans _____ live to be 100 years old. (I'm sure.)

2 Some of us _____ live to be over 130 years old. (It is possible.)

3 Humans _____ go to Mars this century. (It is possible.)

4 There _____ be hotels on the moon in the next century. (It is likely.)

5 Because of technology, people _____ not need to learn languages in the future. (It is possible.)

6 There _____ be cities under water. (It is unlikely.)

Irregular verbs

BASE VERB	SIMPLE PAST	PAST PARTICIPLE
be	was / were	been
become	became	become
begin	began	begun
break	broke	broken
bring	brought	brought
build	built	built
burn	burned	burned
buy	bought	bought
choose	chose	chosen
come	came	come
cost	cost	cost
cut	cut	cut
do	did	done
drink	drank	drunk
eat	ate	eaten
fall	fell	fallen
feel	felt	felt
find	found	found
fly	flew	flown
forget	forgot	forgotten
forgive	forgave	forgiven
get	got	gotten
give	gave	given
go	went	gone
grow	grew	grown
have	had	had

BASE VERB	SIMPLE PAST	PAST PARTICIPLE
hear	heard	heard
hide	hid	hidden
hit	hit	hit
hold	held	held
hurt	hurt	hurt
keep	kept	kept
know	knew	known
leave	left	left
learn	learned	learned
lend	lent	lent
let	let	let
lose	lost	lost
make	made	made
mean	meant	meant
meet	met	met
pay	paid	paid
put	put	put
read	read /red/	read /red/
ride	rode	ridden
run	ran	run
say	said	said
see	saw	seen
sell	sold	sold
send	sent	sent
set	set	set
show	showed	shown

Irregular verbs

BASE VERB	SIMPLE PAST	PAST PARTICIPLE
sing	sang	sung
sit	sat	sat
sleep	slept	slept
smell	smelled	smelled
speak	spoke	spoken
spell	spelled	spelled
spend	spent	spent
stand	stood	stood
swim	swam	swum
take	took	taken

BASE VERB	SIMPLE PAST	PAST PARTICIPLE
teach	taught	taught
tell	told	told
think	thought	thought
throw	threw	thrown
understand	understood	understood
wake	woke	woken
wear	wore	worn
win	won	won
write	wrote	written

Extra speaking tasks

PAGE 72, 6A, EXERCISE 8

Work in pairs. Read the information and do the task.

Imagine you live in a place where you have to travel by bus for 15 kilometers every day. You live in the countryside and work in the center of a busy city by the ocean. Your office is 1 kilometer from the beach, near a big park. You want to try a different way to travel. Compare the types of transportation below. Think about the cost, the commute time, what you need to carry, where to keep it, and what clothes you might need. Which type of transportation would you choose and why?

Example: A helicopter will be the quickest, but the most expensive. The jet ski would be fun but I still need to walk 1 kilometer to the office.

1 a bicycle

2 a jet ski

3 a hot air balloon

4 a skateboard

5 a camel

6 a helicopter

7 your own idea

PAGE 84, 7A, EXERCISE 8, STUDENT A

What do you think gave someone the ideas for these products? Tell Student B your ideas. Were you correct?

a plastic bottle   plastic made from fish waste

Student B will tell you what they think inspired someone to invent a home security system and a pencil eraser. Listen to their ideas and then tell them if they were correct.

home security system

In 1966, Marie Van Brittan Brown invented a home security system using cameras, a TV, a telephone, and peepholes (little glass holes in the door to look through). She didn't feel safe at home and wanted to know who was at her door.

a pencil eraser

People used to erase pencil marks with bread. Then in 1770, Edward Nairne accidentally picked up some rubber, a material that comes from a tree, and noticed that it was better than bread.

Extra speaking tasks

PAGE 111, 9B, EXERCISE 7, STUDENT A

First situation

Student B is staying at their best friend's house. Their friend goes to work and accidentally locks them in the house. Find out what they would do. Think about these different situations and add your own ideas. Ask them:

What would you do if:

1 you had an important appointment?
2 your friend works nearby / far away?
3 there was no food in the house?
4 you didn't have a cell phone?

Second situation

Your friend offers you a job on a small island. There are no other people on the island. Answer Student B's questions. Use second conditionals to respond.

That sounds awful. I wouldn't take the job. I hate being alone.

PAGE 147, 12B, EXERCISE 6, STUDENT A

Answer Student B's questions using this information and your own knowledge. Answer in full sentences that use the passive voice. Don't say the name of the inventions until your partner has tried to guess them.

Invention 1 (the car): 1886 / Germany

Invention 2 (the television): 1920s / the U.K.

PAGE 120, 10A, EXERCISE 7

Work with another student. Make a story using some or all of these pictures. Take turns saying what happens. Use time expressions and decide on a moral at the end.

A: *One day it was raining. The weather was terrible. It was cold and wet.*

B: *Then my alarm went off. I didn't want to get out of bed.*

Extra speaking tasks

PAGE 84, 7A, EXERCISE 8, STUDENT B

Student A will tell you what they think inspired someone to invent a plastic bottle and plastic made from fish waste. Listen to their ideas and then tell them if they were correct.

a plastic bottle

Engineer Nathaniel Wyeth invented the plastic bottle in 1973. He worked for a plastics company and wanted to make a bottle that didn't break, stayed the same shape, and kept the drinks fizzy.

plastic made from fish waste

Lucy Hughes is a product design student who invented a compostable plastic made from fish skin. She wanted to solve two problems—what to do with fish skins that don't get eaten and how to reduce the amount of plastic in the world.

What do you think gave someone the ideas for these products? Tell Student A your ideas. Were you correct?

a pencil eraser

home security system

PAGE 111, 9B, EXERCISE 7, STUDENT B

First situation

You stayed at your best friend's house. Imagine your friend went to work and accidentally locked you in. Answer Student A's questions. Use second conditionals to respond.

If I didn't have anything important to do, I'd turn on the TV, make some breakfast, and wait for my friend to come home.

Second situation

Student A has been offered a job on a small island. There are no other people on the island. Find out what they would do. Think about these different situations and add your own ideas. Ask them:

What would you do if:
1 there was no internet or electricity on the island?
2 your accommodations were very uncomfortable?
3 it was a beautiful island somewhere hot and sunny?
4 the money was really good?

PAGE 147, 12B, EXERCISE 6, STUDENT B

Answer Student A's questions using this information and your own knowledge. Answer in full sentences that use the passive voice. Don't say the name of the inventions until your partner has tried to guess them.

Invention 1 (paper): about 2,000 years ago / China

Invention 2 (the telephone): 1876 / the U.S.

Audioscripts

1.1

Eva: I'm Eva. I was born in Spain 36 years ago, but I live in Tokyo now. I love it here, it's a very exciting city, there's so much life and so much to do. I get up at 6 and go for a run every day. I take the train to work and I'm always at work by 8. I like to have time for a coffee with my colleagues before work. I usually work 45 to 50 hours a week. It's a long day, but I meet friends several times a week after work and then I feel great again! On the other evenings I usually chat to my friends back in Spain. On the weekends I play soccer in the park.

Meera: My name's Meera. My parents come from a small village in India, but I was born in London in 1995 and have lived here all my life. I'm lucky because my job pays well, so I only work three days a week. I get up at 7, and on the days I don't work, I go for a run before breakfast. I nearly always ride my bike to work. In the evenings, I occasionally meet a friend after work, but generally, I prefer to read a book, listen to music, or watch a bit of TV. I always try to get to the gym on the weekend. A friend and I go for a long bike ride once or twice a month.

1.2

I = Interviewer, A = Arianna

I: I'm here with National Geographic Explorer Arianna Soldati. Arianna, you've lived and worked in several different countries, right?

A: Yeah, right. I'm living in Germany now. Before that, the U.S. and France. And I've studied volcanoes in several places, including Costa Rica, Guatemala, and of course Italy, where I'm from.

I: So you speak, what, three, or four languages?

A: Actually, five.

I: Five? Wow! Amazing! I only speak English and Spanish. Actually, I sometimes feel like a different person when I speak Spanish. Is that the same for you when you speak different languages?

A: Hmm… you know, yeah, that definitely happens. I'm more comfortable in Italian because it's my first language. I don't have to think before I speak. Sometimes that's good, but sometimes maybe I say something without thinking and people understand it in the wrong way.
English is really my second language. In English, I have to think a little more about vocabulary. So I have extra time to make sure people understand me. I feel that is so important in social situations. And, well, in German I'm less confident because I'm still learning it.

I: How about when you're living in different places? Do you change because the culture is different?

A: Absolutely. I've seen that change a lot. For example, living in the U.S. was fun. Actually, the U.S. is the place where I feel my best self because the culture fits me. But one year my parents visited me there and they asked, "What is wrong with you?" They saw me with all my friends and they said I sounded very excited compared to when I'm in Italy. And right now I'm living in Germany, like I said. I'm working at the university for a year. The culture is more serious and quiet—in a good way—so I'm naturally trying to act like other people. So, yeah, I do think I change in different places.

I: One last question on this topic. Do you change when you're with different groups of people? For example, I feel like a different person at work and at home.

A: Yeah, I think the situation really affects how I behave. At work, for example, I try to be reliable and professional. And if I sound really excited, maybe they don't see me as serious. With friends, though, I can be more like myself. Actually, I don't like to mix work situations and friend situations for this reason. And with family, I probably act differently, too. I didn't think about this before, really, but yeah, that's interesting.

1.7

1 That's his book. That's his book.
2 Are they sleeping? Are they sleeping?
3 They're very fit. They're very fit.
4 The ship is coming. The ship is coming.
5 We eat a lot. We eat a lot.
6 I'm heating it. I'm heating it.

UNIT 2

2.1

I = Interviewer, G = Gina

I: Do you have any memories of something that changed your life?

G: Well, the reason I do what I do now is because my mom decided to go caving on a family holiday.

I: Wow!

G: I know! So in my early teenage years, maybe when I was thirteen or fourteen, my mom planned this summer holiday to Cheddar in Somerset. We stayed in this campsite where there was a guy running this outdoor education center. So like caving, canoeing, rock climbing. My mom wanted to try caving, but didn't want to go alone and asked me if I wanted to go, so I did it and I absolutely loved it.

I: Sounds great!

G: It was! And so then we went back several times over the next few years and I saved my money from holiday jobs so I could do more caving and stuff. The whole reason I do what I do now is because I tried caving on holiday. So then I went to university and studied, well actually I studied geography at university and then I started studying caves and climate change there. And so that family holiday changed my life.

Audioscripts

I: Sounds like it! Do you have any other interesting memories from your childhood that you would like to tell us about?

G: Well, when I was eight years old, I fell at the start of the summer holidays and I broke my arm. My parents took me to hospital, but the hospital was too busy so they sent me home and told my parents to bring me back the next day.

I: Oh no! Was it sore?

G: I don't remember that evening, but I guess it was painful. When I went back to hospital the next day, they told me that I now had to stay in for two nights and have an operation.

I: Oh! How did you feel?

G: I felt very scared and took my teddy bear called Pudsey with me. Pudsey is a famous teddy bear in the U.K., as he helps the BBC raise money for children in need. Anyway, Pudsey came into the operating room with me and when I woke up, both of us had our right arm in a bandage!

I: That's nice! What lovely nurses!

G: I think the nurses had a lot of fun with Pudsey. When I had my bandage taken off weeks later, Pudsey came too and had his taken off. It was very cute and it's a nice memory.

🎧 2.3

1 finish
2 decided
3 offer
4 watched
5 needed
6 ask
7 saved
8 start
9 rained

🎧 2.4

I1 = Interviewer 1, I2 = Interviewer 2, N = Nora

I1: Hi Nora, we have some questions for you about things you do to help you learn and remember things better.

N: Great. Ask away!

I1: OK. First question. How do you remember new words in another language?

N: Well, I usually write things down by hand. In general, I write down things I want to remember. I also try to find a word it reminds me of in my own language, English. For example, *rosado* in Spanish makes me think of pink roses.

I1: Ah! Did you use any memory techniques to get ready for school exams?

N: Well, I'm not very good at memorizing. To revise for exams, I color-coded my notes and made lists of information and keywords. I highlighted everything that looked important in yellow pen—and whatever I highlighted, I usually remembered. I used lots of colored Post-it™ Notes in all my books, too. I'd choose a different color for different topics and stick them in important places in my text books.

I2: What were your favorite subjects at school?

N: Oh definitely history and geography—I'm an archaeologist, of course!

I1: Were there a lot of facts to remember in history? How did you do that?

N: I created mind maps, you know? Diagrams to link different ideas. I also wrote lots of lists and topic headings to help me remember a fact or piece of information—for example, I would write "cities" to help me remember to write about ancient cities in my history exam.

I2: Yes! I like using topic headings too. Thanks for talking to us today, Nora.

I1: Yeah, thanks Nora!

🎧 2.5

1 history
2 drama
3 gym
4 geography
5 art
6 math
7 IT
8 biology
9 physics
10 chemistry

UNIT 3

🎧 3.3

I = Interviewer, C = Caroline

I: Today we're talking to successful businessperson Caroline Bennett. Caroline runs a sushi restaurant in London. Tell us about that, Caroline.

C: Hi there. Sure. In the late 1980s, I lived in Japan for a while. While I was there, I fell in love with Japanese society and food. After I returned to London, I was looking for good sushi, but I couldn't find it, so I started a restaurant. People say most restaurants close after five years. Well, I started Moshi Moshi Sushi in 1994. It was difficult sometimes, of course, especially in the last few years. Still, we're doing OK.

I: That's great! Are things different now compared to 1994?

C: Yes, very different! We are always trying to improve because our customers expect it.
In 1994, few people in London were eating sushi, but raw fish is really popular now. So, people know more about it and they expect their sushi to be both delicious and cheap.

I: Sounds hard! And how's your restaurant different from other sushi restaurants?

C: Well, one thing is that we try to do the right thing for the planet. When people think about sushi, many think about eating tuna. About twenty years ago, though, I found it was very hard to get tuna. The reason shocked me. It was hard to get because there are so few blue fin tuna left in the oceans. When I learned that, I took blue fin tuna off the menu.

I: What did your customers think?

C: Some were unhappy, but it was the right thing to do for the environment. In fact, I decided to sell only environmentally friendly fish. It was hard to find, though, so about ten years after I started Moshi Moshi, I started another company that connects people who catch fish and the restaurants that sell it.

I: That sounds like a good idea, but running two companies must keep you very busy. Thinking about eating out in general, can you talk about some other changes during that time?

C: Well, some changes are positive, I think. For example, a lot of people are changing their diets these days. More people are vegetarian or vegan than before. And even people who do eat meat may eat it rarely. And, of course, it seems that many people have food allergies these days. So, I think people want food that is healthy for their bodies and good for the environment. Another positive change is that people want to try new dishes and flavors when they eat out. In a city like London, there are restaurants selling delicious foods from all over the world. I love it! Another example is that people are starting new kinds of restaurants. For example, I know somebody who started a pop-up restaurant in her home. She prepares food for customers in her own kitchen. She serves them in her home, too. That definitely didn't happen in 1994! Not all changes are positive, though. Starting a few years ago, I noticed customers were taking more and more time to finish. What's the reason? Well, they were using their phones to take photos of their foods or use apps. That's a problem for restaurants because other customers are usually waiting to order.

UNIT 4

🎧 4.1

I = Interviewer, AG = Andrej Gcajić, AB = Abby McBride

I: Andrej, do you set yourself goals to work towards, or do you live in the moment?

AG: I'm somewhere in between. I never set goals like "in two years' time, I'm going to be this," but I don't just live in the moment, either. I don't decide exactly when I will do something because it's difficult to plan my work, but I do know what I would like to achieve. For example, in the future I hope to have more animals protected.

I: Do you have work goals?

AG: Well, I would like to be a successful marine biologist. I never dreamed I'd work for National Geographic. I didn't set myself that goal! I don't really set myself work goals. I just want to work—and work better. I'm going to learn more about my science and to educate people so that they will continue our work. It is almost impossible to set goals because everything changes so fast. But I do have one definite plan: I'm moving to the U.S. for work in the summer.

I: And do you have any personal goals?

AG: I'd love to travel to Vietnam. I'm going to spend more time doing things I love—like martial arts, skydiving, and underwater photography. And I'm going to keep using social media to tell people about the places I go and the animals I work with.

....

I: Abby, do you set yourself goals to work towards or do you live in the moment?

AB: Well, I definitely don't set five-year or two-year plans. I think I usually live in the moment. Goals can be helpful, but I like to change them when I need to. Also, I think fun activities are more fun when you don't plan them too much.

I: Do you have any work goals?

AB: One big goal that I always think about is finding new ways to use art and storytelling to help protect wildlife. Recently I've been drawing a lot of seabirds. In one of my next projects, I'm going to draw insects in Patagonia.

I: And do you have any personal goals?

AB: I usually make goals one at a time. Like, I'm traveling in South America soon, so I would like to practice my Spanish. That's one goal. Usually my goals are just things that will make my life better. Like, I'd really love to stop using social media, but I don't know exactly how I'm going to do it because I need it for work!

🎧 4.5

M = Maria, L = Linzi

M: Hi and welcome to my weekly podcast. I'm Maria and as usual, today I'll try to motivate you by speaking to motivated people! Today I'm talking to Linzi. Hi Linzi, you are studying environmental law at university. So, what motivates you?

L: Um, well, I'm not sure! I always push myself to be successful and I like challenges. Plus, my parents always encourage me and my brother is a lawyer, so maybe I'm competitive with him. I dunno. I mean, I know it's not money!

M: Well, in fact, there are lots of studies to show that money is not motivating for thinking tasks.

L: Oh! Why?

M: Well, I'll explain! So, one experiment asked two groups to do the same task. They offered one group the reward of lots of money and one group a little money to do it as quickly as possible. And do you know who was faster?

185

Audioscripts

L: Who?

M: Both groups took the same time!

L: Wow! Why?

M: Well, the task was, like, a puzzle, so people had to, er, think. The experiment showed that people generally do thinking tasks or learn new things for fun.

L: I sometimes think I, like, study for fun!

M: Many people do. On the other hand, there are studies that show getting a reward like money is motivating for tasks that use your body.

L: Oh good! Can you pay me to go to the gym? It's so boring! But, uh, don't tell my coach I said that!

M: Ha! I won't tell anyone! You need to find something you like. I'll help motivate you! What exercise do you enjoy?

L: Y'know, I'm crazy about basketball.

M: So do that then! And try to do it with friends. Exercising with friends or listening to music is very motivating. Do you enjoy studying?

L: Yes, I do. I mean, I don't like working all day every day, but I think my research is important.

M: Feeling like you are making a difference and having a goal is also motivating. I'll tell you my three motivation rules: choose, improve, and have a purpose.

L: Nice song! I'll remember that!

M: Choose, improve, and have a purpose. Good, isn't it? Helps you remember! Choose things you enjoy…

L: What, oh, like basketball?

M: Yup. Like basketball! Do things you can improve…

L: Like my university course?

M: Yes! And purpose—do things do for a reason.

L: Like trying to, like, help change the world—that makes me feel good, so it's, you know, motivating. Thanks.

M: Thank you for your time today, Linzi. Next week I'll give you more ideas to help motivate you…

UNIT 5

5.1

G = Goran, H = Hazam

G: So, I have something exciting to tell you!

H: Oooh! What is it?

G: We are moving to Colombia!

H: Congratulations! What are you going to do there?

G: Rawan's got a job working for a big engineering company. It's a great opportunity.

H: That's excellent. What will you do?

G: Well, if my boss agrees, I'll just continue to work for the same company. I work from home a lot now, so it won't be too different.

H: And what about the kids?

G: They'll go to school. If we stay for a while, they'll learn to speak Spanish, which will be great for their future.

H: Great! What if they miss their friends and grandparents?

G: If we miss people, we'll call them—and we'll come home for holidays.

H: That's good. What if I miss you?

G: You'll just need to come and visit!

H: I'll come visit if you pay for my flight!

5.3

1 I'll travel by bus when I'm in Brazil.
2 If we arrive late, we take a taxi.
3 If I live near the gym, I'll go every day.
4 They'll help you, if you ask them.

5.5

Alexis: The most unusual accommodation I can think of was when I stayed on a Venezuelan traditional fishing boat for a survey I was doing. I lived on that boat with the rest of the fishermen for ten days. The beds were tiny, like, I was basically sleeping on a wooden board with a thin mat, 30 centimeters wide! It was more uncomfortable than sleeping on the floor, particularly when the weather was bad! It was one of the worst sleeping experiences of my life! To save fresh water, we were showering, brushing our teeth and shaving with cold sea water. I was just salty all the time! The hot shower in the hotel at the end of the mission was the best!

Another memorable experience I remember was in Indonesia. I visited one of my friends who was a teacher at the time in a remote village in the countryside. After a long journey, we arrived in this village. There was no hotel so they prepared a room for us at the house of a local farmer. It was a simple house—very basic. They spent a long time making the room prettier, with a lamp, and a mosquito net, etc., which was really kind. The bed was a mattress on the floor, but the funny thing was the blankets and pillows had huge red and pink flowers printed all over them. I slept really well, though, and it was definitely more memorable than staying in a hotel.

Ellie: One of the most memorable places I've stayed was in Lucern, Switzerland. We were on a family holiday with my grandmother. It was winter in Switzerland, which is much, much colder than the tropical Philippines, so we packed all the warm clothes that we had. When we got there, it was freezing and we had to walk uphill through snow to our hostel. But it was worth it. The views from the enormous windows were spectacular! My grandmother stayed in the hostel for the rest of our trip because she didn't want to climb that hill again! In terms of work, I have slept in all sorts of places: in tents and hammocks, and had some awful nights on bus seats and chairs, and woken up lots of times with insect bites! Of all of these, the best memories are the times that I get to sleep in the homes of teammates. It's much nicer to stay with friends than in a hot tent or on a cold bench! Their homes are often less comfortable than a hotel—I usually sleep on the floor—but they are the friendliest places to stay and the ones I like the most!

🎧 5.9

H = Host, G = Guest

H: Hi! Welcome! How are you?

G: I'm good. It was a really long flight. It's great to see you.

H: Here's your bedroom. You can put your bags here. Do you want dinner? I've made fish for the appetizer, then curry for the entrée. And I know you love chocolate cake, so I made that for dessert. It's almost ready. Do you want to take a shower before we eat? Here's a clean towel. The bathroom is at the end of the hall. Make yourself at home. If you want to come down in half an hour, we can eat and catch up. I can't wait to hear about your travels… Oh!

.....

H: Hi! Good to see you! Come on in. Make yourself at home.

G: Great. Thanks. Do you have any coffee?

H: Yes. You can help yourself. The coffee machine is in the kitchen.

G: Can you help me? I don't know how to work this coffee machine!

H: Sure. Here you go.

G: Thanks. Have you got any cookies?

H: Yes. They're in that cupboard.

G: I can't find any.

H: Here you are.

G: Thanks. Do you have any sugar?

H: In that box.

G: Do you have any more? There's none left!

UNIT 6

🎧 6.1

I = Interviewer, S = Salome

I: So, have you ever had a bad travel experience?

S: Well, I haven't had any *terrible* travel experiences, but I've had some pretty difficult ones.

I: What's the worst journey you've ever had, then?

S: When I went backpacking with friends in Peru, we stupidly used a really old guidebook which recommended an amazing six-day trail in the Andes, so we took a long bus ride down to the town where the trail started. But when we got there, we learned it hasn't been possible to do this trail for almost twenty years.

I: Oh, so what did you do?

S: Well, we got a new guidebook and chose an alternative hiking trail, which was the closest we could find. Locals advised us to take a bus back to the capital, Lima, and then take another bus to the town where the trail starts. But Lima was an eight-hour ride in the opposite direction and the new trail looked like it was not so far from where we were. So, instead of listening to the locals, we decided to take small rural buses from town to town directly across the Andes to get there. Big mistake! The Andes is a huge mountain bridge with the narrowest and roughest mountain roads I've ever been on.

I: Ah! So, what happened?!

S: I don't know how many buses we took overall, but every bus was old and packed with people and things. In one bus I sat next to someone with live chickens in a sack. Each of these bus rides were four to eight hours long. I mean, it took almost two days to get to our destination.

I: Oh no! How long was it the other way?

S: Well, in the end it was a whole extra day of traveling. Also, when we finally arrived we really needed to rest after our crazy journey as our backs were sore, so we lost another day. And the worst thing was that one of my friends lost her backpack on the journey.

I: Wow! That sounds stressful!

S: Yeah, it was stressful, but it was also one of the most memorable adventures I've ever had. Apart from the lost backpack and the scary roads, it was really interesting to travel with the locals who live in these remote mountain communities and see their way of life. Oh, and the scenery was spectacular!

I: Has it changed the way you do things when you travel?

S: Well, since that journey, I've never traveled without a *new* guidebook and I always listen to the advice of the locals!

I: Yeah, that makes sense…

Audioscripts

🎧 **6.4**

Tim: Hi, I'm Tim Dee. Thanks for coming to hear me talk about my new book, *Greenery*, which is about the spring in Europe and about the birds that come to Europe every spring after spending winter in Africa. I've been a birdwatcher for most of my life and always love seeing the swallows arrive in spring. Long ago people knew that swallows came to Europe in the springtime and left in the autumn, but no one knew where they went. Some people thought they flew to the moon, or went underwater for the winter. The truth is almost as unbelievable. Every swallow hatched from an egg in Europe flies south into Africa for winter. The same birds return on similar journeys north the following spring to find food, good weather, and to start a family. They fly over 300 kilometers every day, and feed on flies as they go. Some swallows manage to fly 10,000 kilometers, from South Africa all the way to northern Scandinavia.

I wanted to follow the swallows in my book from my new home in South Africa to my old home in England—and on to Norway.

Human travel might be physically easier than flying is for a bird, but it is more complicated and less enjoyable. Tickets are expensive and we have to get to an airport and carry heavy bags, but birds don't need bags! Does anyone enjoy checking in and queuing to go through security…and then spending hours sitting in a tiny little seat with only airline food to eat?

And while humans need clocks and timetables, the swallows just know when to leave their winter home. Swallow time is the right time for them. However, climate change is making spring come earlier in Europe and swallows keep arriving from Africa earlier than before.

Birds don't need to take a passport, either. Swallows are always at home—and their homes are anywhere they feel like landing. I always like the thought that South Africans think of swallows as South African birds, and British people think of them as British, but they are birds of the world. They don't care about maps and borders.

That's actually what I've found the most incredible about swallows. They don't need to ask for directions or use GPS, they just know the way. Baby birds often go the wrong way the first time they fly, but if they live through their first winter, they'll know where to go the next year. To begin with, they just know they have to go south. I really miss seeing the swallows when they leave and look forward to them coming back…

🎧 **6.6**

1
A: It's so annoying when people don't understand my accent.
B: Sorry, could you say that again please?
2
A: I find it to be exceptionally infuriating when people say I am incomprehensible.
B: Sorry, could you repeat that?

🎧 **6.7**

1
A: What time does your flight arrive tomorrow?
B: Sorry? What did you say?
A: What time does your flight arrive tomorrow?
2
A: I've booked a seat on the bus tomorrow. I need to pack my bags.
B: Sorry. I don't understand.
A: I've booked a seat on the bus tomorrow. I need to pack my bags.
3
A: I'm traveling to Venice tomorrow. I've rented a mini-van with my friend Vanessa.
B: Sorry? Could you repeat that please?
A: I'm traveling to Venice tomorrow. I've rented a mini-van with my friend Vanessa.

UNIT 7

🎧 **7.1**

Alem: A story that inspired me was one I read about some Turkish waste collectors who opened a library with books that they found in trash cans. They first shared the books with friends and family, but soon they had 6,000 books, so decided to share them with the local community. They think it's wonderful.
Beatriz: The place where I feel inspired is Lake Falkner in Argentina. It's absolutely beautiful and very peaceful. I go there to hike, and my favorite place to stop and look at the view is the beach which runs alongside the lake.
Zena: A person who inspires me is Edwina Brocklesby. She started running at 50 and did an Ironman triathlon at the age of 74. Imagine swimming 3.8 kilometers, cycling 180 kilometers, and then running 42 kilometers! She's amazing! I've just finished the book that she wrote.

188

Ma = Marwan Mu = Musa

Ma: Hi Musa. How are you?

Mu: I'm annoyed, I just rode my bike along the river and I saw so much trash. People just throw things away without thinking. Potato chip bags, plastic bottles, plastic bags... Everywhere!

Ma: I know. It makes me sad. There didn't use to be so much plastic pollution in the river. It was so beautiful, but now it's a mess.

Mu: I wish I could change it, but nobody cares about the environment!

Ma: You *can* change it! I saw this inspiring story about the beach in Mumbai, India. It used to be full of trash...plastic bags, bottles, cups, toothbrushes...everywhere. Then this local lawyer, Afroz Shah, decided he was going to clean it up. He just went out with his neighbor one day, then more people joined him. In the end 1,000 people volunteered! Politicians, famous actors and actresses, schoolchildren.

Mu: Wow! That's incredible.

Ma: Let me find a photo on my phone. Look, turtles are laying eggs there now! All because one man started picking up some trash one day.

Mu: Wow! That is amazing! What a difference!

Ma: We could do that!?

Mu: Hmmm. But why don't people take responsibility for their own trash? They should just respect the environment and put things in the trash cans!

Ma: Yes! I totally agree.

Mu: People should also reduce how much plastic trash they create. I used to use plastic toothbrushes but I buy wooden ones now. And I reuse my water bottle and take a bag with me everywhere.

Ma: Me, too. I used to buy so many shower gel bottles but I changed to a bar of soap.

Mu: But we still need to do something with all the plastic we've used and thrown away. I read an article the other day that said we don't recycle 91% of all plastic!

Ma: 91%! That means that we only recycle 9% of our plastic! But I think more companies are selling things made from recycled plastic.

Mu: Yeah, true! Actually, my shoes are made from plastic bottles. Do you like them?

Ma: Ooh. Yeah! They're cool.

Mu: So, anyway, that story about Mumbai beach has got me thinking, we really need to do something. Do you want to clean up the path along the river with me? Maybe on Saturday? We can ask a few other people too.

Ma: Good idea. I'll ask my friends at work. They ride along that path every day.

Mu: Awesome! Thanks for telling me that inspiring story!

Mu: Yes. Well it inspired me too! Thanks for changing the world with me!

Mu: Ha! I'm not Afroz Shah!

Ma: Yet...

UNIT 8

🎧 8.3

I = Interviewer, A = Anne

I: Today we have Anne Jungblut, a research scientist, with us. Hi Anne. Can you tell us what you like about your job?

A: Well, the Natural History Museum is a really interesting place to work because we have all the exhibitions and we also do research and teaching. One of the things I love most is discovering new things, like things we didn't know before. That's cool. And I get to travel to amazing places. I've just got back from a trip to the Arctic. Every day is different.

I: Sounds amazing! What did you do before you worked at the Natural History Museum?

A: Well, I've worked here since 2010, but before that I did some research at universities in Canada, Australia, and Germany. After high school I studied biology, you know, the science of plants and living things, in Germany. Then I did another year in Australia to improve my English, then worked as a researcher in Canada. When I was at university in Germany, I once worked as an admin assistant during the holidays. But more often, I tried to get jobs as a research assistant at the university to learn something new.

I: What was your dream job when you were a child?

A: When I was a child, I wanted to be an Egyptologist, you know, someone who studies ancient Egypt. When I was in high school, when I was like 12, 13, 14, before I got into biology, I was super-interested in Egypt—it's thousands of years of history! My mum took me to an exhibition about Egypt at a museum and I just loved it. I had a pencil case with an Egyptian mummy and I learned how to write in hieroglyphs—you know, the ancient Egyptian symbols?

I: The ones that look like drawings?

A: Yes, that's them!

I: Are you still interested in Egypt?

A: I think that was more when I was little, but I still find it very interesting to find out and learn about ancient history. I always love going to the museums when I'm traveling. I'd also still like to visit Egypt. I haven't been there yet!

I: What is your dream job now?

A: Well, I've already got my dream job, but it would also be amazing to be an astronaut. It's the ultimate job of finding out and exploring new things.

I: Ha, yes. It would be incredible, wouldn't it? Though I think I'm happier with both feet on the ground! Well, thanks for chatting to us.

Audioscripts

UNIT 9

🎧 9.1

Federico: My health? Well, I think I'm in pretty good shape. I don't get sick much, but when I do, it's the standard traveler illnesses. It's kind of, you eat something and then you get ill! When I'm away, I think about what I eat, and I try to eat a bit less. I also try to be sensible about sleeping, eating, and drinking. I've only ever ended up in a hospital once and that was when I stupidly got heatstroke! I should know better! I flew to Canada and it was a long flight and I didn't drink enough water. I think I got to camp at 1 a.m. and at 6 a.m. we were having breakfast and starting work. I was tired, I was thirsty, it was hot, and by lunch I was exhausted. I went to hospital and they gave me an IV drip, y'know, a needle and a tube with water, and salts, and sugar in your arm! Then, I was back in my tent sleeping. I was stupid because it's my job to look after myself and stay healthy. I mean, heatstroke! I mustn't do that again! Take my advice. You should drink lots of water if it's hot and you shouldn't stay in the sun all day!

If I was with my kids, I'd be more sensible! I look after them much more than I do myself! When they're sick, I make this magic drink. It's just lemon juice and sugar, but when you add the hot water, if you do it right, it fizzes! They love it. Kids often don't like taking medicine, so I have to mix their tablets with jam or Nutella.

What you eat is important. So is when you eat. A lesson I learned from work trips is that you must eat when it's time. It's sometimes difficult to take a break, but you shouldn't ignore your body. It's also very important to exercise and to find exercise you like. You don't have to think of it as "hard work," just make time to stay fit. So maybe at 6 p.m., do 30 minutes of exercise, but, trust me, just climbing the stairs or cleaning can be very good exercise too.

I'm actually surprised that I haven't had any other health problems when I'm away. There have been lots of scary times when snakes, bears, crocodiles, or spiders might have attacked me, but I've always been OK!

🎧 9.6

1 I can do it on the weekend.
2 I've made some time tomorrow.
3 He isn't available right now.
4 I won't be able to until next year.
5 I'm sorry I don't have time at the moment.

UNIT 10

🎧 10.1

Malee: I remember my first comedy show well. I'd practiced for weeks so I felt ready. But when I got on stage I couldn't remember anything. I'd forgotten all my jokes! I just stood there, staring at the audience for what felt like a long time! Thankfully, I'd written a few notes on my hand before I went on, so finally, I looked at them and started talking. Once everyone laughed at my first joke I relaxed and everything was OK. In fact, I loved it!

Kofi: During the speeches at my wedding we noticed something moving under the table. It was my cousin's three-year-old son, Ebo. He had hidden under the table as part of a game with the other children! My wife picked him up and asked him to say a few words. As soon as he got the microphone, Ebo started singing "Happy Birthday." He had obviously thought the big party was for our birthday. All the guests loved him and our family still tell this story about the surprise song at our wedding.

Nam: When I was at school, we had to put on a show and I had to play a few songs on my recorder with some other students in my class. The night before the show I felt very anxious because I hadn't learned the songs, but it was too late to learn them. So, the next day, I stood on stage and moved my fingers, but didn't blow into the recorder. As soon as the concert had finished I went to find my mom. Luckily, she said nobody had noticed.

🎧 10.4

I = Interviewer, A = Andrej

I: What do you do in your free time?
A: Well, what I love best is photography. As you know, I also play in a rock band, but when I want to relax at home, I watch a film or play video games.
I: Oh cool. What's your favorite type of film?
A: I like drama. I love real stories, like you have to see *Only the Brave* if you haven't already. It's about firefighters putting out wildfires in America. I almost cried—and I never cry! It's a great movie. I love classics, like *The Shawshank*

Redemption. And I love adventure or mystery TV series like *Lost* – the one where they get stuck on the desert island. Yeah, I also like science fiction. So that's why I love everything about Stephen King – his books, his stories, his movies, his TV series... I loved *Under the Dome*. It's about a town that gets covered by a dome, like a huge roof, and the people can't leave and no one can come in. The dome stops radio signal and electricity getting to the town. It was, like, three seasons and I watched them all in maybe ten days! I rarely read books for entertainment as I spend almost twelve hours a day looking at scientific papers. If I do, it has to be fiction. But when I'm reading a book, even if I get into it, I always have something different on my mind. So, to relax, give me a video game!

I: Oh. Why do you like video games?

A: Well, they're fun because it's not only me. Half of my team from work play too. A lot of the scientists I know here in the Balkans like video games. I call it team building! I like them because everything happens so fast and you don't have time to think about different issues...

UNIT 11

🎧 11.3

Anne: So, I'll start by talking about the challenges of my working environment. I work in the polar regions, so it's really different to our normal environment because of things like coldness and the light. We can't wash properly, like we don't shower or wash our hands for weeks and we have to use baby wipes. It's also hard to drink enough. The air is very dry at very low temperatures, and we do a lot of hiking. Therefore, we all need to watch out that we drink enough water all day. We aren't able to get fresh vegetables and fruit in our field camps, but we get very good supplies of frozen and tinned vegetables and food. I can live off chocolate because you burn lots of calories when it's cold!

Although it's challenging to work in the freezing cold, it's not like you see it in the movies. But it's still cold. And we live in tents, so it's warm, but it's not like being warm in a house. I mean, maybe it can be five, six degrees plus in the Arctic. But then in Antarctica, it can be minus five, minus 10 outside. And yeah, it's about having the right clothing and knowing what your body can take. You have to look after yourself. On my first trip, I couldn't sleep well at first because I was cold, but I now know that I need to wear lots of layers, including socks. I just know I can sleep better if I'm warm. And I don't worry what I look like!

We are here to do science, we only have a limited amount of time to do the work and we can't take many things home with us. It is very expensive and difficult to go to Antarctica and therefore we often only have a few weeks to do everything. So sometimes we have very, very long days. And then we also have 24-hour daylight. I quite like the daylight. I'm able to work late since the light gives me energy. Sometimes I work until 3 or 4 a.m. for a few days, then I sleep well. But if we do this, we can feel exhausted, so we need to find ways to be able to get enough sleep. For example, I have to wear my hat over my eyes to sleep.

Some people tell me that my work is a brave thing to do, but it's not dangerous if we look after our body and mind. But if you plan ahead you will be able to live just fine. Before I go there, I think about what I can't live without, which includes good gloves, and some luxury items including plenty of chocolate, nice tea and coffee, as well as a selection of books to read.

UNIT 12

🎧 12.1

W = Woman, M = Man

W: So, technology is changing our world in many ways, but there are still certain things we need humans for, right?

M: Right!

W: Well, maybe wrong! Do you like pizza, for example?

M: Love it!

W: How about pizza made by a robot?

M: What?

W: Yep! Several companies are developing pizza-making robots. One company, called Picnic, has a robot that can make 300 pizzas an hour.

M: That's much faster than pizzas can be made by humans, surely?

W: Exactly. Robots have been created that can deliver pizzas to customers, too!

M: So, no people are needed at all? Amazing!

W: Here's another thing. How often do you get a letter that was written by hand?

M: Hmm, my grandmother used to write to me a lot, but these days, I hardly get any.

W: But you miss them, right? In these days of emails and texts, when you get a handwritten letter, it feels special. But guess what?

M: Letters will be written by robots!

W: Not *will* be. It's already happening! A company called Bond has a robot that writes with a pen in any style. If you send the company an example of your writing, letters can even be written in your handwriting.

Audioscripts

M: Wow!

W: For most of us, a house is the most expensive thing we will ever buy, but that might change in the future.

M: How? No, wait. Let me guess. Robots?

W: You got it! Houses that are built by robots could be much cheaper because they can be made really quickly. For example, a company called ICON has a robot that uses 3D printing to build a small home in less than a day. And another company—FBR—can build you a home with three bedrooms and two bathrooms in just three days—using, you guessed it, a robot.

M: Extraordinary. Still, only humans can do creative things like produce art, right?

W: Well actually, a robot called CloudPainter won a competition in 2018 for producing paintings similar to works by famous artists from history. And robots can do more than just copy human art. They've created completely new art, too.

M: So, I guess in the future, it's likely even more things will be done by robots?

W: Yeah. Perhaps we need to start looking for a new job! Maybe we'll have to ask a robot to help us find one!

🎧 12.2

1 The earliest battery was created around 220 years ago in Italy.
2 The first modern photograph was taken in France in 1826 or 1827.
3 Light bulbs were invented by two people in the year 1879.
4 Electric refrigerators have been used to keep food fresh since the 1920s.
5 The first electric computer was built in the U.S. in the 1940s.
6 These days, smartphones are carried by over 3.5 billion people around the world.
7 It is likely that powerful new technologies will be developed in the future.
8 Voices that sound human can now be produced by computers.

🎧 12.4

1 programs
2 documents
3 messages
4 laptops
5 houses
6 emails

🎧 12.6

I = Interviewer, IM = Isaí Madriz

I: Have you ever had a problem when your technology didn't work?

IM: Oh, sure. Once I was on a trip—a long expedition. We had a big storm and the wind made a hole in my tent while I was sleeping. When I woke up, I was lying in water. My batteries were all damaged, so I had no power. Luckily, I had a small solar panel that gets energy from the sun. I could use it to charge my devices, but it was really slow.

I: How do you think, or hope, that technology might change in the future? To keep you safer or help you do your work better?

IM: Hmm. Well, batteries may last longer and have more power. And cameras will probably get smaller but have more memory for photos. They probably won't get cheaper, though!

🎧 12.7

I = Interviewer, P = Paola

I: Paola, I know you use technology for your work, too. What problems have you had with it?

P: Actually, my phone is a kind of a problem. I can use it for everything, which is great, but maybe I use it too much, you know? I worry when I don't have it near me. I think a lot of people feel that way. I also think it's bad that people don't talk anymore, they just text or email. Sometimes it takes, like, 100 messages to understand something. But maybe a two-minute call could help everybody to understand.

I: Yeah, I agree with a lot of what you just said. So, uh, what technology do you want to see in the future? Do you think these problems might get better, for example?

P: Hmm. I think—I hope—people will try to find a balance. You know, using technology for work and fun, but also spending time with friends and family without technology.

I: What about new technology?

P: Well, my wish is for a machine that can help people understand what animals are thinking and feeling.

I: Wow. That would be incredible. Do you think that could happen, though?

P: Well, I hope so, one day. Then I'll be able to understand how corals feel and what they need.

Acknowledgments

The *Voices* publishing team would like to thank all of the explorers for their time and participation on this course—and for their amazing stories and photos.

The team would also like to thank the following teachers, who provided detailed and invaluable feedback on this course.

Asia

SS. Abdurrosyid, University of Muhammadiyah Tangerang, Banten; Hằng Ánh, Hanoi University of Science Technology, Hanoi; Yoko Atsumi, Seirei Christopher University, Hamamatsu; Dr. Nida Boonma, Assumption University, Bangkok; Portia Chang, SEF Education, New Taipei City; Brian Cullen, Nagoya Institute of Technology, Nagoya; David Daniel, Houhai English, Beijing; Professor Doan, Hanoi University, Hanoi; Kim Huong Duong, HCMC University of Technology, Ho Chi Minh City; Natalie Ann Gregory, University of Kota Kinabalu, Sabah; Shawn Greynolds, AUA Language Center, Bangkok; Thi Minh Ly Hoang, University of Economics—Technology for Industries, Hanoi; Mike Honywood, Shinshu University, Nagano; Jessie Huang, National Central University, Taoyuan City; Edward Jones, Nagoya International School, Nagoya; Amelie Kelly, Dongguk University, Seoul; Ajarn Kiangkai, Sirnakarintrawirote University, Bangkok; Zhou Lei, New Oriental Education & Technology Group, Beijing; Louis Liu, METEN, Guangzhou; Jeng-Jia (Caroline) Luo, Tunghai University, Taichung City; Thi Ly Luong, Huflit University, Ho Chi Minh City; Michael McCollister, Feng Chia University, Taichung; Ms. Ly, Hanoi; Robert McLaughlin, Tokoha University, Shizuoka; Hal Miller, Houhai English, Beijing; Jason Moser, Kanto Gakuin University, Yokohama; Hudson Murrell, Baiko Gakuin University, Shimonoseki; Takayuki Nagamine, Nagoya University of Foreign Studies, Nagoya; Sanuch Natalang, Thammasart University, Bangkok; Nguyen Bá Học, Hanoi University of Public Health, Hanoi; Nguyen Cong Tri, Ho Chi Minh City University of Technology, Ho Chi Minh City; Nguyen Ngoc Vu, Hoa Sen University, Ho Chi Minh City; Professor Nguyen, Hanoi University, Hanoi; Dr. Nguyen, Hoa Sen University, Ho Chi Minh City; Nguyễn Quang Vịnh, Hanoi University, Hanoi; Wilaichitra Nilsawaddi, Phranakhon Rajabhat University, Bangkok; Suchada Nimmanit, Rangsit University, Bangkok; Ms. Cao Thien Ai Nuong, Hoa Sen University, Ho Chi Minh City; Donald Patterson, Seirei Christopher University, Shizuoka; Douglas Perkins, Musashino University Junior and Senior High School, Tokyo; Phan The Hung, Van Lang University, Ho Chi Minh City; Fathimah Razman, Northern University, Sintok, Kedah; Bruce Riseley, Holmesglen (Language Center of University of Muhammadiyah Tangerang for General English), Jakarta; Anthony Robins, Aichi University of Education, Aichi; Greg Rouault, Hiroshima Shudo University, Hiroshima; Dr. Sawaluk, Sirnakarintrawirote University, Bangkok; Sun Yanwei, Yun Gu School, Hangzhou; Dr. Supattra, Rangsit University, Lak Hok; Dr. Thananchai, Dhurakijbundit University, Bangkok; Thao Le Phuong, Open University, Ho Chi Minh City; Thap Doanh Thuong, Thu Dau Mot University, Thu Dau Mot; Kinsella Valies, University of Shizuoka, Shizuoka; Gerrit Van der Westhuizen, Houhai English, Beijing; Dr. Viraijitta, Rajjabhat Phanakorn University, Bangkok; Dr. Viraijittra, Phranakhon Rajabhat University, Bangkok; Vo Dinh Phuoc, University of Economics,

Ho Chi Minh City; Professor Wadsorn, Bangkok; Dr. Nussara Wajsom, Assumption University, Bangkok; Scott A. Walters, Woosong University, Daejeon; Keano Wang, B910 Solutions Education Consulting Co. Ltd.; Yungkai Weng, PingoSpace & Elite Learning, Beijing; Ray Wu, Wall Street English, Hong Kong.

Europe, Middle East, and Africa (EMEA)

Saju Abraham, Sohar University, Sohar; Huda Murad Al Balushi, International Maritime College, Sohar; Salah Al Hamdi, Modern College of Business and Science, Muscat, Victor Alarcón, EOI Badalona, Barcelona; Yana Alaveranova, International House, Kiev; Alexandra Alexandrova, Almaty; Blanca Alvarez, EOI San Sebastian de los Reyes, Madrid; Emma Antolin, EOI San Sebastian de los Reyes, Madrid; Manuela Ayna, Liceo Primo Levi, Bollate, Milan; Elizabeth Beck, British Council, Milan; Charlotte Bentham, Adveti, Sharjah; Carol Butters, Edinburgh College, Edinburgh; Patrizia Cassin, International House, Milan; Elisabet Comelles, EIM—Universitat de Barcelona, Barcelona; Sara De Angeles, Istituto Superiore Giorgi, Milan; Carla Dell'Acqua, Liceo Primo Levi, Bollate, Milan; John Dench, BEET Language Centre, Bournemouth; Angela di Staso, Liceo Banfi, Vimercate, Milan; Sarah Donno, Edinburgh College, Edinburgh; Eugenia Dume, EOI San Sebastian de los Reyes, Madrid; Rory Fergus Duncan, BKC-IH Moscow, Moscow; Ms. Evelyn Kandalaft El Moualem, AMIDEAST, Beirut; Raul Pope Farguell, BKC-IH Moscow, Moscow; Chris Farrell, CES, Dublin; Dr. Aleksandra Filipowicz, Warsaw University of Technology, Warsaw; Diana Golovan, Linguist LLC, Kiev; Jaap Gouman, Pieter Zandt, Kampen; Maryam Kamal, British Council, Doha; Galina Kaptug, Moonlight, Minsk; Ms. Rebecca Nabil Keedi, College des Peres Antonines, Hadath; Dr. Michael King, Community College of Qatar, Doha; Gabriela Kleckova, University of West Bohemia, Pilsen; Mrs. Marija Klečkovska, Pope John Paul II gymnasium, Vilnius; Kate Knight, International Language School, Milan; Natalia Kolina, Moscow; David Koster, P.A.R.K., Brno; Suzanne Littlewood, Zayed University, Dubai; Natalia Lopez, EOI Terrassa, Barcelona; Maria Lopez-Abeijon, EOI Las Rozas, Madrid; Pauline Loriggio, International House London, London; Gabriella Luise, International Language School Milan, Milan; Klara Malowiecka, Lang Ltc, Warsaw; Fernando Martin, EOI Valdemoro, Madrid; Robert Martinez, La Cunza, Gipuzkoa, Mario Martinez, EOI Las Rozas, Madrid; Marina Melnichuk, Financial University, Moscow; Martina Menova, SPĚVÁČEK vzdělávací centrum, Prague; Marlene Merkt, Kantonsschule Zurich Nord, Zurich; Iva Meštrović, Učilište Jantar, Zagreb; Silvia Milian, EOI El Prat, Barcelona; Jack Montelatici, British School Milan, Milan; Muntsa Moral, Centre de Formació de Persones Adultes Pere Calders, Barcelona; Julian Oakley, Wimbledon School of English, London; Virginia Pardo, EOI Badalona, Barcelona;

William Phillips, Aga Khan Educational Service; Joe Planas, Centre de Formació de Persones Adultes Pere Calders, Barcelona; Carmen Prieto, EOI Carabanchel, Madrid; Sonya Punch, International House, Milan; Magdalena Rasmus, Cavendish School, Bournemouth; Laura Rodríguez, EOI El Prat, Barcelona; Victoria Samaniego, EOI Pozuelo, Madrid; Beatriz Sanchez, EOI San Sebastian de los Reyes, Madrid;

Acknowledgments

Gigi Saurer, Migros-Genossenschafts-Bund, Zurich; Jonathan Smilow, BKC-IH, Moscow; Prem Sourek, Anderson House, Bergamo; Svitlana Surgai, British Council, Kyiv; Peter Szabo, Libra Books, Budapest; Richard Twigg, International House, Milan; Evgeny Usachev, Moscow International Academy, Moscow; Eric van Luijt, Tilburg University Language Center, Tilburg; Tanya Varchuk, Fluent English School, Kyiv; Yulia Vershinina, YES Center, Moscow; Małgorzata Witczak, Warsaw University of Technology, Warsaw; Susanna Wright, Stafford House London, London; Chin-Yunn Yang, Padagogische Maturitaetsschule Kreuzlingen, Kreuzlingen; Maria Zarudnaya, Plekhanov Russian University of Economics, Moscow; Michelle Zelenay, KV Winterthur, Winterthur.

Latin America

Jorge Aguilar, Universidad Autónoma de Sinaloa, Culiacán; Carlos Bernardo Anaya, UNIVA Zamora, Zamora; Sergio Balam, Academia Municipal de Inglés, Mérida; Josélia Batista, CCL Centro de Línguas, Fortaleza; Aida Borja, ITESM GDL, Guadalajara; Diego Bruekers Deschamp, Ingles Express, Belo Horizonte; Alejandra Cabrera, Universidad Politécnica de Yucatán, Mérida; Luis Cabrera Rocha, ENNAULT—UNAM, Mexico City; Bruna Caltabiano, Caltabiano Idiomas, São Paulo; Hortensia Camacho, FES Iztacala—UNAM, Mexico City; Gustavo Cruz Torres, Instituto Cultural México—Norteamericano, Guadalajara; Maria Jose D'Alessandro Nogueira, FCM Foundation School, Belo Horizonte; Gabriela da Cunha Barbosa Saldanha, FCM Foundation School, Belo Horizonte; Maria Da Graça Gallina Flack, Challenge School, Porto Alegre; Pedro Venicio da Silva Guerra, U-Talk Idiomas, São Bernardo do Campo; Julice Daijo, JD Language Consultant, Rua Oscar Freire; Olívia de Cássia Scorsafava, U-Talk Idiomas, São Bernardo do Campo; Marcia Del Corona, UNISINOS, Porto Alegre; Carlos Alberto Díaz Najera, Colegio Salesiano Anáhuac Revolución, Guadalajara; Antônio César Ferraz Gomes, 4 Flags, São Bernardo do Campo; Brenda Pérez Ferrer, Universidad Politécnica de Querétaro, Querétaro; Sheila Flores, Cetys Universidad, Mexicali; Ángela Gamboa, Universidad Metropolitana, Mérida; Alejandro Garcia, Colegio Ciencias y Letras, Tepic; Carlos Gomora, CILC, Toluca; Kamila Gonçalves, Challenge School, Porto Alegre; Herivelton Gonçalves, Prime English, Vitória; Idalia Gonzales, Británico, Lima; Marisol Gutiérrez Olaiz, LAMAR Universidad, Guadalajara; Arturo Hernandez, ITESM GDL, Guadalajara; Gabriel Cortés Hernandez, B-P Institute, Morelia; Daniel Vázquez Hernández, Preparatoria 2, Mérida; Erica Jiménez, Centro Escolar, Tepeyac; Leticia Juárez, FES Acatlán—UNAM, Mexico City; Teresa Martínez, Universidad Iberoamericana, Tijuana; Elsa María del Carmen Mejía Franco, CELE Mex, Toluca; José Alejandro Mejía Tello, CELE Mex, Toluca; Óscar León Mendoza Jimenéz, Angloamericano Idiomas, Mexico City; Karla Mera Ubando, Instituto Cultural, Mexico City; Elena Mioto, UNIVA, Guadalajara; Ana Carolina Moreira Paulino, SENAC, Porto Alegre; Paula Mota, 4 Flags, São Bernardo do Campo; Adila Beatriz Naud de Moura, UNISINOS, Porto Alegre; Monica Navarro Morales, Instituto Cultural, Mexico City; Wilma F. Neves, Caltabiano Idiomas, São Paulo; Marcelo Noronha, Caltabiano Idiomas, São Paulo; Enrique Ossio, ITESM Morelia, Morelia; Filipe Pereira Bezerra, U-Talk Idiomas, São Bernardo do Campo; Florencia Pesce, Centro Universitario de Idiomas, Buenos Aires; Kamila Pimenta, CCBEU, São Bernardo do Campo; Leopoldo Pinzón Escobar, Universidad Santo Tomás, Bogotá; Mary Ruth Popov Hibas, Ingles Express, Belo Horizonte; Alejandra Prado Barrera, UVM, Mexico City; Letícia Puccinelli Redondo, U-Talk Idiomas, São Bernardo do Campo; Leni Puppin, Centro de Línguas de UFES, Vitória; Maria Fernanda Quijano, Universidad Tec Milenio, Culiacán; Jorge Quintal, Colegio Rogers, Mérida; Sabrina Ramos Gomes, FCM Foundation School, Belo Horizonte; Mariana Roberto Billia, 4 Flags, São Bernardo do Campo; Monalisa Sala de Sá, 4 Flags, São Bernardo do Campo; Yamel Sánchez Vízcarra, CELE Mex, Toluca; Vagner Serafim, CCBEU, São Bernardo do Campo; Claudia Serna, UNISER, Mexicali; Alejandro Serna, CCL, Morelia; Simone Teruko Nakamura, U-Talk Idiomas, São Bernardo do Campo; Desirée Carla Troyack, FCM Foundation School, Belo Horizonte; Sandra Vargas Boecher Prates, Centro de Línguas da UFES, Vitória; Carlos Villareal, Facultad de Ingenierías Universidad Autónoma de Querétaro, Querétaro; Rosa Zarco Mondragón, Instituto Cultural, Mexico City.

U.S.A. and Canada

Rachel Bricker, Arizona State University, Tempe; Jonathan Bronson, Approach International Student Center, Boston; Elaine Brookfield, EC Boston, Boston; Linda Hasenfus, Approach International Student Center, Boston; Andrew Haynes, ELS Boston, Boston; Cheryl House, ILSC, Toronto; Rachel Kadish, FLS International, Boston; Mackenzie Kerby, ELS Language Centers, Boston; Rob McCourt, FLS International Boston; Haviva Parnes, EC English Language Centres, Boston; Shayla Reid, Approach International Student Center, Boston.

Credits

Credits

Text: p52: Lydia Sweatt. July 14, 2016. 19 Quotes About Motivation. Retrieved from https://www.success.com/19-quotes-about-motivation/; p52: Stephen Hawking. (n.d.). However difficult life may seem, there is always something you can do, and succeed at. It matters that you don't just give up. Retrieved from https://www.goalcast.com/2017/07/25/stephen-hawking-quotes-inspire-you-think-bigger/stephen-hawking1-copy/; p52: Chris. (AUG 11, 2017). No One Will Motivate You. Only You Can Motivate You. Retrieved from https://thesaleshunter.com/no-one-will-motivate-you-only-you-can-motivate-you/; p34 Source: Donald McRae. (2019, April 03). Ed Jackson: "I want to be the first quadriplegic to climb Everest." Retrieved from https://www.theguardian.com/sport/2019/apr/03/ed-jackson-rugby-interview-everest; p134 Source: MILLIMETRES TO MOUNTAINS ED JACKSON. (n.d.). Retrieved from https://therpa.co.uk/news/2019/10/millimetres-to-mountains-ed-jackson/